FELIX FRANKFURTER

Judicial Restraint and Individual Liberties

TWAYNE'S TWENTIETH-CENTURY AMERICAN BIOGRAPHY SERIES

John Milton Cooper, Jr., _General Editor_

FELIX FRANKFURTER

Judicial Restraint and Individual Liberties

Melvin I. Urofsky

TWAYNE PUBLISHERS • BOSTON
A Division of G. K. Hall & Co.

Twayne's Twentieth-Century
American Biography Series No. 12

Published by Twayne Publishers
A division of G. K. Hall & Co.
70 Lincoln Street
Boston, Massachusetts 02111

10 9 8 7 6 5 4 3 2 1 (hc)
10 9 8 7 6 5 4 3 2 1 (pb)

The paper used in this publication meets the minimum requirements
of American National Standard for Information Sciences—Permanence
of Paper for Printed Library Materials, ANSI Z39.48-1984. ∞™

Printed and bound in the United States of America.

Library of Congress Cataloging-in-Publication Data

Urofsky, Melvin I.
   Felix Frankfurter : judicial restraint and individual liberties /
Melvin I. Urofsky.
      p.   cm.—(Twayne's twentieth-century American biography
series; no. 12)
   Includes bibliographical references and index.
   ISBN 0-8057-7774-1 (hc : alk. paper).—
   ISBN 0-8057-7792-x (pb : alk. paper)
   1. Frankfurter, Felix, 1882–1965. 2. Judges—United States—
Biography. 3. Judicial process—United States. 4. Civil rights—
United States.   I. Title.   II. Series.
KF8745.F7U76   1991
347.73'14'092—dc20
[347.30714092]   91-11730

FOR MAEVA AND DANNY MARCUS

Libiamo ne' lieti calici,
Che labellezza infiora
E la fuggevol, fuggevol ora.
S'in ne brii a volutà. . . .
Libiamo, amore, amor frai calici
Più caldi baci acaldi bacia vrà.

—Verdi, *La Traviata*

CONTENTS

INTRODUCTION

On 4 January 1939, Harvard Law School professor Felix Frankfurter picked up the phone to hear his good friend, the president of the United States, tell him of his nomination to the Supreme Court's "scholar's seat," the chair previously occupied by Horace Gray, Oliver Wendell Holmes, Jr., and until his death a few months earlier, Benjamin Nathan Cardozo. The next day a group of top New Dealers gathered in the office of Secretary of the Interior Harold L. Ickes to celebrate the appointment. Attorney General Frank Murphy came, as did Missy LeHand and Harry Hopkins from the White House and Securities and Exchange Commission chairman William O. Douglas. Tommy Corcoran, the president's special assistant, brought two magnums of champagne, and as they toasted the appointment, all of them heartily agreed with Ickes's characterization of the nomination as "the most significant and worth-while thing the President has done."[1]

The joy of New Deal insiders mirrored that of liberals in the government and academe. "Frankfurter's whole life has been a preparation for the Supreme Court," exulted the *Nation*. "His appointment has an aesthetically satisfying inevitability. No other appointee in our history has gone to the Court so fully prepared for its great tasks."[2] The poet Archibald MacLeish, his close friend, proclaimed that Frankfurter's great devotion to civil liberties, as evidenced over the previous 20 years, would be the hallmark of his tenure on the bench.[3] From within the Court, a satisfied Harlan Fiske Stone described the new nominee as "eminently qualified."[4] Even some conservatives applauded Roosevelt's choice. The *New York Times* predicted approvingly that "he will serve no narrow prejudices, that he will be free from partisanship, [and] that he will reveal the organic conservatism through which the hard-won victories [that] won liberty in the past can yield a new birth of freedom."[5]

In his own eyes and those of many others, Frankfurter's appointment epitomized the opportunities that American democracy offered those with talent and industriousness. Professor at the prestigious Harvard Law School, his career included successful stints in government service and in defense of liberal causes both before the public and in the courts. At Harvard he trained a generation of men in the intricacies of the new administrative law. The best of his students he sent to Holmes and Louis Brandeis as law clerks, and during the New Deal he placed his "boys" in every important agency in the government. Moreover, as a scholar Frankfurter wrote a number of incisive articles on the Supreme Court and coauthored what many considered the definitive study of how the modern Court operated.[6] Here was the man, his admirers believed, who could not only serve as a great jurist but also lead the Court away from the conservatism that had marked so much of its recent past. Frankfurter, too, believed that his entire career had been preparation for the large tasks that now awaited him in the marble temple.

But it is impossible to identify those traits or experiences that will make a "great" judge, as Frankfurter himself admitted.[7] Some men for whom expectations were low, such as Hugo L. Black, have gone on the Court and become giants; others of whom much was expected have proved disappointing. Frankfurter, unfortunately, falls into the latter category. The man who had studied the Court and its members for more than 25 years, who had written so brilliantly about the interaction of judicial decision-making and changing social and economic conditions, who had learned at the feet of Holmes, Brandeis, Stone, and Cardozo about the importance of collegiality on the bench, could never apply that knowledge effectively. Instead of being the herald of a new jurisprudential age, Frankfurter fought a valiant but ultimately ineffective rearguard action to divert the Court from what he considered a disastrous path. A quarter-century after his death, his opinions are all but ignored by both the courts and academia.[8]

This book attempts to explain why that happened. Frankfurter formed his views of proper jurisprudence during the progressive years and the 1920s, years when conservative judges used their authority to strike down reform legislation and enshrined the values of contract and property under the aegis of substantive due process. The Court and the country paid for this folly in the constitutional crisis of 1937: Franklin Roosevelt, with a mandate from the people to go ahead with the New Deal, found himself stymied by a bare majority of the Supreme Court, men who had not been elected, who were not accountable to anyone, and who stood immune to political retribution.

For Frankfurter, the answer to the crisis could be found in judicial restraint and institutional deference. The legislatures represent the majoritarian will, and courts should not second-guess the wisdom of their policies. Unless a statute violates a clear constitutional prohibition, courts should not void a law because judges disagree with its premises. Professor Frankfurter believed this in 1922; Mr. Justice Frankfurter still believed it four decades later when he retired from the bench.

In theory, there is nothing wrong with this philosophy; it expresses a justifiable, logical theory of the proper role of courts in a federal system. But as Holmes pointed out in 1881, the life of the law has not been logic but experience, and the law is vital only so long as it remains tied to the reality of that experience.[9] Roscoe Pound in his sociological jurisprudence, Louis Brandeis in his data-laden briefs, and Felix Frankfurter in his scholarly and popular articles on the Court in the 1920s and 1930s, all reiterated this view.

The two ideas, judicial restraint and a law based on experience, do not necessarily conflict. In the hands of a Holmes or Brandeis, judicial restraint is an effective tool that allows state legislatures to experiment in meeting particular social and economic problems. But Holmes and Brandeis differed significantly in their endorsement of legislative prerogatives: Brandeis did so because he often believed in the reforms under review; Holmes believed in law as the expression of majoritarian sentiment.[10] Moreover, both men believed that courts should defer to the legislative will in reviewing economic policies but should play a different role when legislatures attempt to restrict individual liberties.

Frankfurter never saw this distinction, and his inability to do so may have been at the heart of his failure. Until World War II economic issues dominated the Court's docket; since the war, questions of civil rights and civil liberties have occupied the justices' attention. The old battles, which came to a climax in the 1937 Court-packing plan, had been won, and Frankfurter's critiques of the Court's judicial activism in the 1920s and 1930s had played a part in that victory.

For most of the 23 years Frankfurter sat on the bench, the Court had to respond to demands for an expansion of judicial protection of liberty. Frankfurter, as much as any of his colleagues on the Court, personally opposed illiberalism and intolerance in any form and had courageously battled against bigotry in his academic years. But Frankfurter's position seemed more and more conservative, if not reactionary, as the years went by. His views of judicial restraint and institutional deference had been formed before he went on the Court, and there is no evidence that he altered his ideas in response to the great changes taking place around him. As Hugo Black, William O. Douglas, Earl Warren, and William Brennan forged a modern jurisprudence of constitutionally protected individual rights and liberties, Frankfurter determinedly held on to the old battle cries, emphasizing process regardless of the issue. He seemingly forgot his own warning, written just before his nomination to the bench, that people must have open minds, since in a world that changed so rapidly rigid views could only lead to disaster.[11]

Frankfurter, however, should not be simply adjudged a failure and dismissed as inconsequential. He played a key role in defining the major debate of the postwar era—the extent to which the Bill of Rights applied to the states as well as to the federal government. He accepted the notion, first suggested by

Brandeis, that the Fourteenth Amendment somehow applies the first eight amendments to the states; but in contrast to Hugo Black's view of "total incorporation," Frankfurter expanded on Benjamin Cardozo's theory of partial or "selective incorporation." Ironically, the balancing of values required under selective incorporation demanded that courts take on a powerful and activist role. Balancing, which to Frankfurter constituted the heart of judging, brought the personal predilections of judges to the fore. As Professor Frankfurter had noted years earlier, "The process of constitutional interpretation compels the translation of policy into judgment, and the controlling conceptions of the justices are their 'idealized political pictures' of the existing social order."[12] In this as in so many other things, Justice Frankfurter should have remembered what Professor Frankfurter had learned.

Felix Frankfurter stood at the center of one controversy or another throughout most of his life, and the storms have not stilled with his death. Revelations of his and Brandeis's extrajudicial activities triggered a debate over the proper role of the men and women who don the black robe. The liberal activism of the Court in the 1960s and 1970s made Frankfurter the darling of conservatives like former Attorney General Edwin Meese and columnist and critic Bruce Fein, who held him up as a model of judicial self-limitation. The process jurisprudence he championed as the most value-neutral means of deciding questions has itself come under attack for merely masking the determinative values that are in fact at work. In a generation that has seen courts as the only bulwark against majoritarian subversion of individual rights, Frankfurter's judicial deference very often appears to be abdication of judicial responsibility.

Frankfurter entered public life during the administration of Theodore Roosevelt; he sent his resignation from the Court to John F. Kennedy. His life, which was predominantly focused on the Supreme Court and constitutional law, is of interest for its achievements, of which there were many, as well as for its failures. In it we can examine the major constitutional issues of this century up until the time of Frankfurter's retirement in 1962, and we can note the great changes that have taken place—some of which he supported, others of which he opposed.

This work focuses on Frankfurter and his philosophy and practice of judicial restraint. It touches on his pre-Court and extrajudicial activities only slightly, primarily as they relate to this central theme. The Court years are also treated selectively; the work is not meant as a definitive examination of every issue on which Frankfurter wrote, spoke, or voted.

In examining these questions, however, the biographer cannot escape the Frankfurter personality, which proved so dazzling to students, friends, and oftentimes even foes. In death as in life, Frankfurter just does not elicit neutral feelings. Biographer Michael Parrish relates that he started out liking and admiring Frankfurter and then came to dislike him intensely; only after a long time did he reach a middle point, a guarded affection. I, too, began my work thinking of

Frankfurter as a great man; the more I learned, the less I cared for him. My middle point might better be described as "guarded respect," and that judgment informs this study. I hope, as any scholar would, that I have been fair to my subject; but history, like law, is far from value-free.

I have accumulated a number of debts in writing this book. John Milton Cooper, the general editor of this series, invited me to contribute a volume, and suggested I do Frankfurter. At Twayne, Anne Jones, the senior history editor, helped me maneuver the obstacle course of turning a manuscript into a book.

In the past few years I have had the benefit of discussing the Supreme Court in general and Felix Frankfurter in particular with a group of men who had the rare opportunity of clerking for justices of the Supreme Court when Frankfurter sat on the bench. Some clerked for him, and some for other justices, but all had interesting stories that they shared with me. I also want to thank Michael Parrish, who generously took time from his own work on Frankfurter so we could discuss "our Felix." My wife, Susan, as always, showed great patience with me while I wrote.

The book is dedicated to two friends with whom Susan and I have shared many wonderful times.

1

THE APPRENTICESHIP

Born on 15 November 1882 into a petit bourgeois Jewish family, Felix
Frankfurter spent his first years in brilliant, decadent Vienna, then in
the twilight of the Hapsburg empire. In 1894 the family emigrated to
America and to the first stop of most Jewish immigrants, New York's
Lower East Side. But Emma Frankfurter, who tyrannized her husband
Leopold and for many years dominated her son, determined that, despite
Leopold's lack of business talent, the family would make it up out of the
ghetto and into the middle class. Within five years the Frankfurters had
moved uptown to Yorkville; more importantly, their precocious son had
discovered that academic achievement could provide him his own road
for upward mobility.

From P.S. 25 Frankfurter entered City College in 1901, and from
there he went to the citadel of American law, Harvard Law School, then
in the heyday of James Barr Ames, Samuel Williston, John Chipman
Gray, and Joseph Beale. Ever since Christopher C. Langdell introduced
the case method of instruction in the early 1870s, Harvard had pioneered
in the "scientific" study of law and had become a preeminent national
law school.

Although initially awed by the tradition and mystique of the place,
as well as by the social standing of many of his classmates, Frankfurter

1

soon recognized that the faculty cherished sharp, aggressive minds far more than family pedigree.[1] And no one was sharper than the young New York Jew who led his class for three years, made the *Harvard Law Review*, and became John Gray's research assistant. He also established lifelong friendships with men such as Sam Rosensohn, Morris Raphael Cohen, Grenville Clark, and Elihu Root, Jr.

Frankfurter took away from Cambridge a set of intellectual ideas as well as a conception of American society from which he never departed. At Harvard he imbibed the spirit of Gray's brand of legal skepticism, a precursor of what would later be called "legal realism." Holmes had argued as early as 1881 in his Lowell Lectures that the life of the law was experience, not logic, and Gray explored the various nonlegal factors that affect judicial decision-making.[2] Frankfurter also imbibed the idealism of Louis D. Brandeis, then at the height of his legal career in Boston; the young student sat in the audience in May 1905 when Brandeis spoke before the Harvard Ethical Society on "The Opportunity in the Law." That evening Brandeis called upon lawyers to stop serving narrow private interests and to be instead the "people's attorney."[3] While at Harvard, Frankfurter also developed a set of social habits, including a taste for good food, wines, and clothing.

On graduation in 1905 he took a job, at $1,000 a year, with one of the major Wall Street law firms, Hornblower, Byrne, Miller & Potter. The firm had never before accepted Jews into its employ, but the young man came with such a brilliant record that the partners offered a job. They did, however, suggest that he anglicize his name. Frankfurter spent a few unhappy months in private practice before he received an invitation in 1906 to join the office of the new U.S. Attorney for New York, Henry L. Stimson.[4] Frankfurter gladly took a cut in salary, as he later recalled, so he "could practice law without having a client."[5] From then on in his extraordinary career, Frankfurter's client would be the public.

The time spent with Stimson proved exceedingly instructive, well worth the $250-a-year reduction in income. The U.S. Attorney's office dealt with an enormous variety of cases, ranging from smuggling to violation of the antitrust laws to habeas corpus proceedings for immigrants detained at Ellis Island. This was indeed intoxicating work, far more interesting and varied than anything Frankfurter had done at Hornblower, Byrne. One day he would be prosecuting petty swindlers and the next day jousting with the Havemeyer sugar trust. Under Stimson's tutelage, Frankfurter learned how the legal machinery worked and eventually gained what few other law teachers of his time would have—an extensive familiarity with the apparatus and procedures of government law.

Stimson believed in very careful preparation and told his assistants that "you must prepare the other fellow's case at least as well as he prepares it, usually better, so there are no surprises."[6] Stimson also set a very high standard of conduct, refusing to use wiretaps or allow raids without proper search warrants, and impressed on his assistants the need to respect the rights of the accused. Frankfurter always treasured his years with Stimson and later recalled that he "had nothing but a wonderful time being Mr. Stimson's personal assistant. . . . It was really a very rich life. Professionally it couldn't have been better."[7]

Henry Stimson was the first of Felix Frankfurter's hero-mentors, a role later filled by Louis D. Brandeis and Franklin D. Roosevelt.[8] A patrician who dedicated his life to public service, Stimson had little of the parochialism and prejudices that so often seem to afflict the upper class. Frankfurter later declared: "I don't see how a young fellow coming to the bar could possibly have had a more desirable, more deepening, and altogether more generous influence during his formative years than to be junior to Henry L. Stimson."[9]

Stimson influenced Frankfurter in a number of ways apart from setting high standards in legal practice. Stimson reassured the younger man of his ability and built up his self-confidence, while introducing him to the movers and shakers, such as Theodore Roosevelt, among whom Stimson moved as an equal. At the same time Frankfurter developed a talent for flattery and for cultivating the friendship of people who could prove useful to him. Stimson was the first recipient of Frankfurter's flattery; he would not be the last.[10]

Of equal importance, Frankfurter learned that, on the legal jousting fields, powerful corporations enjoyed an immense advantage over the government's undermanned and overworked staff. Even when the evidence clearly supported charges of illegality, the corporate barons could hire teams of lawyers to delay and even defeat justice.[11] The behavior of well-known attorneys such as John G. Milburn and Robert S. Lovett disgusted Frankfurter, and he determined that he would never become a "leader" of the bar since it would require bootlicking the industrial magnates.[12] In such cases he could hardly fail to recall Brandeis's plea for more lawyers willing to serve the public.

Stimson left the U.S. Attorney's office in 1909, shortly after William Howard Taft was sworn in, and took Frankfurter with him, first into private practice and then on an ill-fated campaign for the New York governorship in 1910. By then relations between Taft and Theodore Roosevelt had become strained; in an effort to heal the growing breach within the Republican party, Taft asked Stimson to become secretary of war. With Roosevelt's blessing, Stimson accepted; he took Frankfurter to Washington with him as counsel in the department's Bureau of Insular Affairs, which handled legal matters concerning America's overseas territories.

Felix Frankfurter, not yet 30, arrived in Washington in 1911 with, as one biographer put it, "the aplomb of a sophisticated political veteran."[13] It is true that his experience with Stimson, both in the U.S. Attorney's office and in the gubernatorial campaign, had given him a rare look at the inner workings of government, as well as the opportunity to meet a number of important people. His own innate shrewdness had also developed his sense of place and person and his ability to size up a situation, talents that proved particularly useful in Washington. He somewhat self-consciously began to keep a diary, recording his observations about the conversations with the mighty. "Ran into the Solicitor General, Mr. Lehmann, and had good talk with him about the Supreme Court vacancy, Taft and the Sherman Law," ran a typical entry.[14]

Stimson and Frankfurter began their new responsibilities with a trip on the USS *North Carolina* to Cuba, Haiti, San Domingo, and then to the opening of the Panama Canal. Just as he had in the U.S. Attorney's office, Frankfurter served as Stimson's "special assistant on all sorts of things."[15] He also had some specific duties relating to the administration of American territories; in his first appearance before the Supreme Court, he successfully defended the government of Puerto Rico against a suit by former landowners seeking to recover rents and profits on old property claims.[16]

We need not examine in detail Frankfurter's work in the War Department, but it should be noted that in general he accepted unquestioningly the paternalistic imperialism espoused by Stimson, tempered by a belief that the United States should adopt the policy of moving its possessions toward some form of autonomous government. He seemed not to have been touched or bothered either by the anti-imperialism endemic among many liberals or by antimilitarism. In the War Department he came into daily contact with army officers, all of whom he initially called "General" because he could not distinguish between a lieutenant and a colonel. He realized that while some could legitimately be considered heroes, such as the legendary chief of staff, Gen. Leonard Wood, others, such as his immediate superior, Maj. Gen. Clarence Edwards, were "extremely superficial," with narrow political vision.[17]

More important than his work in the War Department, Frankfurter extended his circle of acquaintances to include men who would be very important in his future. A letter of introduction from his old professor, John Chipman Gray, allowed him to meet Oliver Wendell Holmes, thus beginning a friendship that would last until the jurist's death a quarter-century later and that Frankfurter would always cherish. The younger man went often to the Holmes house and there listened to that "wonderful stream of exciting flow of ideas in words." Frankfurter adored Holmes—who stood, in Frankfurter's view, for the best of Brahmin culture—and he let Holmes know his feelings. The older man in turn enjoyed Frankfurter's company and hearing the latest political gossip and once told him that "it will be many years before you have occasion to know the happiness and encouragement that comes to an old man from the sympathy of the young. . . . I am quite sincere in saying you have done a great deal for me in that way and I send you my gratitude and thanks."[18]

Frankfurter lived in a house at 1727 Nineteenth St. owned by the brilliant Robert G. Valentine, then commissioner of Indian Affairs. Other boarders included Winfred T. Denison, as assistant attorney general, Loring C. Christie, a Canadian who had graduated from Harvard Law School and was Denison's assistant, and Lord Eustace Percy, then posted to the British embassy. At almost any time of the day or night, exciting conversation could be found at the "House of Truth," as Justice Holmes dubbed it. Holmes and his wife came there, as did many government officials, reformers, artists, and writers. There Gutzon Borglum sketched out his proposed presidential monument in the Black Hills of South Dakota, and the writer Herbert Croly expounded on his vision of American life. Walter Lippmann, soon to join with Croly in founding the *New Republic,* was a frequent visitor, as was Louis Brandeis, then at the peak of his reform career.

Much of the talk was political; although Frankfurter and others held positions in the Taft administration, they had little respect for the President, his policies, and especially his politics. Nearly all of them supported Theodore Roosevelt in the 1912 election, and Frankfurter even wanted to quit his job to campaign for the colonel, a rash choice that Stimson convinced him would do neither him nor Roosevelt much good.

Besides, Stimson declared, he needed Frankfurter "in clinching the important but little understood reforms upon which you and I have been working during the past eighteen months."[19]

Not everyone shared the enthusiasm for Roosevelt. Louis Brandeis had become Woodrow Wilson's chief advisor on economic matters, and in opposition to the New Nationalism's acceptance of monopoly and its proposal to create a countervailing federal regulatory power, he argued for creating strict rules of competition to prevent the growth of large business.[20] Brandeis tried to talk Frankfurter out of his infatuation with Roosevelt and the New Nationalism and to assure him that progressivism would best be served by the election of Wilson.[21]

With Wilson's election, Frankfurter faced the agonizing question of what he would do after 4 March 1913. Stimson would return to his New York firm, but the thought of private practice had no appeal for his assistant. "I can't quite become a crusader for the rule in Shelley's case," he told his friend Emory Buckner, "or shipwreck a friendship . . . through disagreement on a picayune point of pleading." To another friend he condemned private practice as "putting one's time in to put money in other people's pockets."[22]

The quandary ended, at least temporarily, when the new secretary of war, Lindley M. Garrison, asked Frankfurter to stay. Garrison, Frankfurter said, seemed to be "a real man, and he wants me to help on two or three questions that have become very near to me."[23] So he stayed in government service, and the House of Truth continued to attract intelligent and influential people, as well as young people passing through Washington. One of these was the bright, attractive Marion Denman, who had recently graduated from Smith College. Witty, agnostic, the daughter of a Congregational minister with roots going back to colonial times, she immediately caught Frankfurter's attention. He fell in love with her and determinedly set out to win her, a task that took him six years.

But without Stimson, and working under the burden of not having been a Wilson supporter, Frankfurter did not enjoy Washington as much as he had earlier. He recognized that he had no future in the Democratic administration and did not care much for the new president. Then in the summer of 1913 his friend and housemate, Winfred Denison, wrote to Edward Warren, a professor at Harvard Law School, suggesting that Frankfurter would be ideal for the faculty. Warren wrote back that the faculty had met to consider the idea and concluded that, "to a man, we want Frankfurter."[24]

The faculty's enthusiasm, aside from that of those who recalled Frankfurter's outstanding academic record, derived from a talk he had given the year before at the twenty-fifth anniversary dinner of the *Harvard Law Review*. He had called for a law alive to changing economic and social conditions. The "facts" of an industrializing world are constantly changing, and so the law cannot be static. "So called immutable principles must accommodate themselves to facts of life, for facts are stubborn and will not yield." Courts have to stop imposing their own views of economic theory on legislation that has been designed to deal with the real, rather than an abstract world. Legislators might make mistakes, but legislation by its nature is often experimental, and "the Constitution was not intended to limit this field of experimentation."[25]

The ideas were hardly revolutionary; they echoed the sentiments of Holmes, Brandeis, and one of Harvard's latest acquisitions, Roscoe Pound, a botanist turned legal philosopher who expounded the ideas of "sociological jurisprudence."[26] But the *Law Review* talk demonstrated to faculty members that Frankfurter, already something of a legend at Harvard, fully shared their progressive views on the need to keep the law abreast of the times.

The only problem, Warren explained to Denison, was that there were no openings; money would have to be raised to create a new position. Denison broached the idea to Frankfurter for the first time, and the dean of Harvard Law, Ezra Thayer, approached Stimson for aid in securing the necessary funds. Throughout the fall and winter of 1913–14 an elaborate dance proceeded as Frankfurter and his friends debated the wisdom of whether, if the funds could be raised, he should accept a professorship.

Nearly all of them advised against it. Stimson considered academic life insulated from the real world; "American problems are brewing" in Washington, not Cambridge, "and you must not lose touch with it." Holmes, who had not particularly enjoyed his own brief stint at Harvard, wrote that "academic life is but half-life—it is withdrawal from the fight in order to utter smart things that cost you nothing." Learned Hand and Herbert Croly, as well as Theodore Roosevelt, also spoke against the idea.[27]

Frankfurter himself did not claim any talents as a scholar, but he sensed that great changes in the law could be influenced by teachers, and that "the big public aspect of what should be done by our law schools" might provide an opportunity for useful service. In this he received constant encouragement from Louis Brandeis, who quietly prodded Stimson and others to raise money, a task that he felt disqualified from because of his own recent tilts against the banking community.[28] When Frankfurter worriedly maintained that he did not have the necessary qualifications, Brandeis quietly responded, "I would let those who have the responsibilities for selecting you decide your qualifications and not have you decide that."[29]

In the end, after much consultation and soul-searching, Frankfurter decided to accept. He did not want to go into private practice, and he did not want to stay in Washington. Moreover, he did not see Harvard as a permanent commitment; rather, it would give him time to think about the future while participating in the intellectual give-and-take he loved so much. He would be back in Cambridge, where he felt most comfortable, and from which he would be able to continue his courtship of Marion Denman. Not least, he believed that opportunities to do good work for law and reform could be found in the law schools. In the summer of 1914 he packed his bags and moved to Cambridge, where he spent the remaining weeks before the fall term in the law library, catching up on the cases decided since his graduation eight years earlier.

Anyone who thought that Frankfurter would retire into an academic cloister did not know him; even before classes met he began pursuing an extracurricular schedule that, by itself, would have buried an ordinary man. He was involved from the beginning with the *New Republic,* and although he turned down Herbert Croly's invitation to be one of the journal's editors, along with Walter Lippmann and Walter Weyl, he in essence became a fourth editor, writing numerous pieces and often sitting in on editorial meetings.[30] Along with Croly and Weyl, he took a day off from the stacks on 4 August 1914 to journey to Sagamore Hill, where Theodore Roosevelt had invited them to explain some labor problems to him. That day, however, the conversation focused on the tense situation in Europe.

When the war broke out a few weeks later, Louis Brandeis assumed the leadership of the fledgling American Zionist movement and brought in as one of his lieutenants Felix Frankfurter. It seems clear that Frankfurter never had any great emotional attachment to either Judaism[31] or Zionism, and his involvement in the movement lasted only as long as Brandeis provided leadership.[32] When Wilson named Brandeis to the Supreme Court in 1916, Frankfurter took a leading role in mobilizing progressive sentiment in favor of the nomination and in rebutting conservative charges against the "people's attorney."[33]

With Brandeis on the Court, Frankfurter inherited the role of attorney for the people. He took over the defense of progressive legislation for the National Consumers' League, for which Brandeis had presented the nontraditional, fact-laden brief in defense of an Oregon wage law in the famous case of *Muller v. Oregon* (1908).[34] After that decision, the Court had proven fairly sympathetic to protective legislation. Brandeis had defended the Oregon minimum wage law before the high court in 1914, but the death of Justice Horace Lurton and the increasing influence of the conservative bloc had led the Court to reschedule argument on the minimum wage, as well as on a 10-hour law, for January 1917. Frankfurter took over the cases as unpaid counsel and completed the unfinished briefs with the aid of Josephine Goldmark and Florence Kelley, two of the Consumers' League leaders and trusted associates of Brandeis. A correspondent for the *Nation* reported his impression of Frankfurter's oral argument before the high court: "That august tribunal listen[ed] intently to the plea of a small, dark, smooth-faced lawyer, mostly head, eyes and glasses, who looked as if he had stepped out of the sophomore classroom of a neighboring college. He lectured the Court quietly, but with a due sense of its indebtedness to him for setting it right where it had been wrong. . . . He was becomingly tolerant when the gray-haired learners asked questions which seemed to him unnecessary, and gentle when he had to correct a mistaken assumption."[35] He won a solid 5–3 victory in the 10-hour case, where a clear line of precedents supported such legislation, but the justices split 4–4 on the wage law,[36] leaving it intact until the issue presented itself again in another context.

All this activity, in addition to his regular teaching duties, led the political theorist Harold Laski to marvel that "Felix is a world in himself," and also to worry about his friend's pace. "He is always nervously restless, dashing here and there in a kind of creative fertility that drives me to despair. . . To [go to] New York three times in one week is a drain I wonder whether even he can stand."[37]

Although these were exciting years as he started his academic and public service careers, Frankfurter also found them troubling in many ways. In his personal life, his father died, and in wooing Marion Denman he had to fight to get out from under his mother's smothering influence, a fight he did not completely win for several years.[38] As President Wilson tried to steer a path through the shoals of international events, Frankfurter deplored both the naïveté of William Jennings Bryan's pacifism and the shrill militarism of Theodore Roosevelt. When the United States entered the war in April 1917, he, like many other progressives, was relieved that a decision had finally been made and believed that the war experience would foster democracy both at home and abroad.

In 1914 Frankfurter had accepted a commission as a major in the army reserves in the Judge Advocate General's office. A few days after Wilson's war message, Secretary of War Newton D. Baker summoned Frankfurter to Washington. A former progressive mayor of Cleveland, Baker had headed the National Consumers' League and thus knew Frankfurter well. Baker wanted him in the same job he had had with Stimson, a general-purpose assistant. He first asked Frankfurter to prepare a memorandum on the handling of conscientious objectors. Baker then sent him to Gibraltar along with the former American ambassador to Turkey, Henry Morgenthau, who naively believed that he could detach the Ottomans from the Central Powers and negotiate a separate peace. They were also to look into the problems of the Jewish colonies in Palestine to ascertain the best means of providing relief to the economically hardpressed settlers. To nearly everyone's relief, the mission collapsed after six weeks of talk with the British in Gibraltar. From Frankfurter's point of view, the only saving grace of the trip had been meeting the Zionist leader Chaim Weizmann, who impressed him enormously.[39]

Baker next named Frankfurter as secretary and counsel to the Mediation Commission, which President Wilson had established to deal with strikes in defense-related industries. Along with his assistant, Max Lowenthal, and Secretary of Labor William B. Wilson, Frankfurter traveled west where strikes had crippled the Arizona copper mines.[40] Rather than deal with the miners' complaints, management had branded the strikers as radicals and pro-German and had organized its own henchmen in the small mining towns to get rid of labor activists. The worst case was in Bisbee, Arizona, where the Phelps Dodge Company had persuaded the town's merchants and its sheriff to round up and deport over 1,000 striking miners and their sympathizers. Sheriff Harry Wheeler organized a posse, loaded the strikers into cattle cars, and dumped them, without food or water, in the middle of a New Mexico desert. Phelps Dodge then arranged what could only be described as a kangaroo court to rid Bisbee of any remaining union members, as well as citizens who protested against the company's high-handedness. Even Gov. William Campbell, who had shown no previous sympathy for the strikers, desclared his shock at this lawlessness.

Frankfurter and Lowenthal lived for several months in a railway car while they and other commission members patiently negotiated a settlement. Frankfurter was less than happy with the final agreement, which he believed did not protect worker interests sufficiently, but it satisfied the mine owners and the American Federation of Labor (AFL) representatives, whose main concern seemed to be to freeze out the militant Industrial Workers of the World (IWW). Even if the final agreement had been better, the commission had no enforcement powers, and after it left the companies enforced the agreement as they saw fit.[41]

The Mediation Commission had better luck in resolving some other disputes on the West Coast, but it was never as successful as Frankfurter remembered it decades later.[42] At best, its presence temporarily ameliorated some of the worst employer abuses, but it had neither the power nor the mandate to impose significant labor-management reforms. Moreover, the war hysteria against aliens and radicals, fostered in part by the Wilson administration, played right into the hands of management, which consistently portrayed labor activists as radicals. In fact, Frankfurter himself would up smeared by that brush.

Tom Mooney and Warren Billings, IWW members and labor organizers, had been tried and convicted of murder in San Francisco for their alleged role in the 1916 Preparedness Day bombing that killed 10 people and wounded 40 others.[43] Their trial took place amid not only the war frenzy whipped up by the Hearst-owned *Examiner* but against the background of a history of labor unrest in the city. The prosecutor portrayed the case as a confrontation between respectable law and order on the one hand and radical anarchy on the other. The jury convicted the two men, and the presiding judge promptly sentenced them to hang.

The two might have been executed quickly had it not been for the public protests of the anarchists Emma Goldman and Alexander Berkman, who uncovered evidence that the prosecution's chief witness had lied. Goldman and Berkman used their anarchist connections overseas to organize mass protests, including one before the American embassy in Russia that led the Kerensky government to ask Woodrow Wilson to intervene. Wilson gave this task to the Mediation Commission, and he specifically asked Frankfurter, as the commission's counsel, to look into what had happened.

Frankfurter had never heard of Mooney and in fact had to ask how the name was spelled. When he got to California and began interviewing people, he soon realized that the prosecution had not only exploited the wartime hysteria against radicals but had built its case against Mooney on perjured testimony. Frankfurter drafted the commission's report to the president, urging a pardon for Mooney and a retrial. He did not argue

Mooney's guilt or innocence but declared that such trials undermined the nation's moral standards. "We are in this war," he declared, "to vindicate the moral claims of unstained processes of law, however slow, at times, such processes may be. These claims must be tempered by the fire of our own devotion."[44]

The Mooney report, as well as Frankfurter's earlier condemnation of the Bisbee deportations, evoked the outrage of conservatives. Theodore Roosevelt was particularly upset by the Bisbee report because it singled out for criticism Jack Greenway, a former Rough Rider whose wife, Isabella Selmes, had long been a close friend of the Roosevelt family. The aging ex-president, who had once been one of Frankfurter's heroes, now accused him in a public letter of "an attitude which seems to me to be fundamentally that of Trotsky and the other Bolshevik leaders in Russia."[45] A few years later Solicitor General of the United States James M. Beck continued the attack on Frankfurter, eliciting an extensive public defense by the Harvard professor of his role in the case.[46]

Despite the attack on Frankfurter and the Mediation Commission, Woodrow Wilson recognized that the members had tried to be fair in their handling of some very difficult situations. The inability of the commission to operate more effectively, Frankfurter believed, reflected the administration's general ineptitude in gearing up for the war.[47] Resources had to be mobilized and the government's power utilized to harness different interests and make them work cooperatively. "The confusion of authority," he lamented to Brandeis, "the haphazardness, the multiplicity of agencies without a central direction, cannot go on much longer."[48]

Part of the problem derived from the inexperience of the United States in waging such a war, although its leaders could have learned a great deal from the experience of the Allies in their mobilization efforts. Equally important was the Wilson administration's ideological opposition to big government and its unwillingness to recognize that the successful prosecution of the war demanded large-scale, centralized power. When Newton D. Baker asked Frankfurter for a frank assessment of the War Department's efficacy in early 1918, he got more than he expected.

The secretary was trying to do too much, Frankfurter told Baker, and as a result had become the great bottleneck in the procurement process. Moreover, trapped in a morass of detail, he had failed to provide overall leadership in meeting the problems of production and distribution. Frankfurter recommended strengthening the War Industries Board and getting the War Department out of the business of overseeing production and distribution of war materials. Moreover, the joint use of the

Mediation Commission by the War and Labor departments did not work because the two agencies had different and often contradictory expectations. A new agency, headed by a single administrator, should be created to deal with wartime labor difficulties. Two days later Justice Brandeis, in response to a request from the White House, weighed in with a similar proposal.[49]

The administration, under heavy criticism for its ineffective management of industrial resources, finally took the necessary steps to put the nation's economy on a war footing. It reorganized and strengthened the War Industries Board and made the financier Bernard Baruch "czar" of war production. While Wilson's advisors generally agreed on what had to be done for the production end, they differed widely on what to do about labor. Frankfurter's plan had the simplicity of providing a labor czar equivalent to the industrial czar, but it ran into the immediate opposition of business and labor interests alike. Businessmen feared that a strong labor administrator would force them to adopt wages and hours guidelines, as well as recognize labor unions. The AFL, with the help of Secretary of Labor Wilson, had placed its people in key spots in the existing labor agencies and did not want to lose the power it had to affect government policy. The final arrangement did set up two new agencies but did not give either of them the power Frankfurter had recommended; the existing labor boards kept much of their authority.

To mediate strikes, President Wilson set up the War Labor Board, jointly chaired by William Howard Taft and Frank Walsh. While the board proved effective in negotiating settlements to a number of labor disputes, it had no authority to set policy guidelines. As a result, the chaos over labor standards continued to plague administration efforts to increase war production. Finally, in May 1918, Wilson created the War Labor Policies Board, composed of representatives from all government agencies with production responsibilities, and named Frankfurter its chairman.

Frankfurter now had his opportunity to influence government policy, and he intended to make the most of it. Just as the War Industries Board reflected the aspirations of businessmen, so the War Labor Policies Board would serve as a countervailing force, reflecting the hopes of organized labor. In a bulletin issued a few weeks after he took office, Frankfurter declared that "in seeking standardization [of wages and working conditions] the precedents of unionized industry are being followed."[50]

Despite such statements and Frankfurter's work in Bisbee and on behalf of Tom Mooney, a number of labor leaders distrusted the new agency and its head. In his earlier work with the Mediation Commission,

Frankfurter had come across as intensely patriotic and a tough negotiator, someone who would not hesitate to invoke the flag to force unacceptable contracts on workers. Leaders of powerful unions, such as the machinists, whose workers had benefited from generous wartime agreements, feared that management had concocted the War Labor Policies Board to force a maximum wage. They preferred to keep the decentralized system then in effect, which could be manipulated by strong unions to their members' benefit, rather than cede power to a centralized program, regardless of its efficiency and the contribution it made to war production.

Those opposed to the War Labor Policies Board, whether union or management, need not have been concerned. Frankfurter did not have time to overcome interagency jealousies and develop a unified policy for the government. A conference of all the various federal labor boards did not convene until October 1918, and efforts to establish uniform policies died with the armistice. Frankfurter had greater success in organizing the regional boards in the metal and building trades that promulgated wage standards for both government and private industry.[51] The board also tackled the problem of the eight-hour day, which had become a central demand of American labor, and in doing so pitted Frankfurter against the powerful head of U.S. Steel, Judge Elbert H. Gary.

Actually, the giant Morgan-sponsored firm had been a pioneer in such industrial reforms as accident prevention, health programs, sanitation, and insurance, and its wages had risen steadily for a decade. But the steel industry in general, and U.S. Steel in particular, had a long record of antiunion activities, and even wartime patriotism did not lead the big steel makers to drop their animus and offer to work with the unions. Management acknowledged its responsibilities, but in the manner of ancient feudal lords looking after their serfs.[52]

In May 1918 Secretary of Labor Wilson directed Frankfurter to tackle the problem of wage differentials in industry, including the standardization of the workday.[53] The steel makers still had a 12-hour day, with the infamous 24-hour crossover every two weeks when the night and day shifts switched. Frankfurter wrote Judge Gary early in July suggesting a meeting and hinting that since the War Labor Policies Board would enforce any new standard, it would be to the industry's benefit to cooperate.[54] Gary delayed the meeting all that summer but finally came to Washington to see Frankfurter on 20 September; Gary would look back on the meeting as one of the most frustrating and humiliating experiences of his life.

Calmly and methodically, Frankfurter lectured one of the most powerful industrial barons of his time on the trend toward an eight-hour day, its adoption by enlightened employers, and its sanctioning by the government. Gary, in turn, angrily denounced the whole concept as a fraud to get higher wages. At one point, he asked:

"Professor Frankfurter, you work more than eight hours every day."

"That happens to be so," Frankfurter agreed.

"I work more than eight hours every day. You and I work more than eight hours every day. Why shouldn't these men in the factories?"

"Ah, Judge Gary," said Frankfurter, "but think what interesting jobs you and I have."[55]

When Frankfurter questioned whether the steel leaders would disobey a government mandate, Gary knew the game was up. Saying that he would have to consult with his colleagues, he promised to do what he could.[56] Five days later U.S. Steel announced that it would adopt the basic eight-hour day on 1 October; Frankfurter triumphantly telegraphed the news to Secretary Wilson.

Frankfurter knew that given the shortage of workers during the war, it would be impossible for steel makers to abandon the 12-hour shift, and in fact they did not. They kept the longer shift but paid workers an hourly premium for the last four hours. Frankfurter rather naively believed that once the war ended, the industry would adopt a true eight-hour day. In fact, just the opposite happened. No sooner had the armistice been announced than steel companies began informing the government and labor that the wartime agreements were dead. The resulting dissatisfaction among workers spread until it erupted in the bitter and violent steel strike of 1919.[57]

The crisis attitude of the war evaporated within hours upon news of the armistice, and with it any hope that the government would continue to use its powers to pursue the progressive labor agenda of minimum wages, maximum hours, and union recognition. President Wilson and most of his advisors had never been that comfortable with the powerful government they had had to create during the war, and they set about dismantling the wartime agencies as fast as they could. When congressional leaders asked about administration plans to convert industry back to a peacetime basis, they were told that the reconstruction would take care of itself.[58]

Those who, like Frankfurter, hoped that the war agencies would at least be kept going to cement wartime gains soon lost heart. In January a disgusted Frankfurter wrote to his friend Learned Hand that "the starch is out of the administration, [and] cold feet prevail on a wide area." Wilson had gone in pursuit of his vision of world order, and "his paralyzed subordinates . . . have practically announced bankruptcy and have invited the Republicans as receivers. God help us!"[59] In February Frankfurter resigned.

Before he could return to Harvard, however, Frankfurter found himself drawn into the peacemaking process. He had, in fact, already been sent overseas in March 1918 by Col. Edward M. House, Wilson's shadowy confidant, to explore the attitude of European labor groups toward the president's Fourteen Points peace proposal. At the time he had accurately perceived that the French and British governments had little sympathy with Wilsonian ideals, but he believed that the masses stood solidly behind the American president; unfortunately, they had no means of organization by which to express their support. Frankfurter claimed that Wilson could tap this vast reservoir of goodwill if he mobilized the labor unions in the Allied countries—in effect, going over the hands of the elected political leaders.[60]

Frankfurter's involvement with the peace negotiations, however, resulted not from his ties to the Wilson administration but from his ongoing relationship with American Zionism as one of Louis D. Brandeis's most trusted lieutenants. Frankfurter had not been visibly active in Zionist activities during the war years because of his jobs in the War Department and then as head of the War Labor Policies Board. But he had stayed in touch and had quietly played an important role in the movement. During the touchy negotiations over Woodrow Wilson's endorsement of the Balfour Declaration, Frankfurter argued against bringing direct pressure on the President for all-out approval, since Wilson would just dig in his heels and refuse to budge.[61]

Although the Balfour Declaration had seemingly promised Palestine to the Jews after the war, the Zionists recognized that the British policy could be defeated at the peace conference. Nascent Arab nationalism might have to be placated, while the French would certainly not hand over a geographically crucial area to their arch rivals for influence in the Middle East. Moreover, Protestant missionary groups, with their allies in the State Department, objected to placing "the tomb of the Founder of Christianity under the domination of his murderers."[62] Finally, how could the Wilsonian principle of self-determination allow the establishment of a Jewish homeland in a predominantly Arab area?

In January and February 1919 the air was filled with rumors and counterrumors about the future of Palestine. Brandeis finally decided that he needed someone he could trust in Paris to keep an eye not just on international developments but on the European Zionists as well. As soon as Frankfurter had cleared his office at the War Labor Policies Board, Brandeis dispatched him to Paris to hold, as Frankfurter later described it, "a 'watching' brief for Zionists before the Peace Conference."[63] He also kept an eye on the European Zionists.

Frankfurter had met Chaim Weizmann, the acknowledged leader of European Zionism, during the Morgenthau mission two years earlier, and the two men had taken a liking to each other that would survive the Brandeis-Weizmann feud of the next 20 years. While Weizmann acknowledged that American Jewry had become the great reservoir of Zionist strength, the Europeans still considered them parvenus and did not want to admit them as equals. At Paris in the early spring of 1919, Weizmann, Nahum Sokolow, and others ignored American proposals for the economic development of Palestine and for the peace treaty. When the Zionist delegation appeared before the Council of Ten on 27 February, Frankfurter did not go with them. Secretary of State Robert Lansing offered to make more time available for Frankfurter to testify, but Weizmann firmly told him it would be unnecessary.

Yet it was Frankfurter who did much of the crucial drafting of Zionist memoranda and proposals. He knew many of the staff on the American delegation and mingled with them easily, helping to counterbalance some of the anti-Zionist material they received. Had the Europeans trusted him more, much of the internal friction that plagued the Zionists might have been avoided. Frankfurter, by this time an experienced bureaucrat, understood the nuances and requirements of government documents. Many of the Europeans had a less than perfect knowledge of English, yet they insisted on amending Frankfurter's drafts. Worse, their idea of compromise often consisted of adding together the various proposals, with no regard for internal consistency.

Frankfurter believed that Arab friendship and support of Zionism would be necessary for the Jewish colonies in Palestine to grow into a true homeland. Unlike some of his more naive colleagues, Frankfurter understood that British, Arab, and Zionist interests did not necessarily mesh, and that the Zionists, being the weakest of the three, would probably emerge the losers in any conflict. He tried to learn more about the Arabs and through T. E. Lawrence, the legendary "Lawrence of Arabia," arranged for an interview with Prince Faisal. The three met at Faisal's villa, and Frankfurter secured from the prince a letter promising Arab cooperation with the Jews in building up Palestine.[64]

Promises, either from the British or the Arabs, would not make Palestine a Jewish homeland; only the development of a thriving Jewish settlement there could turn the vision of Theodor Herzl, the founder of Zionism, into a reality. Frankfurter thus seized upon the idea of a Hebrew university in Jerusalem, an idea initially propounded by Chaim Weizmann, as a perfect device to build a visible institution as well as foster better relations between the American and European Zionists. He hectored American Zionist officials to send money, and more money, to help get the university off the ground, and he lobbied American officials to secure the safe delivery of funds from the United States to Palestine.

That spring in Paris proved alternately heady and frustrating, exhilarating and depressing. Like many liberals, Frankfurter believed Wilson was stumbling badly in negotiating the peace treaty. He later recalled that he and William Westermann, a Cornell University history professor on the American delegation staff, "used to walk the beguiling streets of Paris by the hour bemoaning what seemed to us the needless compromises made by the Big Four and by President Wilson, swapping our sorrows and encouraging one another's hopes."[65]

But for the most part Frankfurter had little time to worry as he scurried endlessly back and forth between the Zionist and American headquarters, met regularly with foreign officials, negotiated the northern boundary of the proposed Palestinian homeland, convinced Brandeis that it was absolutely necessary for the justice to travel to Palestine and Europe that summer,[66] helped quash a virulently anti-Zionist report,[67] and tried to keep the different Zionist factions from killing each other.[68] Then came the arrival of several American Jewish groups, including Henry Morgenthau bearing an anti-Zionist petition from Reform Jews as well as a delegation of Orthodox rabbis also opposed to Zionism. To compound the difficulties, President Wilson, by now aware of the contradictions between the promise of a Jewish homeland and self-determination, seemed to be backing off from his earlier commitment.

A troubled Frankfurter, trying to keep at least the American government in back of the Zionist proposals, wrote two lengthy letters to Wilson, begging him to reaffirm his earlier promises of justice for the Jews after the war. Wilson, somewhat surprised at the vehemence of Frankfurter's missive, nonetheless gave the desired reassurances.[69]

Although in the ensuing schism between Brandeis and Weizmann Frankfurter would stand with Brandeis, his work in Paris made him better known—and better liked—than any of Brandeis's other lieutenants.[70] He withdrew from active Zionist affairs along with the other Brandeisians following their defeat at the 1921 Zionist convention, but unlike them he never returned to an active role in the movement. Nonetheless, during and after World War II he quietly helped the Zionists in their efforts to save European Jewry and then to secure U.N. support for the establishment of a Jewish state.

When Frankfurter returned to Harvard in the fall of 1919, he was far different from the man he'd been when he left. In 1917 he was still a wunderkind, the bright young law school graduate who had been Mr. Stimson's assistant and pals with the literary and political intellectuals of the House of Truth and the *New Republic*. Progressive politics had been a great game, but while the stakes had been important, it paled in comparison to what he had been fighting for during the war years. He had seen firsthand the violent bigotry directed at suspected radicals and the hatred between labor and management. He had been not only an aide to the secretary of war but an important figure in his own right in the effort to mobilize American resources for the war. He had been an eyewitness to the drama at Paris and had played a key role in moving the Zionist dream closer to reality. The young man from the provinces had been tested under very trying conditions and had succeeded well, some even said brilliantly. Prior to the war Frankfurter had often been in the shadow of others, a sort of apprentice; no one could doubt in 1919 that his apprenticeship had ended.

2

"THE MOST USEFUL LAWYER"

The two decades Frankfurter spent at Harvard Law School between World War I and his appointment to the Supreme Court proved extremely productive as well as personally and professionally satisfying. He established a scholarly reputation as one of the nation's more perceptive observers of the Supreme Court; he maintained his credentials as a leading academic liberal, most notably in his involvement in the Sacco-Vanzetti affair; and his efforts at placing his "boys," combined with his friendship with Franklin Roosevelt, made him a key figure in the heyday of the New Deal. It is little wonder that during this period Louis Brandeis considered Felix Frankfurter "the most useful lawyer in the United States."[1]

Frankfurter returned to Harvard Law School during the Red Scare that tore America apart in 1919 and 1920, and he soon found himself condemned as a radical.[2] Given the hysteria of the time, his defense of labor during the war and his role in the Mooney case would have been enough to brand him as dangerous in the eyes of proper Brahmins. "Old Boston is unregenerate," Brandeis told his wife after meeting with Roscoe Pound. "F.F. is evidently considered by the elect as 'dangerous' as I was."[3] Although Frankfurter did not seek a confrontation with the conservative establishment, neither did he run away from the fight.

He quickly aroused conservative ire when he presided over an Armistice Day rally at Faneuil Hall called to urge the Wilson administration to extend diplomatic recognition to the Soviet Union. Although many in the audience may have been radicals, the meeting had been organized by ultrarespectable members of the Brahmin elite. "I dare say I shall be called a Bolsheviki," Frankfurter told the crowd, but, he then assured his listeners, "I have no patience for the Bolshevik form of government." Military intervention, however, violated American principles, especially the ideal of self-determination. Russians should be left alone to determine their own fate.[4]

In the midst of making plans for his December wedding to Marion Denman, Frankfurter defended clothing workers on strike in Rochester, New York,[5] and filed an amicus curiae (friend-of-the-court) brief in the case of William Colyer and 19 other aliens arrested during the raids of Attorney General A. Mitchell Palmer on suspected "reds."[6] Judge George W. Anderson, an old friend of Brandeis, freed the defendants, and his opinion relied in large part of Frankfurter's broad indictment of the illegal methods employed by the Department of Justice. Frankfurter also signed his name, along with 11 other prominent law professors and attorneys, to a devastating critique of Attorney General Palmer and the illegalities perpetuated under his direction by the Justice Department.

The counterattack came, but not directly. Recognizing that Frankfurter would not be intimidated, conservatives went after his younger colleague on the Harvard Law faculty, Zechariah Chafee, Jr., who had collaborated with Frankfurter in preparing the Colyer brief as well as the indictment of the Justice Department. Chafee had also written several articles for the *Harvard Law Review*, later expanded into his classic *Freedom of Speech* (1920), that criticized the Supreme Court's decisions upholding the Wilson administration's wartime restrictions on speech and the press.[7]

In the spring of 1921 Austen Fox, a conservative New York attorney, and 20 other law school alumni asked the Harvard Board of Overseers to determine Chafee's "fitness to teach" in light of his radicalism and "reckless indifference to the truth." The message was clear: if Chafee could be silenced, so could any other member of the faculty, no matter how prominent. The overseers asked their Committee to Visit the Law School to look into the charges; by a narrow vote, it "acquitted" Chafee by dismissing all of Fox's charges. Frankfurter, who had been advising Chafee throughout the ordeal, recognized the seriousness of the threat and wished that the committee had been more emphatic in its defense of academic freedom.[8] Chafee, thoroughly dispirited by the attack, considered resigning, but Frankfurter called on Holmes and Brandeis to reassure him that the fight had been worthwhile.[9] Chafee stayed on to become the foremost academic champion of free speech in the first half of this century.

Frankfurter, despite the charges, was anything but a radical. This is not to say that he lacked courage; it took a great deal of courage to speak out in defense of aliens and to take on powerful adversaries such as Judge Gary and A. Mitchell Palmer. But his defense of people like Tom Mooney, the Bisbee strikers, and William Colyer grew out of a very conservative belief in the rule of law. Frankfurter had no desire to overthrow the system, or even to change it very much. The immigrant boy who had made good believed in the promise of American life; but, as his friend Chafee had put it, he wanted those who benefited from the system to play fair, to play by the rules. This trait can be seen in one of Frankfurter's most publicized undertakings, the defense of Nicola Sacco and Bartolomeo Vanzetti.

The Sacco-Vanzetti case, perhaps more than any other event, delineated the great schism of the 1920s between official and unofficial America, between the advocates of the traditional "America-that-was" and those of the modern "America-that-would-be." Although Frankfurter entered the case rather late, it would affect him and Marion for the rest of their lives.

The two men had been arrested, tried, and convicted for the April 1920 robbery of the Slater Morrill Shoe Company in South Braintree, in which two payroll guards had been shot to death. Both Sacco and Vanzetti had been armed at the time of their arrest, but both also had witnesses who vouched that they had been far from South Braintree at the time of the robbery. The conflicting testimony should have been enough to raise some doubts among the members of the jury, but as people recognized then and later, Sacco and Vanzetti stood trial not for the payroll robbery but for being aliens and anarchists.[10] The presiding judge, Webster Thayer, and the prosecutor, Frederick Katzmann, both displayed considerable prejudice against the pair, as did at least one of the jurors. Walter Ripley, the jury foreman and a former police chief, indicated his belief in the defendants' guilt even before the trial began. When a friend expressed some doubts, Ripley exploded, "Damn them, they ought to hang anyway."[11]

The irregularities in the trial aroused opposition not only among sympathetic radicals but also among some of Boston's more respectable citizens, including a close friend of both Brandeis and Frankfurter, Elizabeth Glendower Evans, whose prodding finally awoke Frankfurter's interest and involvement in the case. In response to her continuous questions about the trial, he at last went and read the record; what he found, he later recalled, "outraged my sensibilities, outraged my whole conviction of what the administration of justice calls for."[12]

The gross unfairness of the trial, the open hostility of the government toward the defendants, and evidence that the prosecution had encouraged perjury on the part of some its witnesses all affronted Frankfurter's near-religious belief in the integrity of the criminal justice system. He wanted the guilty punished, but those in power had to obey the rules, and in this case they most assuredly had not.

William G. Thompson, a respected member of the Boston bar, had filed a motion with the Massachusetts Supreme Judicial Court calling for a new trial; he urged Frankfurter to write an article exposing the legal irregularities that had occurred. Originally, Frankfurter planned to publish the piece in the *New Republic,* which had taken a major role in defending Sacco and Vanzetti.[13] But when Ellery Sedgwick, the editor of the very proper and prestigious *Atlantic Monthly,* expressed interest, Frankfurter quickly agreed to publish it there. One more article on Sacco and Vanzetti in the *New Republic* would be preaching to the converted; in the *Atlantic,* he could hope to provoke thought among the middle and upper classes, the "best people," whose outrage might elicit some action.[14]

The article appeared in March 1927 and was all that the defenders of Sacco and Vanzetti could have desired. Frankfurter coldly analyzed the trial and painstakingly set out proof after proof that Katzmann, with Thayer's support, had undermined the integrity of the criminal justice system in this case. "The prosecutor systematically played on the feelings of the jury by exploiting the unpatriotic and despised beliefs of Sacco and Vanzetti, and the judge allowed him thus to divert and pervert the jury's mind."[15] Citing one incident after another, Frankfurter built up his case that the trial had been a mockery of justice.

Because of the *Atlantic's* respected position, and because Frankfurter concentrated on the legal irregularities of the trial, his article probably had more impact than any of the hundreds of pieces written on the case in the 1920s. Phrases such as "the unpatriotic and despised beliefs of Sacco and Vanzetti" made it clear that Frankfurter did not share their views. He wrote as a professor of law at the nation's preeminent law school, claiming that, from a legal standpoint, the trial of Sacco and Vanzetti had serious flaws. Whether one believed that the "anarchist bastards," as Judge Thayer called them, were guilty of the crime or not, Frankfurter caused many respectable people to think about what had happened. As Michael Parrish notes, "Frankfurter's dissent reached [deep] into the state's establishment. He stirred doubts among State Street lawyers and Beacon Hill bankers that had to be stilled before the commonwealth could carry out the death sentences."[16] Faced by this concern from the "better" people, Gov. Alvan T. Fuller finally acceded to demands that he appoint a committee to review all the evidence in the case.

The article did not go unchallenged, then or later. Dean John Henry Wigmore of Northwestern Law School, a noted expert on evidence and a friend of Judge Thayer's, exploded in a bitter, racist, reactionary, and totally inaccurate attack on Frankfurter in the conservative *Boston Transcript*. Marion, out shopping, saw the headline "Wigmore Attacks Frankfurter" and came rushing home to find her husband nearly finished with his reply. Frank Buxton, the editor of the *Boston Herald*, held the presses for Frankfurter's reply, which in the words of Frankfurter's colleague at the Law School, Samuel Williston, "pulverized" Wigmore. Harvard's president A. Abbott Lowell, who as a member of Governor Fuller's committee would approve Thayer's conduct, told journalist Norman Hapgood that "Wigmore is a fool! He should have known that Frankfurter would be shrewd enough to be accurate."[17]

Frankfurter, as he later admitted, had been initially indifferent to the Sacco-Vanzetti case. "I don't see," he later recalled, "why my wife and I were so calm about it all. At the time it was just a job I took on, the kind of thing that seems to me to be the most natural thing to do, and all the passion, the venom, the hatred of the community passed over our heads almost without awareness."[18] Once involved, however, both he and Marion came to share the passion, and both suffered enormously from it. High-strung to begin with, Marion fell into a deep depression and had the first of several mental collapses that severely strained their marriage.[19]

Those who had suspected Frankfurter of being a subversive in the Bisbee and Mooney affairs now had further "proof" of his radicalism. Following publication of the article, Frankfurter did not retire to his office in Langdell Hall but became active in attempting to keep the condemned men alive in the spring and summer of 1927. The defense committee filed motion after motion, appeal after appeal, trying to get a new trial. When its efforts failed under state procedures, it tried to get a writ of habeas corpus in federal court on the grounds that Judge Thayer's overt prejudice had denied the defendants due process of law.

But the constitutional criteria for criminal procedure in the 1920s had not yet begun to move toward the rigorous protections developed by the Warren Court in the 1960s. Holmes turned down an appeal with the comment that "prejudice on the part of the presiding judge[,] however strong," did not give the Supreme Court power to interfere.[20] Brandeis, who shared Frankfurter's views on the case, also refused to intervene, but for far different reasons. Close friends and members of his family had been heavily involved; with his permission, Mrs. Evans had sheltered the two men's families in a house Brandeis owned in Dedham. Given these circumstances, Brandeis felt he had no choice but to recuse himself completely from the case.[21]

For the journalist Gardner Jackson and others, the failure to save Sacco and Vanzetti pointed up all the ills of a legal system designed not to secure justice but to protect the rights of property and preserve the status quo. All the efforts of major newspapers and journals and responsible citizens had not been enough to save the lives of two presumably innocent men, who had the misfortune of believing in anarchy during a period of national hysteria.[22]

Although Frankfurter recognized that the system could be perverted by the abuse of prosecutorial and judicial power, he never abandoned his faith in the essential rightness of the system. Despite the charges of his supposed radicalism, Frankfurter's basic conservatism is clear. In the Sacco-Vanzetti case, he attacked not the system but its shortcomings, and he did so in a journal of irreproachable middle-class pedigree. The failure to save Sacco and Vanzetti led Frankfurter to call not for an overthrow of the system but for a strict adherence to proper behavior on the part of judges and prosecutors. Only by clinging to law as an instrument of reason and justice could society be saved from the turmoil of prejudice and revolution.

On 2 June 1927, as Louis Brandeis tidied up his affairs before leaving Washington for the summer, he wrote to Frankfurter apologizing for his oversight in not having his secretary deposit money into Frankfurter's special account earlier in the year. Noting Frankfurter's heavy involvement in the Sacco-Vanzetti case, he added that he had "meant to ask you when we meet whether an additional sum might not be appropriate this year. Let me know." While there is no record of Frankfurter's reply, Brandeis did deposit an additional $500 into the special account two months later.[23] In fact, Brandeis had been secretly subsidizing Frankfurter's reform work since 1916, when the Harvard professor had taken over some of Brandeis's work for the National Consumers' League after he had gone onto the Court; the payments would continue until Frankfurter's own appointment to the bench. Scholars knew about these financial arrangements as early as 1975,[24] but the general public did not learn about them until 1982, with the publication of Bruce Allen Murphy's sensationalized *Brandeis/Frankfurter Connection.*[25]

Both men believed in public service, but Brandeis had made his fortune in lucrative law work before he began his career as a reformer. When Brandeis asked Frankfurter to take over some of his reform obligations, he understood that it would be a drain on his friend's limited professorial salary. Traveling from Boston to New York and Washington, paying for additional secretarial help and the printing of legal documents were expenses that Frankfurter would be hard-pressed to bear. Moreover, Brandeis believed that a man first had to provide adequately for his family; after Frankfurter's marriage to Marion Denman, he had familial obligations that took first priority.

As a professor at Harvard Law, Frankfurter could normally have expected to supplement his salary, which ranged between $6,000 and $10,000 a year during this period, by consulting or taking on cases during the summer recess. But to do this work, he could not have had time for reform activities; to do the reform work precluded paid consulting and would, in fact, probably drive away conservative clients. Frankfurter could live without the extra income, but he could not afford to bear the incidental expenses of *pro bono* work.

Brandeis first broached the subject in November 1916. "My dear Felix," the justice wrote, "You have had considerable expense for travelling, telephoning and similar expenses in public matters undertaken at my request or following up my suggestions & will have more in the future no doubt. These expenses should, of course, be borne by me. I am sending check for $250 on this account. Let me know when it is exhausted or if it already has been."[26] Frankfurter evidently did not want to take the money, perhaps out of pride, perhaps unaware of how burdensome these expenses would be, and sent the check back. A week later Brandeis wrote him again, urging him to take the check:

26

In essence this is nothing different than your taking travelling and incidental expenses from the Consumers League or the New Republic—which I trust you do. You are giving your very valuable time and that is quite enough. It can make no difference that the subject matter in connection with which expense is incurred is more definite in one case than in the other.

I ought to feel free to make suggestions to you, although they involve some incidental expense. And you should feel free to incur expense in the public interest. So I am returning the check.[27]

This time Frankfurter acceded; he in essence would become Brandeis's surrogate for reform for the next 20 years. The arrangement raises questions of propriety regarding both men.[28]

To put the worst possible interpretation on this arrangement, one might argue that Brandeis, constrained by the limits of judicial propriety, could no longer be the political agent he had been before he donned the black robe and so hired Frankfurter to be his surrogate, bombarding the younger man with one letter after another on causes to support, articles to write, people to see.[29] But it is clear that Frankfurter did not have the time to follow up more than a handful of these ideas, nor did Brandeis expect him to. In no letter do we find anything approaching a command that Frankfurter do a particular task. Rather, we find two men who, despite some significant differences, shared basically the same outlook on American society and also shared a passionate commitment to using the law to make that society as free and just and equitable as possible.

Moreover, the money could by no stretch of the imagination be considered a retainer or even a salary supplement.[30] Brandeis never asked for any accounting, nor did he expect one. The money covered reform-related expenses and, with one exception, never went into Frankfurter's pocket. That exception involved heavy medical bills Frankfurter faced for one of Marion's illnesses, and he turned to Brandeis for help, which was immediately forthcoming.[31]

One can argue that Brandeis did little more than make it possible for his protégé to do the type of work they both believed necessary in a democratic society. Anyone who has even cursorily studied Felix Frankfurter will concede that while he could often be obsequious and fawning, he had far too large an ego to be anyone's unquestioning and obedient servant. He willingly adopted some of Brandeis's causes because he believed in them. He wrote articles that Brandeis suggested because he agreed that certain things needed to be said or explained to the public.

And when he felt passionate about a cause, such as the Sacco-Vanzetti case, he did not need Brandeis's encouragement or approval to get involved.

Nonetheless, one can raise legitimate questions about the image that Frankfurter created about himself as an independent, one who acted solely on his own prerogative. On many occasions he proudly trumpeted the independence of the university in general and of law school faculty in particular. Did even so sympathetic and sensitive a patron as Louis Brandeis pull some strings, create some limits to Professor Frankfurter's freedom of action that, had they been public, might have restricted his field of endeavor, undermined his reputation for independence, and limited his effectiveness? Even if one sees the work that Frankfurter did and Brandeis helped to subsidize as "good" work, serious questions remain about the activities of both men, as well as about what we expect from our judges and professors.

What exactly did Frankfurter do to warrant not only Brandeis's financial support but also his encomium? To begin with, Frankfurter took over the task of arguing cases for the National Consumers' League in defense of protective legislation. This role subsided considerably after 1923, when the conservative majority on the Court used the Fourteenth Amendment's due process clause in deciding *Adkins* v. *Children's Hospital* to put a temporary stop to new efforts to expand protective legislation.[32]

Frankfurter also served as a conduit for ideas that Brandeis wanted publicized, either in the law journals or in the popular press, frequently in the *New Republic*. Frankfurter often took ideas that Brandeis expressed and had them published, either over his name or as unsigned pieces; he sometimes used Brandeis's exact words but never attributed either the words or the ideas to the justice.[33] At other times Brandeis would suggest that something needed to be said on a certain topic, such as immigration policy, and Frankfurter would either pass the word on to Herbert Croly of the *New Republic* or write a piece himself.[34] But—and this is important to note—there were even more instances of Brandeis making suggestions and Frankfurter *not* following them up, probably because of the press of other obligations.[35]

Frankfurter also served as a sounding board for Brandeis, but here the relationship was far more complex than that of elder statesman and protégé. Always a reserved man, Brandeis throughout his life had only a few people, other than his wife and brother, in whom he could confide. He found his colleagues on the Court in the 1920s, with the exception of Holmes and Taft, <u>intellectually bland</u> and certainly unsympathetic to his point of view. His sense of judicial propriety precluded discussion of the Court's business with friends such as journalist Norman Hapgood or Sen. Robert M. LaFollette. But he poured out his grievances, explained his strategies, and discussed his colleagues with Frankfurter, especially in the long walks the two men took at Brandeis's summer home in Chatham on Cape Cod.[36]

The younger man proved a perfect companion. Aside from his gift for flattery, Frankfurter certainly understood the law and wanted to learn as much as he could from a man he considered one of the great jurists of modern America. The two shared many common beliefs, saw the law in basically the same way, thought judges should defer to the legislature in policy-making, had both suffered slights because of their religion and reform activities, and had wives who suffered frequent depressions. It is little wonder that Brandeis once confessed to Frankfurter that he viewed him as "half brother, half son."[37]

Frankfurter's position at Harvard Law School also met some of Brandeis's legal research needs. Although Brandeis had a clerk each term (chosen by Frankfurter), he often wanted information that went beyond the specific needs of particular opinions, information that might never be used in a case but that he thought important for one reason or another. In addition to the money Brandeis provided for Frankfurter's reform work, beginning in 1924 he also paid for research assistants on particular projects; some he suggested, and others Frankfurter undertook on his own initiative.[38]

In addition to articles Frankfurter prepared directly or in collaboration with one of his students, he used his seminars to direct research into areas of interest to Brandeis.[39] A letter from Washington would often carry a suggestion such as, "Would it not be profitable to have one of your seminars consider the establishment of official reviewers as a means of freeing the Fed[eral] Courts of patronage?"[40] Often the resulting papers proved quite good, and Frankfurter would arrange to have them published in either the *Harvard Law Review* or another law journal, much to Brandeis's satisfaction.[41] Brandeis thought these articles were not only informative for his own use but authoritative enough to cite in his opinions, and he became the first Supreme Court justice to cite law review articles to buttress his arguments.

Perhaps Professor Frankfurter's greatest service to Brandeis, as well as to progressive thought during the 1920s and early 1930s, consisted of his searing indictments of the conservative, often reactionary decisions of the Supreme Court. Led by Chief Justice Taft, the Court in the twenties consistently blocked efforts by the states to impose any limits on private property rights. In law review articles and in the popular press, Frankfurter subjected the antilabor and probusiness opinions of the Court to searing critiques. Nor did the jovial chief justice escape his sword. Following one antilabor decision, Frankfurter charged that Taft "deals with abstractions and not with the work-a-day world, its men, and its struggles. To him, also, words are things and not the symbol of things. . . . For all the regard that the Chief Justice of the United States pays to the facts of industrial life, he might as well have written this opinion as Chief Justice of the Fiji Islands."[42]

Even when the Court reached a decision Frankfurter approved of, such as nullifying the Klan-inspired Oregon law against Catholic schools in *Pierce v. Society of Sisters* (1925), he cautioned liberals against premature celebration. Justice James McReynolds's opinion in *Pierce* relied on the same type of reasoning that marked the conservative bloc's attack on minimum wage legislation and anti-injunction laws. The occasional use of this reasoning to strike down a bad law was more than offset by the number of times it had been used to invalidate reform legislation.[43]

Probably no decision outraged Frankfurter as much as the 1923 *Adkins* ruling, not only because he had argued the case in defense of the law but because the decision did in fact seem to set the clock back. All the rulings for more than 20 years in favor of protective legislation, all the gains of progressive reformers, were jeopardized by that ruling. "The whole thing we thought gained in 1912 is now thrown overboard and we are just where we were," he lamented.[44] Moreover, the ruling came as a shock to academic observers of the Court, who believed the issue had been settled years earlier.

Frankfurter saw the due process clause as the key to understanding where the Supreme Court had gone astray in recent years. It figured as the villain in his critiques of Court opinions he considered wrong, and he praised Holmes, Brandeis, Stone, and Cardozo for their reluctance to invoke due process merely because they disagreed with a particular public policy.[45] At one time Frankfurter planned to write his magnum opus on the Fourteenth Amendment, a project that Harold Laski joyfully reported to Holmes.[46] Although he wrote many pieces on the Fourteenth Amendment, and even sketched out chapters of the proposed book from time to time, the major work never came to pass.

Frankfurter eventually realized that due process by itself was never the villain: the problem was judges using it to attack legislation they did not like. Throughout this period, Frankfurter wrestled with the problem of the nature of judging and the criteria by which judges should exercise their enormous powers. It was a question he had pondered since he joined the faculty of Harvard Law School. Frankfurter always subscribed to ideas articulated years earlier by James Bradley Thayer, ideas that Frankfurter at the end of his life characterized as "the great guide for judges and therefore, the great guide for understanding by non-judges of what the place of the judiciary is in relation to constitutional questions."[47] In Thayer's view, as expressed in a famous 1893 article, judges have to defer to the legislatures, which directly reflect the popular will.[48] It matters not whether the legislatures act wisely or foolishly; evaluating the wisdom or folly of policy should be left to the people. Judges have a very restricted role and can do no more, in constitutional cases, than determine whether the legislature has transgressed a clear prohibition. If the legislature has the power, then the people's elected representatives—not judges—will decide how to exercise that power. As Frankfurter later said, Thayer's article "is the compelling motive behind my Constitutional views. . . . That [philosophy] is for me the Alpha and Omega of our job."[49]

But should courts merely validate whatever a majority has decided? If so, there can be no justification for a judiciary, and this neither Thayer nor Frankfurter believed. The answer lay in "reasonableness," a word that Frankfurter would later use over and over again in his opinions. According to Thayer, the courts can only invalidate a statute "when those who have the right to make laws have not merely made a mistake, but have made a very clear one, —so clear that it is not open to rational question."[50]

If one takes Thayer seriously, as Frankfurter did, the only grounds for voiding a bill would be legislative incompetence, and judicial duty would always be clear. But legislatures are rarely so obviously incompetent, and so courts have to examine whether legislatures have acted "reasonably." This word often cropped up, however, in the opinions of conservative judges who considered any effort to regulate private property to be unreasonable, and therefore unconstitutional. To eliminate this bias, Thayer anticipated what would later be called "process jurisprudence." If judges use the right procedures, if they ask the right questions, they will be able to determine if in fact the legislature has acted reasonably.

Frankfurter knew, of course, that the law cannot always be easily ascertained, that there are gray areas in which judges have to, in effect,

31

make policy decisions. He and Pound agreed that courts therefore have to be sensitive to the impact of their decisions on daily life. He decried the false notions that "our judges embody pure reason, that they are set apart from the concerns of the community," or that the Constitution itself consists of "sacred words with meaning fixed forever and ascertainable by a process of ineluctable reasoning."[51]

The judicial activism of the conservative bloc on the Court drove Frankfurter to develop his philosophy of judicial restraint, which in the 1920s could be used as a means to support state efforts at liberal reform. In the hands of a Brandeis, judicial restraint provided a flexible tool to deal with changing circumstances; Frankfurter's view of judicial restraint, however, became a rigid and insurmountable obstacle to dealing with changing social concerns.

It is not too much to say that the views Professor Frankfurter developed in the 1920s did not change significantly for the remainder of his life. Like Holmes, he rejected a formalistic, mechanical approach to the law; he did not see law as a fixed body of eternal verities, but as a set of ideas responding to the changing times. The legal realists[52] had taught him that judges respond as men rather than machines in determining the law, and the conservative bloc on the Supreme Court showed him how dangerous this response could be. Brandeis influenced Frankfurter's commitment to law as an agency of reform—but always operating in conjunction with the elective bodies and in accordance with the essential principles of the Constitution.

Although it is clear how these influences affected his jurisprudence, Frankfurter did not merely parrot these views, and in some areas he departed from them. Holmes, for instance, emphasized that the force of the majoritarian will should not be hindered by the courts; Holmes saw the law as little more than the will of the majority. Frankfurter, on the other hand, believed that judicial intrusion saps the ability of the people to govern themselves; courts should not only avoid negating popular reform efforts, they should also not try to undertake reforms on their own. He preached the gospel of "not relying on the Court for the impossible task of assuring a vigorous, mature, self-protecting and tolerant democracy." Such an ideal could only be achieved by the people acting for themselves.[53]

In a series of lectures given at Yale in 1930, Frankfurter brought some of these themes together in what has been described as "one of the most complete statements of his idealized political vision."[54] Frankfurter revived his earlier notion of the need for experts in all branches of government, as well as his belief that "the art of governing has been achieved best by men to whom governing itself is a profession."[55] But, he warned, in unconscious anticipation of Roosevelt's New Deal, government means experimentation, and the federal system allows the states to act as social and economic laboratories for new ideas. This great democratic asset is jeopardized if judges fail to exercise restraint when faced with unfamiliar and perhaps even unwelcome ideas. Nothing in the Constitution prevents experimentation by the states. "In simple truth, the difficulties government encounters from law do not inhere in the Constitution. . . . That document has ample resources for imaginative statesmanship, if judges have imagination for statesmanship."[56] One wonders if, years later, Frankfurter ever remembered these words.

During the 1920s, with conservatives firmly entrenched in Washington and most state capitals, Brandeis and Frankfurter could hope for little more than to keep the progressive flame alive, in both political reforms and judicial liberalism. The stream of suggestions from Brandeis for articles, law review pieces, editorials, and draft legislation produced some written work, and Frankfurter's reputation as a reformer and liberal scholar benefited immensely from their collaboration. With the collapse of the economy in 1929 and strong signs that a new and reform-minded administration could be elected in 1932, the opportunities for effective work increased significantly.

3

FRANKFURTER AND THE NEW DEAL

The sudden and dizzying termination of Republican prosperity and the onset of the nation's worst economic depression in its history undercut the conservative businessmen's claim to having the "right" answers to questions about America's future. Liberals, who had been fighting a desperate rearguard action to preserve at least a few of the gains of the Progressive Era, now took heart as the nation once again seemed willing to listen to their ideas. For Felix Frankfurter the times appeared propitious indeed, and the ambitious Harvard don looked around to see where he could most effectively exercise his considerable abilities.

A major division in Frankfurter's life was marked by his declining the offer made to him in 1932 of a seat on the Massachusetts Supreme Judicial Court. Years later he joked about it and said that there had been two reasons to tempt him to accept Gov. Joseph Ely's invitation. First, in those days all seven members of the state's highest court went "in lock step . . . to lunch at the Union Club in formal dress and top hat. I thought that would be an interesting thing—to go in lock step in top hat to the Union Club for lunch." The other reason was curiosity: he wanted to find out how Chief Justice Arthur P. Rugg managed to suppress nearly all dissenting opinions.[1]

But there were other reasons as well. As he told his friend Thomas Reed Powell, who thought Frankfurter too bright a mind to waste on the state court, he did not think that "a place that had been occupied by Lemuel Shaw and Oliver Wendell Holmes, Jr., was beneath me, or too meager for my powers."[2] Moreover, for a Jew and a man considered by many less than a decade earlier to be a dangerous radical, the offer must have seemed a vindication.[3] Despite his flippancy years later, Frankfurter did give serious consideration to the offer but in the end declined.

Although Holmes called the appointment "admirable" and termed Frankfurter "much more than ordinarily qualified," Brandeis advised strongly against acceptance. While Frankfurter would no doubt be a good judge, he was too young (50) to leave the field of combat for the judicial cloister. Much work remained to be done, and Frankfurter at Harvard Law School could do that work.[4] In addition, confirmation was by no means assured. Although it praised Frankfurter's intellect, the influential *Boston Transcript* declared that he lacked the appropriate "judicial temperament" and should therefore be denied the seat.[5] Former governor Alvan T. Fuller swore that he would rather have his arm cut off than see Frankfurter on the bench. Political considerations also came into play. Governor Ely supported Alfred E. Smith for the 1932 Democratic presidential nomination and had strongly attacked the front-runner, New York governor Franklin D. Roosevelt. By declining Ely's offer, Frankfurter aligned himself with the Roosevelt camp.[6]

On 29 June Frankfurter thanked Ely but declared that, "after much anguish of mind," he believed that he could make a greater contribution to the law by remaining a teacher. When Ely held up announcement of the refusal, Frankfurter had his letter to Ely printed and distributed to the press.[7] With the election of 1932 just over the horizon, Frankfurter eagerly looked forward to new opportunities for expending his boundless energy.

Felix Frankfurter's influence in the New Deal stemmed from a variety of factors, not the least of which was his friendship with President Franklin Delano Roosevelt. The two men had met casually around 1906 when Frankfurter worked for Stimson; as Frankfurter noted, "We became acquaintances, not intimate friends at all, but we knew each other pleasantly."[8] They got to know each other better during the war, when Roosevelt served as assistant secretary of the navy, and they kept in periodic touch with one another in the early part of the 1920s, when Roosevelt's political career seemed to have been cut off by a bout of poliomyelitis. Then in 1928, despite the Hoover landslide in the presidential race, Roosevelt won the New York gubernatorial election, and relations between the two men grew more intimate.[9] Although Frankfurter still harbored some doubts about Roosevelt's abilities as late as the fall of 1932, he soon came to believe fervently in both Roosevelt and the New Deal.[10]

Roosevelt, like so many others, found the Frankfurter personality irresistible and over the years enjoyed his company and storytelling. But as time went on Roosevelt also found that the Harvard professor apparently knew everyone and everything, or someone else who did, and that he brimmed over with ideas. One of Roosevelt's great strengths was his receptiveness to new ideas, and Frankfurter, often prodded by Brandeis, had loads of advice to offer.[11] During the four years Roosevelt served as governor of New York, Frankfurter went to Albany frequently to visit, to offer advice, and on occasion, to bring messages from Brandeis. That Roosevelt valued Frankfurter both as a person and for his abilities is beyond doubt; shortly after his inauguration as president, Roosevelt offered Frankfurter the post of solicitor general, intimating that this would pave the way to a seat on the Supreme Court. After consulting with Brandeis, Frankfurter turned the position down, telling the president he could be of more use to him as an "outsider-insider" than as an official member of the administration, with all the constraints such employment would involve. Roosevelt, not used to being turned down, called his friend "an independent pig," but added, "I guess that's one reason I like you."[12]

Critics both then and later magnified Frankfurter's influence in the New Deal and with the president. Hugh Johnson blamed the Harvard professor and his acolytes for his own failure as head of the National Recovery Administration and denounced Frankfurter as "the most influential single individual in the United States." George Peek, head of the Agricultural Adjustment Administration, complained that "a plague of young lawyers settled on Washington. They all claimed to be friends of somebody or other and mostly of Felix Frankfurter." According to some people, Frankfurter and his "Happy Hot Dogs" were running the government.[13]

That Frankfurter helped place an enormous number of Harvard Law students in key government positions is true, but that Frankfurter's ideas governed early New Deal policy is manifestly false. Although he had a hand in drafting the initial legislation regulating securities, Frankfurter left for England in the late summer of 1933 to take up an appointment as Eastman Professor at Oxford. While he often wrote to the president that year, influence cannot be exercised at such a long distance; Roosevelt had a multitude of voices clamoring for his attention and had to deal with crises immediately. Frankfurter could do little more than applaud those measures he approved of and suggest that the president speak to others before committing himself to certain policies.

In 1933 and 1934 Roosevelt's key advisors, members of the so-called Brain Trust, preferred policies that derived from Theodore Roosevelt's New Nationalism, such as the suspension of the antitrust laws, extensive cooperation between government and business, and an emphasis on bigness—big government, big business, big labor.[14] Although Frankfurter had at one time supported the New Nationalism, by 1933 he had come around to a Brandeisian belief in competition and an essentially small-unit economy. But not until 1935 would the New Deal veer off in this direction, much to the satisfaction of Brandeis and Frankfurter.[15] In the meantime, they worked to place people sympathetic to their point of view in key New Deal agencies.

The list of former Frankfurter students staffing the Roosevelt administration is staggering. To name but a few: Charles Wyzanski, solicitor for the Labor Department; Nathan Margold, solicitor for Interior; Nathan Witt, Lee Pressman, and Alger Hiss in Agriculture; David Lilienthal in the Tennessee Valley Authority (TVA); Dean Acheson in Treasury; and perhaps most important, Benjamin Cohen and Thomas Corcoran who, whatever their nominal titles, served as part of the president's inner circle. In addition, dozens of young lawyers he taught at Harvard Law served in the middle-management levels of the various New Deal agencies. One writer has described Frankfurter as "the proprietor of an organization for filling government positions of every kind, from a Cabinet page to a clerkship," while *Fortune* termed the Harvard professor "the most famous legal employment service in America."[16] These men[17] kept Frankfurter and Brandeis informed of developments in their agencies and came to them for advice on developing matters.[18]

As Professor G. Edward White has reminded us, "There was a time when public service work was perceived as one of the most prestigious and important employment opportunities offered recent graduates of American law schools."[19] This is hardly the case now, and it certainly was not the case prior to the New Deal; only a few lawyers, Brandeis and Frankfurter being the best known, saw public service as a worthwhile calling. Several developments in the late 1920s and early 1930s, however, suddenly made employment in the public sector an attractive alternative to law offices.

The Great Depression not only restricted opportunities in the private sector but also wiped out the status that businessmen and their minions had enjoyed in the 1920s. Just as the industrialists had claimed credit for the earlier prosperity, they now had to take the blame for the widespread hardships. Under Harding, Coolidge, and Hoover, and their ideology of limited and weak government, public service had not appealed to the best and brightest of the law school graduates. Franklin Roosevelt's New Deal, however, made Washington, not Wall Street, the center of the action. The Roosevelt administration planned to solve the economic and social problems that the private sector had been unable to cure, and it needed bright and aggressive people, preferably with legal skills and knowledge of administrative law to help in the task. Frankfurter had been preparing his students for this task for 15 years.[20]

Frankfurter's role as a one-man employment service should be viewed in several lights. To begin with, he believed in public service and had been one of the few members of his law school class to choose public work over the private sector. His own predilections and views of professorial obligations led him to look for places for those students he felt would prefer public work; he does not appear to have done much to place his students in private firms. Frankfurter seems to have started his placement work fairly early; in fact, he told Holmes that one reason he would go to Harvard would be "to help harness the law school to the needs of the fight outside."[21] During his wartime service in the Wilson administration, he managed to place several of the students he had taught in his brief stint at Harvard.[22]

One should also keep in mind that Frankfurter himself had benefited from the advice and help of several mentors—Gray, Stimson, Holmes, and Brandeis—and he now saw himself as having the opportunity to help younger men as he had been helped. Here, as Professor White points out, Frankfurter's Jewishness played a key role. "Put most sharply," White writes, "older, elite gentile law professors had sponsored a 'bright' young Jew in an overwhelmingly gentile professional and social world; now that 'bright' young person, assimilated into the world, could sponsor others."[23] The characteristic Frankfurter protégé, the type he sent as a law clerk to Holmes or Brandeis or whom he recommended to a government agency, had ranked high in his class at Harvard Law, held liberal political views, and was either a product of the upper-class gentile world or an "outsider," like Frankfurter, who by stint of brains and personality had penetrated and now felt comfortable in that environment. [24]

Frankfurter's "boys," both those he placed in government service in the 1920s and 1930s and those who clerked for him in the 1940s and 1950s, also shared one other characteristic—intense loyalty and devotion to their mentor. They helped establish a network of contacts that benefited Frankfurter, themselves, and those whom they chose to sponsor afterward. The idea of an "old boy network," originally limited to a select few who enjoyed wealth and proper breeding, had now been expanded to take in those who, whatever their background, had talent—a network of meritocracy. Not all of those placed in government remained in public service; in fact, very few of them chose government as a permanent career path. But an extraordinary number of them moved in and out of government work and, even when engaged in a university or a private firm, took on government assignments or *pro bono* work. [25]

How much *real* influence Frankfurter enjoyed during the 1930s is difficult to gauge. That he had the ear of the president is undeniable, and anyone with that access is always a power to be reckoned with in Washington. Frankfurter understood, however, that as an "outsider-insider" he could not exercise power directly. He proved most effective when responding to a specific request; Roosevelt and his Cabinet members tended to listen more closely to the professor's advice when they had solicited it. When Frankfurter tried to push something onto Roosevelt, the president got his Dutch up and would not budge. [26]

Apart from his ability to place students in the major New Deal agencies, Frankfurter's influence on substantive issues proved fairly limited. As Nelson Dawson has put it: "The New Deal simply did not do what Brandeis and Frankfurter wanted it to do. It never grappled successfully with bigness. Taxation was not used effectively as an instrument of reform and recovery. Roosevelt never committed himself to a spending program large enough to pull the nation out of the depression. It is difficult to see any significant impact by Brandeis and Frankfurter on these fundamental issues. They tried diligently, but it was a Sisyphean labor." [27] Bruce Murphy takes a far more positive view of their influence and entitles one chapter "The Vision Is Realized." While it is true, Murphy notes, that Roosevelt did not embrace the "true faith" of economic reform propounded by Brandeis and his scribe, "it was much closer than it had been in 1916, closer even than it had been in 1933." [28] Michael

Parrish notes that Frankfurter "never exercised greater influence over Roosevelt than during the years of 1935 and 1936, yet he could hardly claim a complete ideological and political victory over his opponents inside or outside the administration."[29]

Murphy's description of Brandeis and Frankfurter as the "prophet" and his "scribe" catches an essential element of their relationship. Brandeis had the vision, and he knew the shape of the America he wanted: a nation that would foster liberty and justice and provide equal economic, social, and political opportunity to all.[30] While Frankfurter largely shared that vision, he could not, in fairness, be described as a visionary or even an ideologue. He stood perfectly willing to aid Brandeis in his quest because he did believe that the justice had a true vision of an ideal America. Moreover, because he knew so many people, because his former students fed him so much information, because he knew how to draft legislation, Frankfurter could be an ideal and effective lieutenant.[31] But for him, politics always seemed so much more a matter of people than of programs. In the midthirties his loyalty was severely tested when he found his two idols, Brandeis and Roosevelt, on opposite sides of a great political and constitutional divide.

The well-known story of the 1937 Court-packing plan need not be repeated here, but it put Frankfurter in a very difficult position.[32] Brandeis, even though he had voted against the conservatives and their attack on New Deal legislation, believed that the integrity of the Court could not be compromised for short-term economic reform, and he expected Frankfurter to be an ardent and energetic defender of the judiciary. Roosevelt saw his enormous 1936 electoral victory as a mandate to go forward with the New Deal, and the nine old men of the Court as blocking the popular will. During the 1936 campaign the president said little about the Court, but he made it plain that he believed the Constitution had not been meant to be a dead hand "blocking humanity's progress" but rather "a living force for the expression of the national will with respect to national needs."[33]

Frankfurter's own views on the Court had grown increasingly negative as the conservative majority struck down both state and federal reform measures. In regard to one case, he wrote, "I could hardly have believed that disciplined legal minds would reach the conclusion which the majority reached."[34] At the same time, he along with many others recognized the sloppiness with which many of the early New Deal measures had been drafted and the haphazard way in which authority had been delegated. In their rush to reform the economy, New Dealers often ignored basic common sense. During the oral argument in the "hot oil" case, *Panama Refining* v. *Ryan* (1935), an incredulous Brandeis could not believe that the regulations governing interstate shipment of oil under the National Industrial Recovery Act had never been published, and even the lawyer for the government could not say positively that he knew where to get a copy.[35] Brandeis's vehement opposition to bigness and his contempt for what he termed *künststücke*—the overly clever tricks of some New Deal measures, such as nullifying the gold clause[36]— caused Frankfurter further anxiety. If Brandeis became too outspoken on these issues, if his annoyance led him to join the conservatives on the Court, then Frankfurter's influence with Roosevelt might be undercut even as he tried to move the administration away from its emphasis on concentration of power in big government agencies.

By 1935, in fact, the New Deal had begun to adopt measures much more to the liking of Brandeis and Frankfurter, measures that emphasized decentralization, opposition to bigness, and heavy taxation of corporate and individual wealth. But the "Four Horsemen," the conservative bloc on the Court of Willis Van Devanter, James McReynolds, George Sutherland, and Pierce Butler, often joined by Owen Roberts and Chief Justice Charles Evans Hughes, continued to impose their own economic and social values by invalidating reform measures. Then on Black Monday, 27 May 1935, the Court struck down the National Industrial Recovery Act for improper delegation of authority,[37] invalidated the Frazier-Lemke Farm Relief Act,[38] and sharply curtailed the President's power to remove members of independent regulatory agencies.[39]

Brandeis, who wrote the Court's opinion in the Frazier-Lemke case and whose earlier views on presidential power had now been accepted by the Court, believed that the Court had done the country a good turn. He told Ben Cohen to take a message to Frankfurter: "You must see that Felix understands the situation and explains it to the President. You must explain it to the men Felix brought into the Government. They must understand that these three decisions change everything. The President has been living in a fool's paradise."[40]

What the president understood was that something had to be done about the Court, but not until after the 1936 election. In January 1937 Roosevelt cryptically noted in a letter to Frankfurter, "Very confidentially, I may give you an awful shock in about two weeks. Even if you do not agree, suspend final judgment and I will tell you the story."[41] When the president did unveil the Court plan, Frankfurter wrote him as follows:

> And now you have blown me off the top of Vesuvius where you sat me some weeks ago. Yes, you "shocked" me by the deftness of the general scheme for dealing with the mandate for national action which you received three times, in '32 and '34 and '36, and each time with increasing emphasis. You "shocked" me no less by the dramatic, untarnished secrecy with which you kept your scheme until you took the whole nation into your confidence. . . . But beyond that—well, the momentum of a long series of decisions not defensible in the realm of reason nor justified by settled principles of Constitutional interpretation had convinced me, as they had convinced you, that means had to be found to save the Constitution from the Court, and the Court from itself. . . . Any major action to the body politic, no less than to the body physical, involves some shock. But I have, as you know, deep faith in your instinct to make the wise choice.[42]

Roosevelt had not taken Frankfurter into his confidence because he suspected divided loyalty; he did not know whether the professor would support him or Brandeis. Moreover, in a 1934 article chastising the Court, Frankfurter had nonetheless warned critics against tinkering with the number of justices.[43]

Frankfurter's enthusiastic response caught Roosevelt somewhat by surprise, as did a lengthy letter Frankfurter sent a few days later with suggestions on how to explain the Court's constitutional misbehavior to the public.[44] In the bruising and futile five-month battle over the ill-conceived plan, Frankfurter never once suggested that Roosevelt retreat. But neither did he endorse or denounce the plan openly; he wrote the president: "Foolish folk (enemies of yours) are doing their damndest to make me attack the court so as to start a new line of attack against your proposal. They miss their guess. I shan't help them to divert the issue."[45]

What did Frankfurter really believe about the Court-packing plan? While he had condemned the Court for its abuse of power, he had also warned against just this type of "reform." Was he a hypocrite, going along with Roosevelt either out of loyalty or self-interest while he privately condemned the plan to friends such as James Landis and Thomas Reed Powell? Did he keep quiet publicly to avoid a break with Brandeis?

Michael Parrish suggests that Frankfurter's public silence "sprang more from careful political calculation than from cowardice, doubt or hypocrisy. Endorsement of the president's plan by the notoriously radical professor Frankfurter would not generate much support for the measure." Roosevelt realized this and thus did not ask for Frankfurter's open support. Parrish also believes that Frankfurter did in fact support the spirit if not the particulars of the plan, because he believed the danger to the country from a runaway Court to be greater than that of the Roosevelt scheme.[46]

When Chief Justice Hughes, joined by Brandeis and Van Devanter, sent a letter to the Senate Judiciary Committee on 22 March rebutting the president's charges of inefficiency and the need for reorganization,[47] an angry Frankfurter sat down and wrote a blistering four-page letter to Brandeis that he ultimately decided not to send. In it we get what is probably the most accurate expression of his true feelings:

> Tampering with the Court is a very serious business. Like any major operation it is justified only by the most compelling considerations. But no student of the Court can be blind to its long course of misbehavior. I do not relish some of the implications of the President's proposal, but neither do I relish victory for the subtler but ultimately deeper evils inevitable in the victory for the Hughes and the Butlers and their successors. . . . The core of our difficulty with reference to the Court is the immunity which the Court has enjoyed in being supposedly aloof from politics and, therefore, immune from the conditions under which political controversy is conducted. The Court cannot be allowed to enjoy this immunity and at the same time skillfully take advantage, as does the Chief's statement, of all the opportunities for influencing political action.[48]

Although Frankfurter did not send this letter, he made sure that Brandeis learned at least some of what he felt, both in letters and in some of his personal comments.[49]

Roosevelt, it has been said, lost the battle but won the war. While the Senate debated the reorganization measure, the Court capitulated. On 29 March, with Hughes and Roberts now joining the liberal bloc of Brandeis, Stone, and Cardozo, the Court upheld a minimum wage measure almost identical to one it had struck down nine months earlier.[50] Two weeks later, also by a 5–4 vote, the majority approved the Wagner Act, with Chief Justice Hughes writing a sweeping interpretation of the commerce clause.[51] On 18 May Justice Van Devanter resigned, giving

Roosevelt his opportunity to remake the Court, and shortly afterward the justices validated the two major provisions of the Social Security Act.[52] With the Court now apparently in line with the executive and legislative branches, there seemed no more need for the reorganization bill, which Congress buried with relief. The Court fight had ended.

In two lengthy letters he sent Roosevelt that summer, Frankfurter heartily endorsed what the president had done, but he remained unhappy over the need for such drastic action.[53] "To me it is all painful beyond words," he told a friend, "the poignant grief of one whose life has been dedicated to faith in the disinterestedness of a tribunal and its freedom from . . . politics."[54] Part of this grief must also have been caused by the rift that arose between him and Brandeis. The jurist had expected his protégé to deplore the president's plan and to take an active part in defeating it; he correctly interpreted Frankfurter's silence as assent. There is a marked coolness in the letters between the two men after 1937, but Brandeis did not stop his stipend to Frankfurter—a sign, if one be needed, of the independence in a relationship that both men valued.

On 9 July 1938 Benjamin Cardozo died, and speculation about his successor quickly focused on Felix Frankfurter. For reformers, no one else would do. He had befriended labor during the war, and in the great litmus test of the 1920s, the Sacco-Vanzetti case, his had been the most eloquent cry against perverted justice. He had taken over much of Brandeis's task as a people's attorney and had tried to instill in a generation of Harvard Law students a belief in the necessity of public service. While one can question the extent of his influence in the New Deal, he certainly enjoyed both the friendship and attention of the President, who discovered in the Court battle that he could count on Frankfurter's loyalty. Reformers and legal scholars alike deemed Frankfurter the ideal person to join the nation's highest court. In fact, with his considerable intellectual abilities and familiarity with the Court and its business, they expected him to become the leader of a new, Roosevelt-appointed progressive bloc on the Court.

4

THE FAILURE OF LEADERSHIP

The expectation of both Frankfurter and his supporters that he would become a leader of the Court seemed more than justified. He had, after all, been on intimate terms with Holmes, Brandeis, Cardozo, and Stone and had corresponded regularly with Chief Justices Taft and Hughes. He believed that he knew more about the Court's inner workings than anyone else who had never sat on it, and he would take his seat more with the confidence of an insider than as a junior side judge. For the previous 25 years he had studied the Court intensely, indeed obsessively, watching it as he once said, "as closely as a mother would a sick child."[1] His student Alexander Bickel later pointed out that Frankfurter had studied not only the written opinions but "the judges and their impact on one another," as well as the wider range of administrative and procedural concerns that affect the Court and its work.[2]

In fact, even before going on the bench he had been called upon by Harlan Fiske Stone to instruct a new member in the proper judicial protocols. "Do you know Black well?" a troubled Stone asked in early 1938. "You might be able to render him great assistance. He needs guidance from someone who is more familiar with the workings of the judicial process than he is." Hugo Black's tradition-ignoring dissents worried Stone and Brandeis; as Stone noted, "There are enough present-day battles to be won without wasting our effort to remake the Constitution *ab initio,* or using the judicial opinion as a political tract."[3] Frankfurter gladly accepted the invitation and wrote Black that judges "cannot escape the responsibility of filling in gaps which the finitudes of even the most imaginative legislation render inevitable. . . . They cannot decide things by invoking a new major premise out of whole cloth; they must make the law that they do make out of the existing materials with due deference to the presuppositions of the legal system of which they have been made a part."[4] Frankfurter also talked to Black and reported that while the Alabaman was not "technically equipped," he had a "good head" and was "capable of learning if . . . rightly encouraged."[5]

Just as he had "helped" Black, and just as he had taught a generation of Harvard Law students to see the proper role of the Court and the limits of its jurisdiction, so Frankfurter now proposed to instruct his brethren. For 30 years, however, Frankfurter had been either an acolyte to men he recognized as great figures—Holmes, Brandeis, Stimson, and Roosevelt—or a preceptor and mentor to those he considered his intellectual inferiors; the master-disciple relationship was not going to work with men who saw themselves as his equals and were not beholden to him for their positions on the nation's highest court. One of the great tragedies of Frankfurter's career is that a man renowned for his talents in personal relations, who knew so well the high value the justices placed on careful collegiality, could so terribly misread the situation and the characters of those with whom he served.

Frankfurter's inability to manage the Court did not become apparent immediately, and neither did his deteriorating relationship with the man he could reasonably have expected to be his most loyal ally, William O. Douglas.[6] Shortly after taking his seat as Brandeis's successor, Douglas began joining Frankfurter and Stone in an impromptu caucus that met to discuss each week's cases before the Saturday conference, a practice discontinued after Stone became chief justice in 1942. Douglas sent warm endorsements of Frankfurter's draft opinions during the 1938 and 1939 terms. "Superb!" he scribbled on one draft; "you have done a magnificent job," on another.[7] Even when they disagreed on cases, as was bound to happen, their early exchanges were polite, even bantering. After a minor disagreement, Frankfurter wrote feelingly that "what is really important is the warm consideration that we weave in our relationship in the daily work on the Court."[8]

That "warm confidence" soon vanished, and Frankfurter must bear the major responsibility; he insisted on continuing to act as a professor and treated his colleagues as a seminar of somewhat slow second-year students at Harvard Law School. There were, of course, important philosophical differences, but judges have disagreed, often strenuously, without personalizing their differences. Frankfurter, however, took the refusal of his colleagues to follow his lead as a personal affront and unfortunately allowed full play to his considerable talent for invective.

"You probably think me very persnickety or, at least, academic in fussing about your reference to constitutional facts," he wrote Justice Stanley Reed. "Well, the fact is that I am an academic and I have no excuse for being on this Court unless I remain so."[9] In a letter to Justice Robert H. Jackson, in which he expounded at length upon a point of law, Frankfurter concluded, "If all this sounds to you professorial, please remember that I am a professor unashamed."[10] Frankfurter believed that his career as an academic gave him a greater understanding of the Court and its processes than even some of its members could have: "Not even as powerful and agile a mind as that of Charles Evans Hughes could, with the pressures which produced adjudication and opinion writing, gain that thorough and disinterested grasp of the problem [of judicial review] which twenty-five years of academic preoccupation with the problem should have left in one."[11]

In academia in general, and at Harvard Law School in particular, the Socratic method was central to the learning process. Frankfurter loved to argue and stood ever ready to argue about almost anything for the sake of intellectual sport. "Disputation," he admitted, "is one of my great pleasures."[12] At oral argument, he treated lawyers before the bar like students, heckling them as he had done in class. Douglas charged Frankfurter with asking so many questions not to throw light on an issue but to expose his own views in the hope of winning over one or more of the other justices.[13] Frankfurter also carried his professorial air into the Saturday conference, where he tended to treat his colleagues abrasively and constantly quoted Holmes and Brandeis at them to build up his position. "We would have been inclined to agree with Felix more often in conference," Justice William Brennan said, "if he quoted Holmes less frequently to us."[14] Frankfurter's keen political insights were often lost on his fellow justices, who refused to be treated as inferiors. Seeking to gain Stanley Reed's vote in one case, Frankfurter took a condescending approach and told Reed, "It is the lot of professors to be often misunderstood by pupils. . . . So let me begin again." In another case he told Reed that he had taught Harvard students that to construe a statute

47

correctly they should read it not once but thrice, and he advised Reed to do the same.[15]

If Felix were really interested in a case, Potter Stewart recalled, he "would speak for fifty minutes, no more or less, because that was the length of the lecture at the Harvard Law School." Douglas in turn, Stewart noted, could be "absolutely devastating." "When I came into this conference," Douglas said after one of Frankfurter's disquisitions, "I agreed in the conclusion that Felix has just announced. But he's talked me out of it."[16]

Douglas's ire is more understandable in light of the often splenetic nature of Frankfurter's rage at the failure of his colleagues to follow his lead. Although he considered Frank Murphy a man of principle, he did not think Murphy qualified to sit on the high court, and he constantly attacked Murphy's desire to do justice and to write compassion into the law. Frankfurter compared his results-oriented philosophy to what had happened in Germany and charged Murphy with being "too subservient" to his "idea of doing 'the right thing.'" Frankfurter sometimes addressed Murphy as "Dear God," and in a note regarding an FCC case, said even a god ought to read the record before deciding. In a note he passed to Murphy during the 1944 term, he listed as among Murphy's "clients" reds, whores, crooks, Indians and all other colored people, longshoremen, mortgagers and other debtors, pacifists, traitors, Japs, women, children, and most men. "Must I become a Negro rapist before you give me due process?"[17] He called Hugo Black "violent, vehement, indifferent to the use he was making of cases, utterly disregardful of what they stood for, and quite reckless." Black, he told Judge Learned Hand, "is a self-righteous, self-deluded part fanatic, part demagogue, who really disbelieves in law, thinks it essentially manipulative of language."[18] Neither Black nor Douglas, in his view, was a man of principle.

Frankfurter took the business of judging very seriously; although he liked a good joke, he did not enjoy one at his own expense or in the Court precincts. Once after Douglas read a newspaper story that claimed he and Frankfurter were not speaking, he strolled into the conference room and loudly offered to shake Frankfurter's hand. An astounded Frankfurter stood there in fury, but got even madder when Douglas said, "You'll have to hurry, Felix, I'm a busy man."[19]

Far more basic than personality in splitting the Court in the early 1940s were the justices' philosophical differences, which arose over fundamental issues that have still not been resolved. We will examine these issues, especially judicial restraint and the doctrine of incorporation, as we look at specific cases. The division between Frankfurter and his allies on the one hand and the Black-Douglas view on the other can be characterized in several ways—restraint versus activism, process versus results, even Yale against Harvard, for both Frankfurter and Douglas had started down their respective jurisprudential paths during the academic stages of their careers.

Frankfurter had long venerated Holmes and Brandeis and their call for judges to refrain from allowing their own economic prejudices to overrule the proper policy-making role of elected officials. As a professor, Frankfurter championed the Holmes-Brandeis view and in his writings and classes advocated judicial restraint as a basic element of a proper jurisprudential credo. One of his students, Louis L. Jaffe, wrote that Frankfurter could not be characterized as either a conservative or a liberal. "It is of the very essence of his judicial philosophy that his role as a judge precludes him from having a program couched in these terms of choice."[20] Frankfurter's close friend and colleague at Harvard, Thomas Reed Powell, defended Frankfurter when former admirers claimed he had forsaken the liberal path. One facet of liberalism in a judge, Powell suggested, "may be the insistence that courts should not interpose their vetoes except under the strongest constitutional compulsions."[21]

Frankfurter's study of constitutional development emphasized process and led him to believe that courts should limit their jurisdiction to matters of public law. He was not so naive as to believe that personality and prejudice play no role in court decisions, but he did believe that judges have the obligation to work earnestly to keep their personal considerations from affecting their decisions.[22] A critic claimed that, while at Harvard, Professor Frankfurter worried over each case he taught like a terrier, exploring every minute matter of history, procedure, and philosophy and thus losing sight of the larger policy issues involved.[23] A fairer view may be gleamed from what Powell wrote of his own teaching: "My emphasis is on process, process, process, on particulars, particulars, on cases, cases, cases, on the contemporary court, on resolving competing considerations, on watching for practicalities not likely to be expressed in opinions in which the court pretends that the case is being decided by its predecessors rather than by itself."[24] This coldly analytical method, Frankfurter believed, allowed courts and students to let reason triumph over emotion. "I have a romantic belief in Reason," he told Black; to Jackson he said, "One drawback of a professor is that he does believe in reason and profoundly believes that the mode by which results are reached is as important—maybe more important—in the evolution of society as the result itself."[25] (Perhaps Frankfurter should have remembered a little aphorism he once quoted to Powell, that logic "is the art of going wrong with confidence.")[26]

A major problem with the claim of rational objectivity, of course, is that Frankfurter lacked the Olympian detachment of Holmes or the steely discipline of Brandeis that would have kept his emotions in check.[27] He had strong feelings, and one friend called him "a passionate person, who has given up the other passions of his life for the one—the institution of the Court."[28] Douglas claimed that Charles Evans Hughes had said judges base their decisions 90 percent on emotions. Frankfurter, upon hearing this, denounced the idea, but according to Douglas, "no one poured his emotion more completely into decisions while professing just the opposite."[29]

We can see the disastrous effects of Frankfurter's personalization of issues in the disintegration of the Court during the war years. Frankfurter, of course, does not bear the full blame; even had he been a saint, the strong personalities and philosophical factionalization of the Court and the failure of Chief Justice Stone to exercise leadership would have led to deep divisions. There is no doubt, however, that Frankfurter's behavior further poisoned the well of collegiality. The story starts with the flag salute cases.

The *Gobitis* case in 1940 presented no new questions to either the Court or Frankfurter.[30] Whether or not a state could compel schoolchildren to salute the American flag had been an issue in twenty states between 1935 and 1940, as well as the subject of major litigation in seven. Prior to *Gobitis* the Supreme Court had four times upheld state court decisions validating compulsory flag salute laws.[31] Jehovah's Witnesses objected to the flag salute because of their literal reading of Exodus 20:4–5: they equated the salute with bowing down to graven images. Frankfurter, a naturalized American citizen who always took ideals of citizenship and patriotism very seriously, had little sympathy with those who, as he saw it, refused to meet their civic obligations. In a memorandum to Secretary of War Newton D. Baker in September 1918, Frankfurter had condemned conscientious objectors who refused to do even noncombatant service and had suggested they be turned over to the Fort Leavenworth authorities "for treatment."[32]

Frankfurter apparently saw no trampling of First Amendment rights in the flag salute issue; during oral argument of the case on 25 April 1940 he passed a note to Frank Murphy questioning whether the framers of the Bill of Rights "would have thought that a requirement to salute the flag violates the protection of 'the free exercise of religion'?"[33] Chief Justice Hughes assigned the opinion to Frankfurter, who circulated a draft in May. Douglas, who later intimated that he might have voted the other way had Stone circulated his dissent earlier,[34] endorsed not only Frankfurter's original draft but the final version as well. "This is a powerful moving document of incalculable contemporary and (I believe) historical value," he wrote, terming the opinion "a truly statesmanlike job." He scribbled a similar encomium on the recirculation.[35]

In his opinion for the 8–1 majority, Frankfurter framed the "precise" issue in terms of judicial restraint and called upon the Court to defer to the wisdom and prerogatives of local school authorities: "To stigmatize legislative judgment in providing for this universal gesture of respect for the symbol of our national life in the setting of the common school as a lawless inroad on that freedom of conscience which the Constitution protects, would amount to no less than the pronouncement of pedagogical and psychological dogma in a field where courts possess no marked and certainly no controlling competence. . . . To the legislature no less than to courts is committed the guardianship of deeply cherished liberties."[36]

The opinion has an almost formulaic quality that would reappear in many of Frankfurter's later decisions. First, is the legislative end legitimate? The answer appears obvious: of course school boards and the states have a real interest in promoting patriotism and loyalty to the nation, of which the flag is the symbol. Second, are the means chosen unreasonable? If not, then it is not up to the courts to say that a better way exists. Therefore, if the end is legitimate and the means chosen are not unreasonable, the measure—in this case, the flag salute—is constitutional.[37] Frankfurter paid practically no attention to the Gobitis claim that First Amendment rights of free exercise of religion had been violated and, in a nominal bow to balancing, found national unity a far more pressing matter.[38]

It is useful to compare the Frankfurterian approach to later First Amendment analysis. Where Frankfurter's lead question is whether the state has a legitimate interest, modern courts would ask whether speech or free exercise rights had been restricted. If yes, then the next question would be whether the state had a *compelling* interest to warrant that restriction. A merely "legitimate," or even an "important," interest will not justify violation of the First Amendment. If, however, the state does have a compelling interest, then the courts will ask whether the limitation has been imposed in the least restrictive manner. The difference between the two approaches is neither semantic nor one of degree; one view sees regulations of speech or religion in the same manner as economic rules, and the other approach elevates the rights of the individual above the administrative convenience of the state. In terms of balancing, the modern approach places far greater weight on individual liberty than on any but the most compelling governmental interest.

Only Harlan Fiske Stone dissented,[39] and much of the liberal press applauded his opinion and denounced Frankfurter's. Harold Laski, a close friend of Frankfurter, wrote Stone to tell him "how right I think you are . . . [and] how wrong I think Felix is."[40] Harold Ickes, recognizing Frankfurter's concern about the war in Europe (the decision came down during the Dunkirk evacuation), thought the opinion worse than useless, "as if the country can be saved, or our institutions preserved, by forced salute of our flag by these fanatics."[41]

Frankfurter knew that the opinion troubled some of his friends and seemed to run counter to his earlier reputation as a civil libertarian. To Alice Hamilton he wrote that he could appreciate her concern: "After all, my life has not been dissociated from concern for civil liberties."[42] In the files concerning the flag salute cases, there is an undated memorandum in Frankfurter's handwriting that reads: "No duty of judges is more important nor more difficult to discharge than that of guarding against reading their personal and debatable opinions into the Case." In this opinion, however, Frankfurter certainly read into the case his zealous love of country and his belief that all other Americans should be just as patriotic as he was.

The three most liberal members of the Court, Black, Douglas, and Murphy, all voted with the majority, but from the start Murphy at least had been troubled by the decision.[43] Black did not like the law but saw nothing in the Constitution to invalidate the measure. When the Court convened after its summer recess, Douglas told Frankfurter that Black had had second thoughts about his *Gobitis* vote. "Has Black been reading the Constitution?" Frankfurter asked. "No," Douglas responded, "he has been reading the newspapers."[44] There, Black, and everyone else, would have noted the Justice Department reports that in the weeks following the decision hundreds of attacks on Witnesses had occurred, especially in small towns and rural areas; this pattern continued for at least two years.

Behind *Gobitis,* of course, had been the whole issue of how far the protection of the Bill of Rights extended to the states, and what role the courts had in determining the limits of that protection. Frankfurter's mentor and hero, Louis Brandeis, had first intimated that the Fourteenth Amendment's due process clause could mean protection of speech as well as property;[45] by the 1930s the doctrine of incorporation, as it came to be called, had been accepted at least in principle by the Court.[46] Problems then arose in deciding particulars, and here Frankfurter followed the guidelines set down by another of his heroes, Benjamin Nathan Cardozo, in *Palko* v. *Connecticut* (1937).[47] In *Palko* Cardozo had suggested that the Fourteenth Amendment only incorporated those protections that are "of the very essence of a scheme of ordered liberty"[48] and "so rooted in the traditions and conscience of our people as to be ranked as fundamental."[49] In *Gobitis,* despite the 8–1 vote, at least three members of the majority found themselves uncomfortable over Frankfurter's application of *Palko.* In the next few terms this unease expanded and split the Court.

A set of companion cases around this time brought together two unlikely allies, the radical West Coast labor leader Harry Bridges and the ultraconservative *Los Angeles Times.*[50] California state courts had found both in contempt, the newspaper for editorially urging a judge, while sentence was pending, to send two convicted members of a labor "goon squad" to prison, and Bridges for threatening a longshoremen's strike if a state court enforced what he described as an "outrageous" decision in a labor dispute. The two cases presented a direct confrontation between First Amendment rights of free speech and press and Sixth Amendment protection of a fair trial.

The cases had first come up in the 1940 term, when Frankfurter apparently had a 6–3 majority to uphold the state courts. But his preparation, which he claimed included reading nearly all the relevant cases in English-speaking jurisdictions, delayed the opinion, and he lost McReynolds to retirement and Murphy to Black, Douglas, and Reed, creating a 4–4 tie. The case was put over for reargument in the fall of 1941.[51]

That summer Charles Evans Hughes retired, James Byrnes took McReynolds's place, and Robert H. Jackson filled the seat vacated by Stone's elevation to chief justice. Jackson (later to be a close ally of Frankfurter) joined Black's opinion, and for the first time the Supreme Court reversed a state court finding of fact in a case of contempt by publication and extended First Amendment freedom of the press to published comments regarding pending court decisions. Black's opinion, which eventually won over all the bench save Frankfurter, applied the traditional speech test of clear-and-present danger and ruled that the "substantive evil" must have a "degree of imminence extremely high" before courts could punish allegedly contemptuous speech or writings.[52] States would have to show that comments posed a real threat to a fair trial; neither the *Times* editorial nor the Bridges telegram met that test. Judges might find such criticism disrespectful, but "the assumption that respect for the judiciary can be won by shielding judges from published criticism wrongly appraises the character of American public opinion. For it is a prized American privilege to speak one's mind, although not always with perfect good taste, on all public institutions."[53]

The decision infuriated Frankfurter, not only because he had lost the majority by his own pedantic delay, but because the opposition had invoked Holmes, whom he—and only he—really understood. Black, who had not yet arrived at his absolutist position on the First Amendment, applied the same balancing test between state authority and individual liberty that Frankfurter had approved in *Gobitis*. Frankfurter recognized that Black gave far more weight to the First Amendment and thus far less deference to governmental authority; this view could in time lead to courts ignoring the legislature if liberal judges determined to expand civil liberties, just as the old conservatives had expanded property rights. In his dissent he charged the majority with mischievous use of the clear-and-present danger test, which had deprived the state of the proper "means of securing to its citizens justice according to law."[54]

There is a fascinating letter in the Frankfurter files that he wrote to an old friend, the great Harvard historian Samuel Eliot Morison, who had questioned the extent to which the First Amendment protected speech. Frankfurter argued that the Court should have ignored the question of whether the *Los Angeles Times* editorial had been contemptuous and should have asked only whether the Constitution prohibited California from punishing that speech.

> Whether the Commonwealth of Massachusetts, through its appropriate organ, should have put Sedgwick and me in durance vile [prison] for The Atlantic article on the Sacco-Vanzetti case is one thing; whether Massachusetts would have been forbidden to do so by the Constitution of the United States quite another.
> The main function of law is drawing lines. Should an American state really be denied those standards and practices of judicial admin-

istration which are the commonplaces of an England which is more alert to civil liberty even during time of war than we are as a matter of national habit in times of peace?[55]

That Frankfurter showed consistency is admirable; that he showed absolutely no sensitivity to the need to protect unpopular speech is deplorable. One wonders whether he and so many others would have labored so hard to save Sacco and Vanzetti if they could have been sent to jail for suggesting that a judge had been biased.

The break widened at the end of the term when the Court announced its decision in *Jones v. Opelika* (1942), in which Jehovah's Witnesses had refused to pay a municipal licensing fee for peddlers prior to selling their religious tracts.[56] The issue was essentially the same as in *Gobitis*—the extent to which the government's acknowledged power to maintain public order impinges on the free exercise of religion.

Frankfurter again voted with the majority in favor of the state, but this time four judges dissented—Stone, Black, Douglas, and Murphy. Moreover, in an unprecedented step, the latter three appended a statement acknowledging *Opelika* as a logical extension of *Gobitis*, and they believed it "an appropriate occasion" to confess they had been wrong in the earlier case, since the majority opinion, as in *Opelika*, "put the right freely to exercise religion in a subordinate position in violation of the First Amendment."[57] This recantation infuriated Frankfurter, who pointed out that *Gobitis* had not been challenged in the *Opelika* litigation, or even mentioned in conference.

The situation deteriorated further in the October 1942 term as philosophical differences within the Court widened. Stone, unlike Hughes, did not keep a tight rein on the Saturday conference, preferring to allow full discussion, which often degenerated into lengthy and inconclusive debates. Frankfurter, whose 50-minute lectures contributed greatly to the problem, began complaining about the "easy-going, almost heedless way in which views on Constitutional issues touching the whole future direction of this country were floated" at the conferences.[58] Douglas complained that "we have [conferences] all the time these days and they seem eternally long—and often dull."[59] The divisiveness in the conference could be seen in the rising rate of nonunanimous opinions. In the 1941 term nonunanimous opinions had constituted 36 percent of the total, the highest in Court history to that time, but the number jumped to 44 percent in the 1942 term.[60] "I have had much difficulty herding my collection of fleas," Chief Justice Stone confided to a friend; he complained that he himself had had to write an excessive number of opinions, since the justices were "so busy disagreeing with each other."[61]

By now even outsiders could see the split in the Court. The *Wall Street Journal* remarked that the justices tended "to fall into clamorous argument even on the rare occasions when they agreed on the end result."[62] Within the Court, Frankfurter's temper grew shorter and his invective more vitriolic. He began to talk about "enemies" on the bench, especially Douglas, and once yelled at the clerk, "Don't you get the idea that this is a *war* we are fighting."[63] He referred derisively to Black, Douglas, and Murphy as "the Axis."[64]

Whatever Frankfurter's private feelings, public discourse within the Court remained fairly civil. In fact, his colleagues may not have even recognized the extent of his antipathy toward them at this time. Frankfurter's diaries show that often after a seemingly calm discussion of a case, he would return to his chamber to vent his spleen in writing.[65] What had been private and concealed anger, however, broke out into the open in his anguished dissent in the second flag salute case.[66]

In light of the spate of attacks on Jehovah's Witnesses, the apparent shift in Court sentiment, and news of Hitler's "final solution" of the Jewish question in Europe, the Court accepted another case dealing with required flag salutes and free exercise of religion, *West Virginia Board of Education* v. *Barnette* (1943). Both the American Bar Association Committee on the Bill of Rights and the American Civil Liberties Union, a rare alliance, filed amicus curiae briefs in support of the Witnesses. Justice Jackson, who hardly ever voted for minority rights against a public interest argument, this time joined the liberals to strike down the mandatory salute and wrote one of the most eloquent opinions of his judicial career, declaring that, "if there is any fixed star in our constitutional constellation, it is that no official, high or petty, can prescribe what shall be orthodox in politics, nationalism, religion or other matters of opinion or force citizens to confess by word or act their faith therein."[67]

Frankfurter's impassioned dissent, if taken literally, nearly denies the Court any role in enforcing the Bill of Rights; Douglas's denunciation of the dissent in his memoirs seems to be warranted. "The Frankfurter philosophy was fully exposed," he wrote. "Although free exercise of religion was guaranteed by the First and Fourteenth Amendments, the legislature could nonetheless regulate it by invoking the concept of due process, provided they stayed within reasonable limits."[68] Indeed, despite

Frankfurter's comment that he belonged to "the most vilified and per-secuted minority in history,"[69] he dismissed judicial protection of minor-ities. The framers of the Bill of Rights, he said, "knew that minorities may disrupt society."[70]

Frankfurter worked for weeks on the dissent; in apologizing to Jack-son for holding up the decision he described his dissent as "the expression of my credo regarding the function of this Court in invalidating legisla-tion."[71] He reiterated the formula he had used in the earlier decision, that "this Court's only and very narrow function is to determine whether within the broad grant of authority vested in legislatures they have ex-ercised a judgment for which reasonable justification can be offered."[72] Frankfurter could not pass over Jackson's eloquent depiction of the meaning of free exercise of religion as lightly as he had in *Gobitis,* but he took a minimalist approach. The First Amendment provides "freedom from conformity to religious dogma, not freedom from conformity to law because of religious dogma."[73] Claims of conscience by themselves can never justify exemption from valid laws that have a reasonable basis. Since, as Sanford Levinson points out, the state could always create the nexus of a reasonable justification for its action, the courts would never impose any serious review on state action.[74]

Frankfurter's pride in his dissent and the importance he attached to it led him to an active extrajudicial campaign to publicize his views. He sent copies to retired chief justice Hughes and suggested to President Roosevelt that a copy be placed in the Hyde Park library, since it would "furnish to the future historian food for thought on the scope and mean-ing of some of the Four Freedoms—their use and misuse."[75] He wrote friends in the press such as Bruce Bliven of the *New Republic* and Frank Buxton of the *Boston Herald* and pointed out that Learned Hand and Louis Brandeis had agreed with his *Gobitis* opinion. But, he noted, "those great libertarians," Black and Douglas, had also agreed, "until they heard from the people."[76]

There is a bitter sadness here, due in part to Frankfurter's recogni-tion that he had lost the opportunity to lead the Court into what he considered its proper jurisprudential role, namely, a limited jurisdiction in mediating between the elements of the federal system. What is also regrettable is the failure of a man who had studied the Court for over a quarter-century, a man who, in his own words, "knew all there was to know . . . on what had gone on behind the scenes,"[77] a man who had argued brilliantly that the Court had to be sensitive to changes in the larger society, but ultimately, a man who allowed his views to become so rigid as to deny him flexibility or room for change and maneuver.[78]

His heroes, Holmes and Brandeis, had argued for judicial restraint, but they had done so in cases primarily involving economic questions. Holmes in *Lochner* and Brandeis in *New State Ice* had called upon courts not to interpose their economic views in place of legislative policy. But it had also been Holmes and Brandeis who initiated the modern jurisprudence of free speech.[79] Brandeis was the first to suggest that the Fourteenth Amendment incorporates parts of the Bill of Rights, and that courts have a special obligation to scrutinize legislative actions that restrict those rights.[80] Another one of Frankfurter's judicial heroes, Benjamin Nathan Cardozo, was the first to express the doctrine of incorporation in a systematic fashion,[81] and Harlan Fiske Stone, in his famous *Carolene Products* footnote, called for a heightened level of review when basic rights are at stake.[82] The tragedy of Mr. Justice Frankfurter is that he became a prisoner of an idea—judicial restraint—and failed to distinguish between the regulation of economic and property rights and limitations upon individual liberties.

As for the charge that Douglas and Black "heard from the people," one might recall Holmes's comment in *Lochner* that the case was decided "upon an economic theory which a large part of the country does not entertain."[83] One might also note Brandeis's famous talk on "the living law," and his charge that courts had been "largely deaf and blind" to the great revolutionary changes then taking place and had "continued to ignore newly arisen social needs."[84] Much of the agitation over the judicial system during the Progressive Era resulted from popular perceptions that the courts and the law had not kept up with the times. In *Gobitis* the Court had made a mistake and in doing so had unleashed ugly passions and prejudices.[85] That it rectified its error ought to be seen not as pandering to popular tastes but as a sign of strength and self-confidence. The Court has, after all, adhered to other unpopular opinions when it believes them to be right.[86]

The major issue before the courts in the first half of the twentieth century had undoubtedly been the extent to which legislatures could regulate property rights; a difference of opinion on this issue between a majority of the Supreme Court and the majority of the American people led to the crisis of 1937. The old battles ended, though, and by the time Justice Douglas delivered the coup de grace in 1955,[87] the Court had essentially removed itself from passing on matters of economic regulation. The major issue in the second half of the century has been the tension between legislative power and individual rights. Here the courts, despite some bumpy spots, have for the most part ridden in tandem with an increasingly liberal society, which has in fact seen the courts as holding a special warrant for the protection of constitutional liberties. In the transition, Justice Frankfurter could never break away from views formed years, even decades, before he went on to the bench.[88] Douglas, and especially Black, proved the better judges in terms that Professor Frankfurter would have applauded, such as the ability to recognize that the Constitution, in order to serve the needs of a changing society, has to remain a flexible document.[89]

The divisions in the Court widened perceptibly in the October 1943 term, when for the first time in history a majority of the Court's decisions—58 percent—came down with divided opinions.[90] "The justices not only continued to disagree but to be disagreeable on occasion in doing so."[91] Court watchers had been aware of the growing divisiveness; now even those who did not follow the Court closely could hardly fail to see that internal strife burdened the nation's highest tribunal. On 3 January 1944 the Court handed down decisions in 14 cases, but the justices agreed unanimously in only 3. The other 11 elicited 28 full majority or dissenting opinions, and 4 shorter notations of partial disagreement or concurrence. In one case, *Mercoid Corp.* v. *Mid-Continent Investment Co.* (1944), Douglas wrote the majority opinion, Roberts and Reed concurred, Jackson and Frankfurter dissented in separate opinions, and Black, joined by Murphy, entered a concurrence that was in effect a "dissent from the dissent," in which he lambasted Jackson and Frankfurter.[92]

Whether one believes in the principles of law enunciated in cases like *Mercoid* or *Barnette,* the decisions did introduce an element of instability. "Those bozos," complained one federal court judge, referring to the high court, "don't seem to comprehend the very basic characteristic of the job, which is to keep some kind of coherence and simplicity in the body of rules which must be applied by a vastly complicated society."[93] Learned Hand, who shared much of Frankfurter's frustration and anger at "the Axis," complained that "they are sowing the wind, those reforming colleagues of yours. As soon as they convince the people that they can do what they want, the people will demand of them that they do what the people want. I wonder whether in times of bland reaction—

59

[and] they are coming—Hillbilly Hugo, Good Old Bill and Jesus lover of my Soul [Murphy] will like that."[94]

The 1944 term saw more of the same; three out of every five decisions called forth multiple opinions. Frankfurter complained to Justice Wiley B. Rutledge near the end of the term about "an increasing tendency on the part of members of the Court to behave like little schoolboys and throw spitballs at one another."[95] It is unclear whether he included himself in that description.

The story from 1946, when Stone died, to 1962, when a stroke forced Frankfurter to retire, is for the most part a playing out of the same scenario, with a few dramatic moments but no major changes in the script. According to one Frankfurter biographer, after the "siege" of the first five years on the bench Frankfurter would "mentally divide his colleagues into three categories—adversaries, allies, and potential allies."[96]

A major shift within the Court came with the appointments of Earl Warren as chief justice in 1953 and William J. Brennan as associate justice three years later. At first Frankfurter expressed great enthusiasm for Warren, whom he believed to be a clever politician (capable, therefore, of protecting the Court as Taft and Hughes had done) who was somewhat weak in the law, and thus open to his tutelage, and for Brennan, a former student of his at Harvard. Frankfurter never seemed to learn or to stop hoping; he repeated the same pattern of flattery, attention, cajoling, and endless attempts at instruction, but it did no good.[97] As Warren grew accustomed to the Court, he relied more on his own judgment and began to resent Frankfurter's constant stream of advice. "All Felix does is talk, talk, talk," Warren told his colleagues. "He drives you crazy!"[98] The new Chief moved within three years from a centrist position in the Court's makeup to alignment with the liberal wing, and for this he earned Frankfurter's condemnation.[99]

Even when Frankfurter had constructive comments to make, his didactic manner rubbed his colleagues the wrong way, especially Douglas. As Dennis Hutchinson has shown, Frankfurter began making suggestions for improving and strengthening Court procedures around 1946 and at the beginning of every term would circulate a lengthy memorandum enumerating and explaining his proposed changes.[100] One can recognize in one section of the 1956 term memorandum all the irritating features discussed above: "Even before I came on the Court, I had good reason to believe that the course of proceeding leading to adjudication was not all that it might be. My grounds for feeling that the deliberative process was inadequate derived from the intimacies I had enjoyed over the years with Justices Holmes, Brandeis, and Cardozo."[101]

In his "October greeting" for the 1960 term, Frankfurter made several suggestions for improving and speeding up the voting and announcement procedures. In particular he wanted the per curiam decisions issued immediately, rather than allowing a single justice to hold up the announcement if he wanted to think about it some more. Frankfurter then asked for a conference to discuss his proposals. Douglas had his answer printed and circulated:

> With all due respect, I vote against a meeting to discuss the proposals. The virtue of our present procedures is that they are very flexible. If anyone wants a *per curiam* held over, it is always held. If anyone wants to pass and not vote on a case until a later Conference, his wish is always respected. If anyone wants to circulate a memorandum stating his views on a case, the memo is always welcome.
>
> If we unanimously adopted rules on such matters we would be plagued by them, bogged down, and interminably delayed. If we were not unanimous, the rules would be ineffective. I, for one, could not agree to give anyone any more control over when I vote than over how I vote. . . . We need not put ourselves in the needless harness that is proposed.[102]

When Frankfurter renewed the suggestion the following year, Douglas expressed his continued opposition in even stronger terms.[103]

There were, as Professor Hutchinson notes, a number of worthwhile ideas in these annual memoranda, but Frankfurter's abrasiveness often prevented a fair hearing. Moreover, Frankfurter himself often held up decisions for weeks and even months as he laboriously prepared his elaborate opinions. At the end of the 1948 term, Douglas (who always wrote quickly) was the one to complain about delays; he suggested that a case be reassigned if a justice held up his opinion more than three months after the case had been decided at conference. "I do not think," he told the brethren, "in fairness to each other and the litigants, one of us [Frankfurter] should be allowed to serve his own personal ends by holding cases beyond that time."[104]

Once again Frankfurter, who prided himself on understanding the importance of personal relations and individuality on the Court, had misjudged the issue. His proposal can be seen as part of his emphasis on procedure, on getting the rules and the process right, in the belief that right procedure always will produce the right result. Douglas's chilly response is undoubtedly correct: the nature of judging could not always be girdled by rules, there had to be room for flexibility and the accommodation of a justice's second thoughts or his desire to rethink and perhaps rediscuss a difficult issue rather than rushing to judgment because of an artificially imposed time limit.

There would have been some tension under the best of circumstances between Frankfurter and his strong-willed colleagues on the nation's highest court. Other justices, however, holding equally strong views, have managed to remain on civil and even cordial terms with their associates who adhere to diametrically opposite opinions. With the exception of the anti-Semitic McReynolds, Brandeis got along well with the conservatives who dominated the Court during most of his 23-year tenure. On the modern Court, Chief Justice William Rehnquist and Justice Brennan could not have been further apart doctrinally, yet got along quite well. Frankfurter, for all that he could be charming, solicitous, witty, and outgoing, was also duplicitous and conniving, and these characteristics triggered confrontation.

Frankfurter tended to divide the world into disciples and mentors. While possibly an appropriate attitude for a professor, it boded ill for his relationships with persons who did not care to be treated as students. This attitude had led to a break between Frankfurter and two of his most gifted protégés, Ben Cohen and Thomas Corcoran, who, after seven years of doing top-level work for the President of the United States, refused to be treated any longer as two of Frankfurter's brighter students. "Felix is incapable of having adult relationships!" Cohen complained; Frankfurter could relate well to his mentors and his students, but not to his peers.[105]

Another consideration is that Frankfurter's success as a professor spoiled him for his work as a justice. He did, as even Douglas conceded, know more about the Court than anyone else. He had been on intimate terms with Holmes, Brandeis, and Cardozo, and he therefore assumed that he had some special knowledge denied to others, even to those who sat on the bench. He could not understand why his colleagues resented his efforts to share his knowledge with them; he saw it as his duty to instruct, just as he had done while at Harvard.

Third, Frankfurter's intellectual arrogance, combined with a nastiness some of his students had seen years earlier, led him to alienate nearly all of his colleagues at one time or another. He would flatter them so long as they agreed with him, but at the first sign of independent thought he would explode. During his tenure on the bench, no one—with the possible exception of Robert Jackson—escaped his scorn. Typical are the comments he scribbled on an opinion by Wiley Rutledge that went against his advice: "If I had to explain all your fallacies I would have to write a short book on (1) federal jurisdiction (2) constitutional law (3) procedure generally."[106]

Frankfurter's high-flown lectures on the purity of the Court often angered those who saw the hypocrisy—for there is no other word for it—in his own secretive political activities. His loudly proclaimed adherence to judicial restraint did not hide from either the bench or the law reviews the fact that he could write his own views into opinions just as "the Axis" did. Douglas was not alone in describing Frankfurter as "a real conservative who embraced old precedents under the guise of bowing to 'the law,' but who actively chose the old precedents because he liked them better."[107]

Justices of the Supreme Court, as we well know, do not give up their emotions and prejudices when they don the black robe, although we do expect them to keep their private feelings somewhat in check. For all his constant reference to Holmes and Brandeis, Frankfurter could never separate his judicial from his private views as they did. He personalized every battle, so that within five years of going on the bench he had divided his colleagues into "we" and "they"—allies and enemies. It is possible that the country—and the Constitution—benefited from the philosophical tensions and debates generated by the clash of views between Frankfurter and the other justices. Unfortunately, the Court and its members suffered for more than two decades from the personal animosities generated by this prima donna of the law.

5

THE JUSTICE AT WAR

Throughout his life, Felix Frankfurter never made a secret of his enormous love for America or of his gratitude at what it had allowed an immigrant boy to achieve. On his deathbed Frankfurter told his chosen biographer, "Let people see . . . how much I loved my country."[1] His law clerks recalled the diminutive justice bouncing down the halls of the Supreme Court whistling "Stars and Stripes Forever," albeit offkey. This intense patriotism colored his entire life as well as his jurisprudence, and during the Second World War Frankfurter, both on and off the bench, stood ready to do everything to help his beloved country.

As war clouds loomed ominously over Europe in the late 1930s, no question existed in Felix Frankfurter's mind over whether the United States should aid Great Britain. A confirmed anglophile, his year as Eastman Professor at Oxford had if anything enhanced his view that England and the United States stood apart as two nations indivisibly linked by common ties of heritage, language, and politics. His role as Brandeis's aide in the Zionist movement left him fully aware of British shortcomings, especially in regard to its Palestine policy, but that consideration paled before the threat of Nazi domination of Europe.[2] Only the British could resist Hitler, but to do so they needed American help. Frankfurter assumed that Roosevelt would eventually bring the country into the fight against fascism and saw the timing of his own appointment as part of the war against the totalitarians. While Hitler preached racial anti-Semitism and condemned Jews as pariahs, Franklin Roosevelt had named a Jew to America's highest tribunal.[3]

But would Justice Frankfurter be able to help the President? He realized that as a Jew, and as the only foreign-born member of the Court, he had to be circumspect. Although Frankfurter's protégés could be found throughout the government, none of them enjoyed the same relationship with him that he had had with Brandeis as the older man's surrogate. Moreover, where Brandeis had been quite able to allow an intermediary to carry his advice to the White House, Frankfurter could not; he had to be there himself.[4]

First, however, the new justice had to find out just how far he could go in continuing to serve the President. A month after he took his seat on the Court, Frankfurter wrote to his commander in chief resigning his commission as a major in the army reserve. Roosevelt immediately refused to accept the resignation and declared that "it is more essential than ever that you remain in the Army." A delighted Frankfurter, "recognizing a military order," quickly agreed and signed his next letter to the White House, "Obediently and martially yours, Felix Frankfurter, Lieutenant Colonel *in spe*, J.A.G.-Res."[5]

From the correspondence between Frankfurter and Roosevelt, as well as from other evidence,[6] it is clear that the justice continued to advise the president on a number of issues, although it should be noted that Frankfurter was not the only member of the Court to make regular trips to the White House during the war years. William O. Douglas, Frank Murphy, and Robert Jackson had all been close to Roosevelt and part of the higher echelons of the New Deal administration; they, as well as Frankfurter, were frequent visitors at the White House during the war.[7] None of them, evidently, saw any incongruity in members of the judicial branch advising the executive.

One of Frankfurter's greatest assets, of course, was his wide array of friends and acquaintances. If Roosevelt needed to find out about something or somebody, he could always ask Felix; sometimes the justice could be positively brilliant and quite persuasive regarding both lesser and major posts in the administration. His encomium to his good friend Archibald MacLeish led Roosevelt to name the poet and playwright the librarian of Congress in 1939.[8] Frankfurter also helped the president when the latter badly needed to replace the isolationist Harry Woodring as secretary of war in 1940.

In late April 1940 Frankfurter went to the White House for lunch.

Roosevelt obviously wanted to talk about conditions in the War Department and about the need to replace Woodring, who, aside from his foreign policy views, had proved an incompetent administrator when faced with the task of preparing the nation for possible war. Roosevelt said he had been considering former New York City mayor Fiorello LaGuardia, Secretary of the Interior Harold Ickes, and New York governor Herbert Lehman. Frankfurter objected to all three.

After mulling the problem over, Frankfurter came up with a solution. Roosevelt should name Henry L. Stimson, Frankfurter's first mentor, who had previously served as secretary of war under Taft and as secretary of state in the Hoover administration. Stimson had ability and experience; the fact that he was a Republican would underscore Roosevelt's belief that the current crisis transcended partisan differences. But could Stimson, at 73, shoulder the physical and mental demands of the office? Frankfurter recognized the problem and with typical resourcefulness set about to implement the plan.

First he arranged for Stimson to lunch at the White House so that Roosevelt could see for himself the older man's condition and sound out his views. Then Frankfurter suggested that if Stimson could be named to the War Department, he should use his experience primarily to shape policy; the heavy burden of daily administration should be shouldered by Robert Patterson, whom Frankfurter had known as "the first man in his class" at Harvard Law School, and who had recently been appointed to the Court of Appeals for the Second Circuit. "Some things click—they seem just right—and I cannot help but feel that the combination of Stimson and Patterson would take off your shoulders a very great burden."

Frankfurter dispatched Grenville Clark to sound out both men on whether they would be willing to undertake the work and also to seek assurances that both were, in fact, physically able to do the work. Stimson raised certain conditions, one of which was that he would be able to pick his own assistant. But when Clark informed him of Frankfurter's plan, Stimson quickly agreed; he could think of no better person for the job than Patterson. Clark reported back to the justice, who went to the White House on 3 June 1940 to sell the President on the plan. Roosevelt immediately saw the benefits and said Frankfurter had "struck fire" with the plan. He had no problems with Stimson's conditions;[9] he only wished he knew more about Patterson. Frankfurter took care of that, having already asked Clark to draft a memorandum detailing Patterson's career and abilities. Less than three weeks later, Roosevelt named Stimson and Patterson to head the War Department. Frankfurter telegraphed the president, congratulating him on "this new manifestation of leadership for a free people."[10]

The appointment of the two men gave Frankfurter access to one of the most important departments of the government; both Stimson and Patterson, one a former mentor and the other a former student, consulted with him often during the war years. When the administration needed to calm the black community during the election, Frankfurter put forward the name of William L. Hastie, whom he had earlier described as "not only the best colored man we have ever had [at Harvard] but he is as good as all but three or four outstanding white men that have been here during the last twenty years." Frankfurter helped Stimson find other aides as well and met with him often to discuss issues, much as he had 30 years earlier during the Taft administration. According to Bruce Murphy, Frankfurter also served as an intermediary between the cold, formal Stimson and the ebullient president.[11]

Later in the year Frankfurter helped draft the lend-lease bill, which allowed the United States to supply ships and war supplies to Great Britain on long-term credit. While isolationists never challenged the constitutionality of the measure, Roosevelt, beset by other problems, might have felt some relief that a justice of the Supreme Court had vetted it. Frankfurter not only helped Benjamin Cohen with the technical details but, drawing on his accumulated political knowledge about Congress, spent many hours advising the President's staff on how best to put the measure across. It was he who suggested that the bill be numbered H.R. 1776. America had once gained her independence by fighting Great Britain; now, according to the justice, we have "to seek independence through interdependence," a phrase the president relished and recounted often. Immediately after the bill's passage in late February 1941, Frankfurter sat down and wrote a lengthy memorandum outlining what American industry would have to do to help achieve the goals of the program.[12]

Had anyone asked, of course, Frankfurter would have denied any extrajudicial activity. When John Maguire, a former colleague at Harvard Law School, wrote asking Frankfurter's assistance in getting the President to commute a death sentence, the justice declined. "You above all ought not to be surprised," he wrote, "that since I have been down here I have kept within the orbit of my judicial job with finicky scrupulousness; that on no matter even remotely connected with law or politics would I dream of making any suggestion to the President, and certainly not on a matter which, in some of its phases, came before this Court. You see, I take the tripartite separation of our Government seriously."[13]

In fact, throughout the war Frankfurter responded to requests from the White House and just as often put forward ideas of his own. The dinner-seminars at his Washington apartment, 1511 30th Street, N.W., brought together high officials from different departments who discussed common problems while their host moderated, listened, and then suggested solutions. Although he continued to accuse his colleagues Black and Douglas of political machinations, he sanctimoniously preached that "when a priest enters a monastery, he must leave—or ought to leave—all sorts of worldly desires behind him. And this Court has no excuse for being unless it's a monastery."[14]

If Frankfurter had honestly believed this, he would have been unable to reconcile his incessant extrajudicial activity with the principle of separation of powers. No doubt he believed that his role as a presidential advisor did not conflict with his responsibilities as a judge sworn to give impartial judgment. Those who benefited from his advice, and they were many, no doubt found this potential conflict irrelevant to the larger task of winning the war; this was how Frankfurter rationalized it as well. The day after Pearl Harbor, the justice told his law clerk, Philip Elman, "Everything has changed and I am going to war. I am going to need you as no justice has ever needed a law clerk." Although Elman had some doubts about the propriety of his boss's politicking, he swallowed them and "we both went to war."[15]

If patriotism justified Frankfurter's extrajudicial activities, it also informed his vote on key cases during the war, as well as during the cold war that followed. In the flag salute cases (discussed in chapter 4) Frankfurter poured out his love of country in both opinions, triumphantly in the one, bitterly in the other. How could anyone question the need and right of the state to inculcate love of country among its children? Religious principles are all very well, but do not these people recognize that they can practice their religion only because of the freedoms America offers? It did not seem too high a price to pay for that freedom to require people to salute the nation's symbol.

Individual liberties are always, to some degree, circumscribed in wartime. What is surprising is not that the Court upheld the flag salute in *Gobitis,* but that it reversed itself in *Barnette,* which was decided in the middle of the conflict. The Court's record during the rest of the war is mixed, but it did, among other things, approve the worst invasion of civil liberties in the nation's history, the forced evacuation of men, women, and children of Japanese descent from the West Coast and their internment in concentration camps.

The members of the wartime Court all remembered quite vividly the excesses of the Wilson administration during World War I, and some, such as Frank Murphy and Robert Jackson, had taken steps during their terms as attorneys general to make sure that such excesses would not be repeated should the United States enter another such conflict.[16] Nonetheless, the justices still recognized the government's need to protect itself.

Under this rationale, the Justice Department sought to revoke the citizenship of naturalized citizens of German and Italian origin who either displayed disloyal behavior or had secured their citizenship illegally or under false pretenses. Within a year after American entry into the war, the government had initiated over 2,000 investigations and secured the denaturalization of 42 people. The case testing this campaign, however, did not involve a Nazi or a fascist sympathizer, but a Communist, William Schneiderman.[17] Born in Russia in 1905, he had come with his parents to the United States in 1908. He applied for citizenship in 1927; by then he had already joined several Communist party groups. In 1932 he ran for governor of Minnesota as the Communist party candidate. In 1939 the government moved to strip Schneiderman of his citizenship on the grounds that his Communist activities in the five years prior to the naturalization process showed that he had not been truly "attached" to the principles of the U.S. Constitution. Schneiderman, in turn, argued that he did not believe in using force or violence, and that in fact he had been a good citizen: he had never been arrested and had used his rights as a citizen to advocate change and greater social justice.

Schneiderman's case came before the Court in early 1942, by which time the United States had entered the war and publicly acknowledged the Soviet Union as an ally. Wendell Willkie, the Republican candidate for president in 1940, represented Schneiderman and eloquently pleaded with the Court not to establish a legal rule that a person could be punished for alleged adherence to abstract principles. The government, recognizing how embarrassing a victory might be, privately suggested to Chief Justice Stone that the Court delay its decision. Although Stone understood the Justice Department's quandary, he believed more important issues were at stake, namely, that the political branches should not interfere in the business of the Court. Moreover, Stone believed that people like Schneiderman, who did not support American institutions, ought not to avail themselves of American citizenship. At the conference on 5 December 1942, Stone led off discussion of the case with a forceful statement that the government ought to have the power to rid the nation of agitators who not only did not believe in the Constitution but worked actively to overthrow the government. [18]

Given his idolization of Holmes and Brandeis, Frankfurter might have been expected to speak in defense of Schneiderman, as Holmes had done so eloquently for another immigrant who held unpopular views, Rosika Schwimmer, a Quaker who had been denied citizenship because she refused to bear arms. "If there is any principle of the Constitution that more imperatively calls for attachment than any other," Holmes wrote in a dissent joined by Brandeis, "it is the principle of free thought—not free thought for those who agree with us but freedom for the thought we hate."[19]

But Frankfurter supported Stone's view. Knowing that his position might appear contradictory in light of his professed reverence for Holmes and free speech, he explained it in conference at length and with great emotion. This case, he began, "arouses in me feelings that could not be entertained by anyone else around this table. It is well-known that a convert is more zealous than one born to the faith. None of you has had the experience that I have had with reference to American citizenship." He had been in college when his father received his naturalization papers, "and I can assure you that for months preceding, it was a matter of moment in our family life." He went on to talk about his work in the U.S. Attorney's office in dealing with naturalization cases and confessed that, "as one who has no ties with formal religion, perhaps the feelings that underlie religious forms for me run into intensification of my feelings about American citizenship."

For Frankfurter, "American citizenship implies entering upon a fellowship which binds people together by devotion to certain feelings and ideas and ideals summarized as a requirement that they be attached to the principles of the Constitution." While mere membership in the Communist party did not constitute grounds for either denying or revoking citizenship, Frankfurter believed that Schneiderman's actions had gone far beyond paying dues. Schneiderman had committed himself to the "holy cause," and "no man can serve two masters when two masters represent not only different, but in this case, mutually exclusive ideas."[20] Frankfurter voted to affirm the conviction, but only he, Roberts, and Stone did so.

After several delays, the Court finally handed down its decision in the spring of 1943. Frank Murphy's opinion for the majority conceded that naturalization constituted a privilege granted by Congress, but that once that privilege had been granted, a person became a citizen and enjoyed all the rights guaranteed by the Constitution, including freedom of thought and expression. Membership in the Communist party had not been illegal at the time Schneiderman took out his papers, and the government had not proven his current membership "absolutely incompatible" with loyalty to the Constitution.

Frankfurter gave Murphy a hard time during the circulations of the majority opinion. One day he suggested that Murphy might want to add to his opinion the statement that "Uncle Joe Stalin was at least a spiritual co-author with Jefferson of the Virginia Statute for Religious Freedom." A few days later Frankfurter sent a note, signed "F. F. Knaebel," offering Murphy the following as a headnote for the decision: "The American Constitution ain't got no principles. The Communist Party don't stand for nuthin'. The Soopreme Court don't mean nuthin', and ter Hell with the U.S.A. so long as a guy is attached to the principles of the U.S.S.R."[21]

Stone, joined by Frankfurter and Roberts, entered a vigorous dissent that seemed strange coming from the man who had stood alone in the first flag salute case. "My brethren of the majority," he said, "do not deny that there are principles of the Constitution . . . civil rights and . . . life, liberty and property, the principle of representative government, and the principle that constitutional laws are not to be broken down by planned disobedience. I assume also that all the principles of the Constitution are hostile to dictatorship and minority rule."[22]

Some comments by Frankfurter are quite revealing here. Shortly after Murphy circulated his draft opinion, he stopped to talk with Frankfurter and confessed that while everybody should have freedom of opinion, Congress did have the right to set conditions for citizenship. Murphy conceded that the opinion "skates on the thinnest possible ice—awfully thin," but he did not like the idea of cancelling a person's citizenship 10 years after it had been conferred. Frankfurter casually dismissed the issue as none of the Court's business. If Congress had set conditions, "then it is our business to enforce what Congress had commended and not overrule the legislative power."[23]

Frankfurter totally missed the point, one so obvious that even the Court's newest justice, Wiley Rutledge, had immediately spotted it. If citizenship could be cancelled because of strong—or weak—beliefs held by an individual, then no naturalized citizen could be secure in his rights. As a naturalized citizen himself, Frankfurter believed he owed full and complete loyalty to the United States, and so did every other naturalized citizen, with no less passion. Communists could not share that love of country that true patriots had, and therefore could be stripped of their citizenship. The notion of full freedom of belief, it would seem, did not apply in this case.

In a letter to the chief justice offering suggestions for the dissent, Frankfurter said that it was "plain as a pikestaff" that political considerations, the need to not antagonize Russia, had been the "driving force behind the result in this case." Had the record come up with reference to a Bundist rather than a Communist, the opposite result would have been reached.[24]

In fact, such a situation came up a year later, when the Court unanimously reversed the denaturalization order of a German-American citizen the Justice Department had accused of endorsing Nazi racial doctrines. Frankfurter voted to reverse because he believed the government had failed to carry the necessary burden of proof, but in his draft opinion he did not mention the earlier decision in *Schneiderman*. At Stone's suggestion, Frankfurter added a sentence distinguishing this case from *Schneiderman*, but the original omission led Murphy, joined by Black, Douglas, and Rutledge, to file a concurrence that ringingly endorsed freedom of expression for all citizens, native-born as well as naturalized, including the right to criticize their country.[25]

Deference to Congress on naturalization issues led Frankfurter to acquiesce in what even he saw as a legislative vendetta—the government's lengthy effort to deport Harry Bridges, the controversial maritime union leader, for alleged affiliation with the Communist party. When the Justice Department had reported that it did not have the necessary authority under the law, Congress changed the law, and the sponsor had announced that the amendment would now permit the deportation of Bridges and "all others of similar ilk."[26]

Five members of the Court—Black, Douglas, Rutledge, Murphy, and Reed—believed that while there might be constitutional problems with the law, it would be easier to thwart the deportation on procedural grounds; Douglas's opinion, couched in a deliberately noncondemnatory tone, did just that.[27] Stone agreed that Congress had attempted "a rotten thing," but along with Frankfurter and Roberts, he dissented, claiming that it had long been settled law that Congress had plenary power in controlling resident aliens. The Court stood powerless to respond to a manifest injustice.

Frankfurter's reputation as a civil libertarian, the would-be heir to the mantle of Holmes and Brandeis, slipped even further in a case arising under the same law that had led Holmes to pen his famous dissent in *Abrams v. United States* (1919).[28] In the first Espionage Act case to reach the Court during World War II, a 5–4 majority reversed the conviction of a native-born citizen who had circulated vitriolic attacks on England, the Jews, and President Roosevelt and urged an alliance with Germany in a race war against the Asiatics.[29] Justice Murphy, writing for the majority, applied a strict interpretation of the clear-and-present danger test. Although some of the pamphlets had reached army officers, there had been no proof that the scurrilous materials had had any effect on the war effort. American citizens have the right to discuss matters as they wish, Murphy ruled, "either by temperate reasoning or by immoderate and vicious invective."[30] Frankfurter joined Reed, Douglas, and Jackson in dissent.[31]

With the exception of slavery, the worst example of racist invasion of civil liberties in American history is the forcible transfer of 110,000 persons of Japanese ancestry—70,000 of them American citizens—away from their homes, jobs, and property to detention centers, ostensibly because they posed a security threat to the West Coast.[32] Although the military had no evidence of a single case of sabotage or even attempted sabotage, government leaders quickly gave in to the public hysteria demanding that something be done. The respected columnist Walter Lippmann informed his readers that "nobody's constitutional rights include the right to reside and do business on a battlefield. There is plenty of room elsewhere for him to exercise his rights." A few days later the less restrained columnist Westbrook Pegler called for every Japanese man and woman to be put under armed guard, "and to hell with habeas corpus until the danger is over."[33]

In fairness, it should be noted that responsible military analysts in early 1942 viewed the Pacific as a Japanese lake; until the Battle of Midway later in the year, it appeared that nothing could stop the Imperial Fleet or prevent an invasion of the West Coast. It should also be recalled that the treatment of Japanese-Americans, unfair as it was, cannot compare with the way the Nazis treated minority groups in the countries they conquered.

On 19 February 1942 President Roosevelt signed Executive Order 9066, authorizing the secretary of war to designate certain parts of the country as military zones, from which any and all persons could be excluded, and in which travel restrictions, including daily curfews, might be imposed. In March Congress enacted the major provisions of 9066 into law and added stringent penalties for those who resisted relocation.

Gen. John L. DeWitt had already begun to act under 9066: on 2 March 1942 he designated the entire Pacific coast as a military area. Three weeks later he imposed a curfew along the coastal plain between 8:00 P.M. and 6:00 A.M. for German and Italian nationals and for all persons of Japanese origin, both Issei (Japanese nationals) and Nisei (American citizens of Japanese ancestry). On 27 March the army prohibited these groups from leaving the coastal area, then on 9 May excluded them from the same area. Issei and Nisei could comply with these contradictory orders only by reporting to designated locations, from which they would be bussed to relocation centers in the interior. Amazingly, the 110,000 men, women, and children affected responded cooperatively for the most part. A number of younger Nisei volunteered to serve in the army, and their units turned out to be among the most highly decorated in the European theater of operations.

The entire operation proceeded on racist assumptions and brought forth such astounding statements as that of Rep. Leland Ford of California that a patriotic native-born Japanese, if he wanted to make his contribution, would "permit himself to be placed in a concentration camp." Without a shred of evidence, the entire Japanese-American population, including native-born American citizens, stood condemned because, as General DeWitt so eloquently put it, "A Jap is a Jap."[34]

The constitutional issue could not have been clearer. Those affected by the relocation plan were never charged with any crimes; they were never accused of anything other than their racial ancestry; they never had any hearings to see if, on an individual basis, they posed a threat to security. In any circumstances, their internment constituted a clear violation of the Fifth Amendment's due process clause. Opposed to that consideration stood the war powers of the president and Congress, as well as the question of how much deference the Court should pay to the other branches. The internment cases caused several of the justices much anguish, but on these issues Felix Frankfurter stood solidly behind the administration's plan, along with Hugo Black and Chief Justice Stone.

The first case to reach the Court involved Gordon Hirabayashi, a native-born American citizen and a senior at the University of Washington, who had been arrested for failing to report to a control center and for violating the curfew.[35] He had been convicted, sentenced to two 3-month prison terms, and then had appealed his conviction on the grounds that the military had exceeded its constitutional authority. Both the federal district court and the appeals court upheld the conviction; the case came to the Supreme Court in the spring of 1943.

Chief Justice Stone strongly supported the army's actions and used all his persuasive powers to mass the Court behind the government. On 30 May he circulated the first draft of his opinion, which included a truly awesome reading of the war powers. Such powers went far beyond purely military matters on the battlefield, comprising any and all "evils that attend the rise and progress of the war."[36] Black and Douglas immediately endorsed Stone's views but made significant suggestions to emphasize what they considered a key element in the Court's decision, judicial deference. Black urged Stone to include a statement making explicit that the Court had no business second-guessing the military, and Stone obliged: "It is not for any court to sit in review of the wisdom of their [the military commanders'] action or substitute its judgment for theirs."[37]

Frankfurter, working as Black's ally, picked up on a second theme of judicial deference and urged Stone to amend the opinion so as to make it clear to the country that "we decide nothing that is not before us." The Hirabayashi case dealt only with the curfew, and so should the Court's opinion; the Court should not address the more controversial aspects of the relocation plan. In his memo Frankfurter wrote: "We decide the issue only as we have defined it—we decide that the curfew order as applied, and at the time it was applied, was within the boundaries of the war power." Stone recirculated the opinion with Frankfurter's language added word for word.[38]

The chief wanted a united Court on this issue, but at least two members had grave doubts. William O. Douglas had grown up in the Pacific Northwest with Japanese-American friends and knew that not all of them, as Stone had insisted in his draft, had strong nationalist attachments to Japan. The lack of due process also troubled Douglas, but he was willing to concur in an opinion that approved the military orders as a temporary expedient; he urged Stone to limit the Court's decision to that holding. Moreover, he wanted the Court to issue a requirement that individuals had to have an opportunity to be classified as loyal citizens.[39]

Douglas circulated a concurring opinion incorporating his views, and Frankfurter exploded. He urged the chief to send at once "for Brother Douglas and talk him out of his opinion by making him see the dangers that he is inviting." The Douglas view would unleash thousands of habeas corpus proceedings, and "it would be for me deplorable beyond words to hold out hopes by any language that we use . . . hopes, which to put it very mildly, are not likely to be fulfilled." Douglas ought to be pulling along with everyone else instead of acting as if he were "in a rival grocery business." Trying to get Douglas to change his mind would probably be useless, Frankfurter concluded, because Douglas "will want to make the spread eagle speech." That same day Frankfurter sent another memorandum to Stone, suggesting a revision in Stone's draft that would close off the habeas corpus option Douglas had suggested.[40]

Frankfurter wisely left the handling of Douglas to Black and Stone, while he personally lobbied Frank Murphy who, alone on the Court, seemed willing to face head on the issue of racism. He termed the discrimination "so utterly inconsistent with our ideals and traditions, and in my judgment so contrary to constitutional requirements, that I cannot lend my assent."[41] Frankfurter pleaded with Murphy not to dissent, for the sake of the Court. As opinion day approached, Frankfurter wrote:

> Do you think it is conducive to the things you care about, including the great reputation of this court, to suggest that everybody is out of step except Johnny, and more particularly that the Chief Justice and seven other Justices of this Court are behaving like the enemy and thereby playing into the hands of the enemy. Compassion is, I believe, a virtue enjoined by Christ. Well, tolerance is a long, long way from compassion—and can't you write your views with such expressed tolerance that you won't make people think that when eight others disagree with you, you think their view means that they want to destroy the liberties of the United States and "lose the war" at home?[42]

The appeal succeeded, and on 21 June, Chief Justice Stone was able to announce an opinion upholding the curfew supported by all the members of the Court. He had labored on it through four drafts and had spent endless hours trying to assuage the doubts of at least five members of the Court about the legality of the detention program. During this time he had had the complete support of Felix Frankfurter in asking the justices to swallow their doubts for the sake of unity in wartime. The final opinion evaded all of the hard issues that the doubters had raised. When Stone circulated his final draft, Frankfurter gave it his blessing: "You have labored with great forbearance and with concentration to produce something worthy of the Torah."[43] But not all of the justices agreed with Stone's broad enunciation of the war powers, or with his cavalier attitude in labeling all Japanese-Americans as potentially disloyal. Douglas, Murphy, and Rutledge entered concurring opinions that came close to dissents; all indicated that they had agreed to what they considered an unconstitutional program because of the allegedly critical military situation. The tone of their opinions indicated that it would be far more difficult to get unanimity if another challenge reached the Court.

Sixteen months later that challenge came, and this time the Court would not be able to evade the larger constitutional issues. Fred Korematsu had been charged with failing to report to an assembly center for relocation.[44] His attorneys claimed that the entire exclusion order violated the Constitution by depriving citizens of their freedom without trial or other guarantees of due process. Moreover, the mass expulsion of an entire group based solely on a racial classification constituted a cruel and unusual punishment forbidden by the Eighth Amendment.

At the conference on 16 October 1944, Stone tried to limit the discussion to a narrow technical question. Korematsu had been convicted of violating the exclusion order, designed to keep Japanese-Americans out of certain militarily designated areas. The only question the Court had to answer, according to the chief justice, was the constitutionality of that exclusion order. Framed this way, the case could be decided on narrow grounds similar to that in *Hirabayashi*.

Stone turned to the senior justice, Owen J. Roberts, who had endorsed the earlier opinion, only to find Roberts dead set against this plan. The combination of exclusion and prohibition orders gave Japanese-Americans a cruel choice—defy the order and be imprisoned, or report to an assembly point and be relocated to a concentration camp. Black and Frankfurter supported the chief, as did Rutledge and Reed. But four justices, Roberts, Murphy, Jackson, and Douglas, planned to dissent on grounds that the military had overstepped its constitutional bounds of authority. Jackson, normally a supporter of strong government, declared, "I stop at *Hirabayashi*."[45]

Stone assigned the opinion to Black, who tried to follow Stone's lead in describing the case in the narrowest possible terms. When Black circulated his draft, Frankfurter responded the same day, "I am ready to join in your opinion without the change of a word." But Frankfurter did suggest that the elimination of one sentence would make even stronger the deference shown by the Court to congressional authority to prosecute the war. Black eliminated the sentence.[46] Black concluded his opinion, however, in a semiapologetic manner: "We cannot—by availing ourselves of the calm perspective of hindsight—now say that at that time these actions were unjustified."[47]

This comment struck Frankfurter as irrelevant; the Court owed deference not to the military but to Congress. He dashed off a brief concurrence declaring that he found "nothing in the Constitution which denies to Congress the power to enforce a military order by making its violation an offense triable in civil courts." Then he saw the draft of Jackson's dissent, which included the sentence, "Our forefathers were practical men, and they had no delusions about war being a lawless business." As Peter Irons notes, Frankfurter wasted no time responding to this "sacrilege." He called in the wife of his law clerk Harry Mansfield, who was completing a graduate degree in history, and put her to work tracking down the Revolutionary War records of each member of the Constitutional Convention. Although Jackson deleted the offending sentence in his final draft, Frankfurter kept in his sentence lauding the Framers and their actual knowledge of what war meant, since "a majority had had actual participation in war." Frankfurter concluded his brief concurrence by declaring that DeWitt's exclusion orders could not "be stigmatized as lawless because like actions in times of peace would be lawless." As for Congress endorsing those orders, "That is their business, not ours."[48]

Given the criticism that he had received from civil libertarians for his earlier opinions, Frankfurter must have welcomed the letter that Alexander Meiklejohn, the noted philosopher and advocate of free speech, wrote him following the *Korematsu* decision. Although Meiklejohn had been asked by the American Civil Liberties Union to keep a watching brief in Washington during the war, he wanted Frankfurter and Black to know that he disagreed with the ACLU's condemnation of the *Korematsu* holding. A grateful Frankfurter responded that "even a judge gets comfort in finding agreement in those very few whose judgment one really values."[49]

In the end only three justices dissented—Roberts, Murphy, and Jackson. Douglas swallowed his dissent when Black agreed to add a paragraph noting that the minority viewed the issues of evacuation and detention as inseparable, and therefore as raising additional constitutional issues.[50] *Korematsu,* according to one of Black's biographers,

> was the worst judicial opinion that Justice Hugo Black wrote in his thirty-four years on the Court. It was devoid of meaningful analysis of the underpinnings of military policy. It was deceptive in its strained narrowing of the constitutional issues that had been presented by Korematsu's attorneys. And it was a philosophically incoherent defense of broad government power by one of the most influential civil libertarians in the Court's history. . . . Although Black did not say so, he had given the military a license to trample on individual rights at will during wartime.[51]

And Frankfurter, who had opposed just this sort of trampling in his days as a reformer, not only went along but encouraged Black and Stone in their views and denigrated the dissenters as unpatriotic! Black never regretted these decisions: Years later he said that if he had been president, he would have done exactly the same thing, and he continued to justify his opinion on grounds of military necessity.[52]

Frankfurter, however, should have known better. He had held frequent meetings with the officials he helped place in the War Department, including John J. McCloy, one of the officials responsible for implementation of the internment program. By the time the cases came to the Court, Frankfurter would have known that the threat of a Japanese invasion of the Pacific coast had evaporated, and that the only questions the War Relocation Authority had to answer involved political, not military risks. But Frankfurter said nothing. He condemned Douglas for the "spread eagle speech" in opposition to the internment; he, in turn, willingly abdicated judicial responsibility in the name of patriotism.[53]

In 1958 the Court decided one more case that had arisen during the Second World War. Albert Trop had been an unruly 20-year-old private stationed with the U.S. Army in French Morocco in 1944 and had twice been thrown in the stockade for breach of discipline. He then deserted, and upon recapture a court-martial had sentenced him to three years at hard labor, loss of pay, and a dishonorable discharge. In 1952, however, after he had resumed civilian life in the United States, Trop applied for a passport and discovered that he had also been stripped of his status as an American citizen. He challenged this in court as a violation of his constitutional rights.[54] The case came to the Supreme Court in 1958, along with a second case in which an American had lost his citizenship after voting in a Mexican election.[55] The Court split on the two cases, with Frankfurter writing the majority opinion in one and a dissent in the other.

In *Perez*, the second case, Frankfurter spoke for a 6–3 majority in upholding congressional power to expatriate under certain circumstances: voting in a foreign election constituted sufficient reason for Congress to act. Chief Justice Warren, joined only by Douglas and Black, dissented, on grounds that the Fourteenth Amendment, by conferring citizenship on all persons born in the United States, raises an absolute bar to the government trying to take away that citizenship. While the Court should defer to Congress in its legitimate exercise of power, here the Court has to enforce the prohibition against illegitimate action.[56]

In *Trop* five members of the Court agreed with the chief justice that stripping citizenship for desertion violated the Eighth Amendment ban against cruel or unusual punishment. Warren's opinion for the majority expressed the activist role he envisaged for the Court in protecting individual liberties, especially his notion that the Court has the obligation to reinterpret constitutional liberties according to the "evolving standards of decency that mark the progress of a maturing society."[57]

All this proved too much for Frankfurter. To begin with, his former student, William Brennan, who had joined the Court only two years earlier, had deserted him, a loss that greatly irritated Frankfurter. Frankfurter unburdened himself of his disappointment to Justice John Harlan, saying that he wished Brennan "was less shallow and thereby less cocksure." While acknowledging his former pupil's honesty, "to me it is a constant puzzle why men like him can't read or rather reflect on what they read."[58]

In his dissent Frankfurter reiterated his credo regarding judicial restraint. "Judicial power," he asserted, "must be on guard against encroaching beyond its proper bounds." The Court should neither formulate policy nor pass on the wisdom of a statute passed under clear legislative authority. Congress, Frankfurter believed, has the power to "deal severely with the problem of desertion from the armed forces" under its war powers (the same powers he had urged Stone to rely on in the Japanese internment cases). "Self-restraint is the essence of the judicial oath, for the Constitution has not authorized the judges to sit in judgment on the wisdom of what Congress and the Executive Branch do."[59] Beyond that, the majority had not only erred in ruling that denaturalization constituted cruel or unusual punishment, it had gone beyond its proper role in creating a new constitutional right, a right to travel, that could not be justified by history, precedent, logic, or the clear words of the Constitution.[60]

Unspoken in Frankfurter's opinions was his sense that Perez and Trop clearly deserved to lose their status as American citizens because they had betrayed their country. By voting in a Mexican election, Perez had, in Frankfurter's view, shown himself to be more attached to the Mexican polity than to the American. Citizenship and patriotism demand that in return for the rights and privileges enjoyed by Americans, they in turn must meet their responsibilities. In wartime citizens have the obligation to defend their country; by deserting the United States when its very existence had been under attack, Trop had forfeited any claims he might have to the mantle of its citizenship.

Robert Burt reads these two opinions as strong support for his view that Frankfurter, the "outsider" become "insider," had lost the special sensitivity to the problems of the underdog and the outcast that had marked the opinions of Brandeis and even, although to a lesser extent, Holmes. Brennan and Warren, on the other hand, showed a sensitivity to the problems of the stateless, those that no one wanted, that should have been especially significant to Frankfurter following the Holocaust, in which the Nazis had stripped German Jews of their citizenship. Burt claims that the majority, even more than Frankfurter, valued the "communion of citizenship" to the point of being unwilling to accept the possibility that citizenship could be involuntarily lost. Frankfurter's passionate patriotism blinded him to this problem.[61]

There is nothing to sneer at in Frankfurter's love of his country. The success enjoyed by the immigrant youth who rose to become a member of the Supreme Court epitomizes the dreams pursued by millions who have come to these shores seeking freedom and opportunity. But one can certainly question whether the relation between a country and its citizens is as simple and unequivocal as Frankfurter saw it, and whether wartime actions taken in the name of national security, policies that run roughshod over the rights of individuals, should be given automatic deference by the courts. What is missing in Frankfurter's opinions is something that a judge always needs: the clearheaded sense of balance that Brandeis had called for to protect individual rights in wartime from the actions of an "intolerant majority, swayed by passion or by fear."[62]

Felix Frankfurter at time of
graduation from elementary
school, 1895. *Harvard Law Art
Collection*

Frankfurter teaching a class at
Harvard Law School, 1917.
Harvard Law Art Collection

Frankfurter as Eastman Professor at Oxford University, 1933. *Library of Congress*

Frankfurter and his wife, Marion, leaving from Boston's Back Bay Station to take up his seat on the Supreme Court, 1939. *Library of Congress*

On Cape Cod in Chatham, Massachu-
setts, 1938: (*left to right*) Frankfurter,
Louis D. Brandeis, Alice Brandeis, and
Marion Frankfurter. *Courtesy of Elizabeth
Brandeis Raushenbush estate*

Frankfurter and James Landis leaving Frankfurter's home at 192 Brattle Street, Cambridge, Massachusetts, ca. 1935. *Library of Congress*

The Warren Court, 1957: (*seated left to right*) William O. Douglas, Hugo L. Black, Earl Warren, Frankfurter, and Harold Burton; (*standing*) William J. Brennan, Jr., Tom Clark, John Marshall Harlan, and Charles Whittaker. *Library of Congress*

Justice Frankfurter ca. 1960. *Library of Congress*

6

FROM CRISIS TO CRISIS

For Felix Frankfurter, the end of the war marked a significant change in his life. His hero, friend, and mentor, Franklin Roosevelt, had died in April 1945, and the new president, Harry Truman, had his own circle of advisors. Frankfurter still knew many people in government, and some of them continued to feed him information or seek out his counsel; a well-known Washington sight during the postwar years was Frankfurter and his former pupil Dean Acheson, now secretary of state, walking to work together in the mornings. But many of the bright young men Frankfurter had helped place in New Deal and wartime agencies had gone into the private sector, and the new men and women who came to Washington, even those from Harvard, had no ties or loyalty to Frankfurter.[1]

Some elements of Frankfurter's life did, of course, remain stable, and by the 1945 term he had established the pattern within his chambers that he would follow for the rest of his time on the bench. He would rise early each morning, read several newspapers, and sometimes jot down stray thoughts either on cases then pending before the Court or on other subjects. He would then leave for the Court, sometimes walking part of the way or else being driven by one his clerks, and upon arriving in the office would dictate memoranda on his earlier thoughts, to be filed for later use.

Just as he had chosen clerks for Holmes, Brandeis, and Cardozo, so his former pupil, Harvard Law professor Henry Hart, chose them for him. Frankfurter played no role in the selection but had delegated to Hart an "unqualified power of attorney . . . to pick men for me."[2] The early clerks put together a lengthy memorandum detailing their responsibilities and what the justice expected them to do. Subsequent clerks added their own handwritten comments or altered some of the procedures when Frankfurter wanted them changed. When the memo became too illegible, it would be retyped, and the process begun anew.[3] Aside from the regular business of the Court, Frankfurter often assigned research projects to his clerks, some of which dealt with cases at hand and some of which merely intrigued him.[4]

Frankfurter, like Holmes, loved his clerks; they were the sons neither man ever had, and he kept them on their intellectual toes. He would grab them at the elbows in a viselike grip, ask them what they thought about a case, and then make them defend their views. One of his favorite clerks, Alexander Bickel, recalled that Frankfurter "gave it to you with both barrels. He was the most unscrupulous debater alive; there were no holds barred; knees in the groin, fingers in the eyes, unfair arguments, shifting of ground; that was as it properly ought to be . . . and you'd walk away from one of these thinking, 'Oh, my God, you left a horrible impression.' . . . And he'd walk into the next room and say to somebody, 'Gee, that's a bright fellow.'"[5] With the exception of those working for Douglas (who had orders not to fraternize with the enemy), Frankfurter went out of his way to meet all of the clerks, and he was a frequent and willing guest at their brown-bag lunches, which he ran as he had run his Harvard seminars.

He once commented that he saw the clerks as "junior partners" whom he took fully into his confidence, provided they in turn measured up to his demands for intellectual acuity. Once a year all of his clerks, past and present, would gather for dinner. At one of them Frankfurter, characteristically, asked them to name the Court's worst opinion from the previous term. Andrew Kaufman identified one that Frankfurter himself had written, and the two men went at it for a while. Another clerk reported that they regarded it as part of their job to disagree with him.[6]

Although aware of his shortcomings, former Frankfurter clerks obviously returned his affection. As Louis Hankin said, "One of the great benefits of being a Frankfurter clerk was that you got to be a former Frankfurter clerk," opening up a lifelong relationship.[7] No matter how busy, the justice always had time to see his boys, to find out how things were going, and to help them. Like Brandeis, he hoped that his clerks would go into teaching, and many of them did. In personal terms, there is little doubt that his relationships with his clerks constituted one of the most satisfying emotional, as well as intellectual, parts of his life.

Other relations on the Court remained less pleasant. Owen Roberts retired in 1945, and three of the Roosevelt appointees, Stone, Murphy, and Rutledge, died, to be replaced by men of decidedly inferior intellect and more conservative views. Frankfurter's philosophy of judicial restraint probably influenced the Court more than at any other time in his 23-year tenure on the bench; the Court repeatedly validated his belief that the judiciary should not second-guess legislative wisdom in matters of economic policy. In fact, his nemesis, William O. Douglas, delivered the coup de grace to the Four Horsemen's economic activism that Frankfurter had railed against in the 1920s and 1930s. "The day is gone," Douglas declared, "when this Court uses the Due Process Clause [to] strike down state laws, regulatory of business and industrial conditions, because they may be unwise, improvident, or out of harmony with a particular school of thought."[8]

Even while winning particular battles, Frankfurter fought a rearguard campaign. The economic issues that had dominated the Court's agenda throughout the first part of the century were giving way to questions of civil liberties and civil rights, a battleground on which Frankfurter's view of judicial deference attracted less and less support. Despite the appearance that his views on judicial restraint guided the Court, Frankfurter won no clear victories and suffered a growing sense of frustration about his inability to lead the Court.

Shortly after the Court adjourned in the spring of 1946, Frankfurter summed up what he considered to have been one of the stormiest five-year periods in the Court's history. If he had to explain these five terms in a classroom, he told Frank Murphy, he would have to say:

1. Never before in the history of the Court were so many of its members influenced in decisions by considerations extraneous to the legal issues that supposedly control decisions.
2. Never before have members of the Court so often acted contrary to their convictions on the governing legal issues in decisions.
3. Never before has so large a proportion of the opinions fallen short of requisite professional standards.[9]

Frankfurter might well have added that never before had collegial relations within the Court been so poor; for that he was in large part responsible. By the end of the war the normal level of polite give-and-take within the Court had been seriously poisoned by the ongoing feuding between Frankfurter, Roberts, and Jackson on one side and Black, Douglas, and Murphy on the other. When the Southern Conference for Human Welfare gave Hugo Black its 1945 Thomas Jefferson Award on 3 April 1945, 900 guests, including Eleanor Roosevelt, gathered at the Washington Statler to pay Black tribute. Douglas, Murphy, Reed, and Rutledge attended; the chief justice, Roberts, Frankfurter, and Jackson pointedly did not. The extent of his bitterness can be seen in two incidents, both seemingly minor, that mushroomed out of all proportion.

During the 1944 term the Court heard a case requiring an interpretation of the Fair Labor Standards Act of 1938, otherwise known as the Black-Connery Act, one of Hugo Black's last legislative accomplishments before his appointment to the bench.[10] The Court had to decide the so-called portal-to-portal question: did the law require that miners' pay be calculated from the time they entered the portal of the mine, or from the moment they actually started to work the coal?[11] In large mines with deep shafts, the amount involved could be substantial. Arguing for the United Mine Workers of America was Crampton Harris, who had once been Black's law partner in Alabama.[12] The Court initially split 5–4 against the union position. Stone assigned the opinion to Jackson; Stanley Reed then changed his mind, and Black, now the senior justice in the majority, designated Frank Murphy to write the decision.[13]

Jackson turned what would have been his majority opinion into a dissent and buttressed his interpretation of the Black-Connery Act by reference to then-Senator Black's own statements in the *Congressional Record*. An angry Black charged that Jackson had quoted him out of context, a view Murphy incorporated into his opinion, but Jackson's dissent still stung.[14] This would have been the end of the issue, but the Jewell Ridge Coal Corporation petitioned for a rehearing on the grounds that Black should have disqualified himself because of the involvement of his former law partner.

Chief Justice Stone saw no merit in this argument. Holmes, Brandeis, and many other justices—including Stone himself—had not recused when the Court heard arguments by lawyers with whom they had at one time or another been professionally involved. It had always been left to the individual justice's sense of propriety whether a conflict of interest existed with a particular counsel in a particular case. The chief justice therefore prepared a per curiam denying the petition; but knowing how strongly Frankfurter and Jackson felt about the issue, he suggested that a statement be added that no question of disqualification is ever open for consideration by the Court. Frankfurter immediately objected, saying this raised new matters; Black insisted that the denial be issued without any explanation. "Any opinion which discussed the subject at all," Black told the conference, "would mean a declaration of war." Stone tried to negotiate a compromise, but to no avail. Jackson believed a simple denial would imply the Court's approval of Black's conduct; encouraged by Frankfurter, he prepared a two-page concurrence to the per curiam, implicitly criticizing Black's conduct.[15] Evidently aware that his signature along with Jackson's might be misinterpreted as merely a personal attack, Frankfurter sent a letter to Black explaining his position:

> It happens to be one of my deepest convictions that the world's difficulties are due to no one cause more than to the failure of men to act on that which they believe to be true. I had no share in creating the situation whereby Bob felt it his duty to make clear the issue of disqualification. But since he had done so, I could withhold joining him only by suppressing my belief in the truth. I do not propose to do that—and that is the sole reason why I join him.[16]

In the ensuing brouhaha in the press, Frankfurter no doubt suffered from conflicting emotions—the pleasure of seeing Black portrayed as an unprincipled judge, and the anguish of having the Court's dirty linen aired in public.[17]

Frankfurter took on Black directly only a short time later. The denial for rehearing came down on the last day of the term, and soon afterwards, Owen J. Roberts decided to retire after 15 years on the bench. During his last few terms, Roberts had grown increasingly close to Frankfurter, who had assiduously cultivated the man who had become, next to Jackson, his strongest ally on the bench.[18] Roberts had had enough of the rancor among the brethren, and also felt himself increasingly out of step with the Roosevelt appointees; in his last term, Roberts dissented 53 times.[19]

Following custom, Chief Justice Stone drafted a farewell letter; in light of the Court's rancorous divisions, it sounded a relatively neutral tone. Stone sent the letter to the senior justice, Hugo Black, asking him to sign it and pass it on to the next most senior member of the Court. But Black objected to two phrases: the expression of the regret the remaining justices supposedly felt at Roberts's departure, and the comment, "You have made fidelity to principle your guide to decision." Black wanted to delete both these phrases, and Stone, hoping for unanimity, told Black to redraft the letter.[20] Black did so and passed the reworked letter on to Stanley Reed, who, assuming it to be Stone's draft, signed and sent it to the next in line. But Frankfurter learned through a conversation with Stone what had happened, and he immediately came to Roberts's defense. He insisted that the members of the Court see both Stone's original draft and Black's revision; when Stone reluctantly agreed, Frankfurter circulated his own memorandum insisting that the original wording be retained. As usual, Frankfurter had to quote from authority: "I *know* that that was Justice Brandeis' view of Roberts, whose character he held in the highest esteem."[21]

In the end, only Douglas agreed fully with Black's draft. Stone, Murphy, Reed, and Rutledge were willing to sign any letter in order to secure harmony, while Frankfurter and Jackson insisted on the original version. Neither Black nor Frankfurter would budge, and so no letter went to Roberts. As Alpheus Mason notes, "Emily Post would have disposed of the Justices' problem in a paragraph . . . but etiquette was not the real issue." This "lilliputian campaign, fought in dead earnest," reflected the sad state that the Court had come to by the summer of 1945.[22] From that poisonous atmosphere, Robert Jackson fled to the Nuremberg trials in Europe, not sure, as he later confessed, whether he would ever come back to the disagreeable climate of the Court.[23]

During the war, Roosevelt and Winston Churchill had pledged that, following an Allied victory, those who had committed crimes against humanity would be brought to justice. To keep this promise, the Allies subsequently convened an international military tribunal in Nuremberg, Germany, the city where the infamous Nazi racial laws had been proclaimed. President Harry S. Truman asked Jackson to serve as the American prosecutor, and Jackson quickly accepted. Jackson saw the Nuremberg trials as not only the greatest challenge of his career but also as the noble endeavor of replacing the vengeance that victors had traditionally inflicted on the vanquished with the rule of law. The trial, Jackson declared in his opening statement, was "one of the most significant tributes that Power has ever paid to Reason."[24]

Not everyone shared this view, and there has been an ongoing debate over the legitimacy of the Nuremberg trials, whether they did in fact represent a rule of law or merely a legal fiction to rationalize vengeance.[25] The Court rejected all efforts by the Nuremberg defendants to file writs of habeas corpus because the tribunal had been created by a four-power agreement and therefore was not subject to review by American courts.[26]

The real impact the war crimes trials had on the Court was not jurisprudential; the trials wreaked havoc among the brethren. Although Jackson had been eager to take on the assignment, he realized that it created both practical and theoretical problems for the Court. His departure left the Court evenly divided in a number of cases; some decisions had to be deferred until Jackson returned to the Court. It also put additional burdens on the other members, a situation deeply resented by Black in particular. Whatever one might have felt about the rightness or wrongness of the war crimes trials, one might well have questioned the appropriateness of a member of the U.S. Supreme Court acting as a prosecutor.

As the trials stretched out for a far longer time than had been anticipated, Jackson grew increasingly uneasy about his role. He knew that Chief Justice Stone disapproved of the war crimes trials, Jackson's role in them, and the extra work caused by his absence.[27] Jackson also knew that Frankfurter shared at least some of Stone's doubt about the propriety of his role, and his letters to Frankfurter took on a strained, self-justifying tone. Frankfurter tried to reassure his friend, urging him to "dismiss all concern," since the complaints "neither in volume nor in quality really amount to a hill of beans."[28] When Jackson remained perturbed, Frankfurter wrote to him again: "Whatever I may think about a Justice of the Supreme Court taking on other jobs—and I am afraid I am impenitent on that subject—I never had any doubt about the profound importance of your enterprise and equally no doubt that you would discharge the task according to the finest professional standards both intellectually and ethically. That you have done so I have said again, and again, and again."[29] Then, on 22 April 1946, Harlan Fiske Stone died, and as Jackson at one time said, "Washington adores a funeral—especially if it ushers in a vacancy."

It was no secret that Jackson wanted the center chair, and supposedly he had been Franklin Roosevelt's first choice to succeed Charles Evans Hughes. At that time it had been Frankfurter who convinced Roosevelt to name Stone, arguing that, with war approaching, naming the

Republican Stone as chief justice would foster national unity.[30] Jackson had then taken Stone's place as associate justice, with Roosevelt's assurances that when Stone, by then almost 70 years old, stepped down, Jackson would take his place. But Harry Truman, not Franklin Roosevelt, now occupied the Oval Office, and Truman, even though he thought highly of Jackson, had serious and legitimate doubts about naming him the chief. The internal strife during Stone's tenure had become general knowledge, and following the *Jewell Ridge* battle, Truman might well have questioned Jackson's ability to unify the Court.

Then on 16 May Doris Fleeson's column in the *Washington Star* carried a report on the confrontation between Black and Jackson over *Jewell Ridge*, with details as could only have been provided by someone who had been at the conference—one of the members of the Court. In addition, Fleeson reported that Truman had been told that if he did appoint Jackson, both Black and Douglas would resign. Less than a month later, Truman named Fred M. Vinson the new chief justice, and the following day the president received a blistering 1,500-word cable from Jackson purporting to set the record straight. In the cable Jackson touched on a number of matters affecting, as he put it, the integrity of the Court. But the heart of the message consisted of Jackson's version of the *Jewell Ridge* controversy and a bitter attack on Hugo Black, whom Jackson accused of meddling with the president's choice of a chief justice.[31] Despite Truman's plea to hold up publication of the cable until he had a chance to talk to Jackson about it, the infuriated justice made its contents public the next day in the form of a letter to the chairman of the House and Senate judiciary committees.

What had riled up Jackson and led him to such an ill-considered outburst? A few years later Robert S. Allen and William V. Shannon published an account blaming Frankfurter for stirring up the pot: "Frankfurter wrote [Jackson] that Black had gone to Truman and declared that he would not serve under Jackson. That accusation was a lie. There was not an atom of truth in it. Black had neither said nor done anything to influence Truman's decision. The story was solely the product of Frankfurter's scheming and devious imagination. But to Jackson, seething and raging in Nuremberg, Frankfurter's letter was like putting an acetylene torch to a powder keg."[32] An outraged Frankfurter personally denied the story to Black and threatened to sue the two columnists for libel. In a letter to Black, Frankfurter declared that "neither directly nor indirectly did I send any communication whatever to Jackson regarding the vacancy created by Stone's death." Whether Black believed Frankfurter at the time is questionable; but later, after he and Felix had grown closer in the late 1950s and early 1960s, Black seemed to have accepted the story.[33] Bruce Murphy is a bit more skeptical and, although admitting that he lacks specific evidence, implies that it would have been perfectly in character for Frankfurter to have done just what Allen and Shannon charged.[34]

In fact, despite his great affection for Jackson and his dislike of Black at the time, Frankfurter did not instigate the incident. Frank Shea, who had been in the Justice Department under Jackson and had assisted in the preparation for the Nuremberg trials, wrote to Jackson on 17 May 1946, recounting the spate of events in Washington and the speculation about Stone's successor. "I understand that for a few hours it seemed a sure thing for you," Shea said. "Then Black got word to the President that there would be a row if you were appointed. At this, [Truman] began to make wide inquiries and to appreciate, perhaps exaggerate, the rifts in the Court." It was this letter from Shea, and not anything from Frankfurter, that pushed Jackson into indiscretion.[35]

Frankfurter apparently played no role in the selection of Vinson; his activity during this time appears to have been limited to trying to sustain his friend's sagging spirits and defending him from attack.[36] Jackson considered resigning from the Court, a thought that horrified Frankfurter, who knew that in the years ahead he would need all the help he could get to fight off Hugo Black's wrongheaded assault on the Constitution.

Two cases decided in the next two terms highlight the growing chasm between Frankfurter and Black. In both instances Frankfurter spoke for the majority while Black dissented, and in both instances Black's view ultimately prevailed.

In March 1946 the Court heard argument in a suit begun by Prof. Kenneth W. Colgrove of Northwestern University against Illinois governor Dwight H. Green, seeking to invalidate all elections held under the state's antiquated apportionment system, which, despite massive population changes, had not been revised since 1901.[37] Under the old system, legislative power remained entrenched in the rural districts; efforts to secure change through state judicial and political methods had failed, so Colgrove appealed to the federal courts. He argued that the Illinois system, which affected the election of congressmen as well as state representatives, violated the Fourteenth Amendment ban against abridgment of the right to vote, as well as guarantees in Article I regarding apportionment of congressmen and the Article IV provision that the

United States "shall guarantee to every State in this Union a Republican Form of Government."

Colgrove also based his case on recent decisions protecting the right to vote. The Court had held that white primary laws designed to thwart black participation in the electoral process violated the equal protection clause,[38] and in a case directly resting on Article I grounds, the Court held that states could not set different criteria for election of state legislatures and congressional representatives.[39] All of these cases, however, had involved the special case of discrimination against blacks, and the Court in 1932 had specifically denied that the Constitution requires compactness, contiguity, or equality of population in congressional districts. Moreover, a majority of the Court expressed the belief that such issues were "political" questions, and were therefore nonjusticiable.[40]

The "political question" doctrine dates back to the Dorr Rebellion of 1842, when defeated rebels attacked the legitimacy of the old government under the guaranty clause of Article IV. Chief Justice Taney denied the claim and held that enforcement of Article IV "belonged to the political power and not to the judicial." In such situations, the courts would not intervene because the judicial branch had neither the authority to resolve the dispute nor the means to enforce such a decision.[41] Although Justice Holmes had indicated that he thought the political question doctrine "little more than a play on words,"[42] it served a very useful purpose in allowing the Court to evade certain types of cases. For an advocate of judicial restraint, however, the political question doctrine could be interpreted as an absolute bar to judicial involvement in the apportionment dispute.

A "bob-tailed" Court of seven justices handed down its decision on 10 June; Chief Justice Stone had died a month after the oral argument, and Robert Jackson, still in Nuremberg, had not taken part. Frankfurter, speaking for himself, Harold Burton (who had taken Roberts's seat), and Stanley Reed, declared that

> the petitioners ask of this Court what is beyond its competence to grant. This is one of those demands on judicial power which cannot be met by verbal fencing about "jurisdiction." It must be resolved by considerations on the basis of which this Court, from time to time, has refused to intervene in controversies. It has refused to do so because due regard for the effective working of our government revealed this issue to be of a peculiarly political nature and therefore not meet for judicial determination.[43]

The Constitution, Frankfurter concluded, had conferred sole authority on Congress to ensure fair representation among the states in the House of Representatives. Courts, he warned, in a famous phrase, "ought not to enter this political thicket."

Frankfurter got his fourth vote, as well as the majority through the concurrence of Justice Rutledge, who disagreed about the nonjusticiability of such issues but agreed to dismiss for want of equity. With the next elections so close, Rutledge believed it would be impossible to implement any workable remedy.[44]

Black, joined by Douglas and Murphy, dissented. Black believed that a clear constitutional violation existed, and that the courts had not only the power but the obligation to protect rights secured by the Constitution. Legislative malapportionment violated his belief in the type of popular sovereignty, implicit in the Constitution, that had been the basis for its adoption.[45] No one, he asserted in his dissent, "would deny that the equal protection clause would also prohibit a law that would expressly give certain citizens a half-vote and others a full vote." Why, then, should the courts tolerate a system that in effect gives certain citizens a vote only one-ninth as effective as that of other citizens in choosing their state and congressional representatives? "Such discriminatory legislation," he concluded, "seems to me exactly the kind that the equal protection clause was intended to prohibit."[46]

Although only four members of the Court found against Colgrove, and only three members actually believed apportionment nonjusticiable, the case served as a barrier to election reforms in the states for the next 16 years. (For the Court's abandonment of the *Colgrove* decision, see chapter 10.) For Frankfurter, *Colgrove* stood for exactly the type of restraint the Court should exercise, but his analysis suffered from a serious flaw. In cases involving supposedly "political" questions, the courts have assumed that if there is a legitimate grievance, then the political process will be amenable to its rectification. But malapportioned legislatures not only constituted the grievance, they barred any change through the political process. As long as a minority of a state's population could elect a majority of the state assembly, it would not voluntarily give up that power, and the majority will would continue to be thwarted.

The most clear-cut example of the increasing jurisprudential gulf between Frankfurter and Black took place in the Court's consideration of a California murder case. Admiral Dewey Adamson (Admiral was his forename), a poor, illiterate black who had twice served time for robbery, had been out of prison for 17 years when police arrested him for the murder of an elderly white widow. The only evidence linking Adamson to the crime consisted of six fingerprints on a door leading to the garbage container in the woman's kitchen, which police identified as his. On the advice of his attorney, a veteran in the Los Angeles criminal courts, Adamson did not take the stand in his own defense. Had he done so, the prosecutor could have brought up Adamson's previous record, and that would have resulted in a sure conviction. But the prosecutor, as he was allowed to do under California law, pointed out to the jury Adamson's failure to testify and claimed that this surely proved his guilt. If he had been innocent, the prosecutor declared, it would have taken 50 horses to keep him off the stand. The jury convicted Adamson, and his lawyer on appeal challenged the California statute as a violation of the Fourteenth Amendment. Allowing comment on the failure to testify was equivalent to forcing a defendant to take the stand; both violated due process.[47]

The case capped the debate that had been going on between Frankfurter and Black for several years on the meaning of the Fourteenth Amendment's due process clause. As James Simon notes, both men started from the same place—opposition to the use of substantive due process by conservative courts prior to 1937 to strike down reform legislation. For Frankfurter, the answer to this abuse of power lay in judicial restraint and appropriate deference to the policy decisions of the political branches. But the due process clause obviously meant something, and as interpreters of the Constitution, courts had to define what this "something" was. Conservative jurists had used it to protect property, but beginning in the 1920s the Court adopted the view that due process also protected civil liberties. Through a process called "incorporation," the due process clause of the Fourteenth Amendment incorporated the protections of the Bill of Rights and applied them to the states.

As early as 1925 the Court, almost in passing, noted that the First Amendment's protection of free speech applies to the states as well as to the federal government;[48] a few years later it also held the press clause to apply.[49] The question now rose whether incorporation meant that all of the guarantees in the first eight amendments apply to the states, or only some. Benjamin Nathan Cardozo, the shy retiring successor to the flamboyant Holmes, held the same commitment to freedom but also believed in the need to draw boundaries. A blanket application of the Bill of Rights would undermine an important aspect of federalism and deprive the nation of diversity and the states of an opportunity to experiment. In late 1937 Cardozo delivered the majority opinion in *Palko* v. *Con-*

necticut and in doing so defined much of the judicial debate for the next generation.[50]

Palko involved a relatively limited question: Does the Fourteenth Amendment incorporate the guarantee against double jeopardy in the Fifth Amendment and apply it to the states? Cardozo said that it does not, for the Fourteenth Amendment does not automatically subsume the entire Bill of Rights. This means that it incorporates some rights, but which ones? Cardozo included all the protections of the First Amendment, for freedom of thought and speech "is the matrix, the indispensable condition, for nearly every other form of [freedom]." But as for the Second through Eighth amendments, the Court should apply only those that are "of the very essence of a scheme of ordered liberty" and "so rooted in the traditions and conscience of our people as to be ranked as fundamental." One test would be whether a violation of such a right would be "so acute and so shocking that our polity will not bear it."[51]

This doctrine of "selective incorporation" lodged enormous power and discretion in the Court. Nothing in the Constitution provided guidance; rather, the justices had to modernize the Bill of Rights and decide which parts applied to the states based on their views (guided at least in part by history and precedent) of what constituted a "fundamental" right. *Palko* made it possible to expand constitutional safeguards without amendment, but it required the justices to develop some hierarchy of values. Frankfurter, a friend of Cardozo's, supported the *Palko* approach, since it coincided nicely with his own views of judicial caution.

Black had just gone onto the Court when the *Palko* decision came down and at first subscribed to it. But he grew increasingly uncomfortable with the philosophy and method of selective incorporation and the great power it lodged in the courts. Black's intuitive commitment to civil liberties derived from his populist background, which often led him to ignore precedent and listen to his own instincts for fair play and justice, instincts that shone through in a 1938 opinion extending the rights of counsel and habeas corpus.[52] Over the next decade he mulled over this problem and finally reached the position he had been seeking in the *Adamson* case.

During these years he and Frankfurter, despite their other differences, had engaged in an ongoing debate over the meaning of the Fourteenth Amendment. Black's reading of history led him to believe that the framers of the amendment, especially Sen. John A. Bingham, had intended to apply all of the protections. Frankfurter's equally detailed reading of history led him to the opposite conclusion, and he doubted whether the states would have ratified the Fourteenth Amendment if in fact it did subject them to such restrictions. Due process requires no more, Frankfurter believed, than that the Court impose standards of procedural fairness on state criminal procedures.[53]

As early as 1939 Frankfurter responded to comments Black made in conference about the applicability of the Fourteenth Amendment to state action. Black had evidently said that he thought the Bill of Rights had been intended to apply to the states from the start, and that the Marshall Court had been wrong in *Barron* v. *Baltimore* (1833) in ruling that it did not.[54] Frankfurter said he could understand that position, but he disagreed with it. "What I am unable to appreciate is what are the criteria of selection," he said. "Which applies and which does not apply."[55] This, of course, was exactly the question Black would wrestle with for almost a decade.

The debate almost came to a head in 1942 in *Betts* v. *Brady*, in which a majority of the Court held that the Sixth Amendment right to counsel did not apply to the states.[56] In conference Black argued passionately that Betts was "entitled to a lawyer from the history of the Fourteenth Amendment," which had been "intended to make applicable to the States the Bill of Rights." He brought up his own experience as a trial lawyer and asked his colleagues how many of them thought that a layman could adequately plan a defense, summon witnesses, and conduct a trial against a trained prosecutor. "If I am to pass on what is fair and right," he declared, "I will say it makes me vomit to think men go to prison for a long time" because they had no benefit of counsel.[57]

Frankfurter responded just as heatedly, claiming that if the Court interpreted the Fourteenth Amendment to apply all of the Bill of Rights to the states, it would destroy the federal system and "uproot all the structure of the states." About a year later Frankfurter sent Black a lengthy letter trying to get him to be more explicit in his evidence for interpreting the Fourteenth Amendment to mean total incorporation. "Believe me," Frankfurter wrote, "nothing is farther from my purpose than contention. I am merely trying to get light on a subject which has absorbed as much thought and energy of my mature life as anything that has concerned me."[58] Frankfurter can be taken seriously here, even if some hyperbole can be discerned. He had given much thought to the meaning of the due process clause, and he did believe that, at a minimum, it requires the states to provide procedural fairness in criminal trials. Moreover, this was exactly the type of intellectual interchange that Frankfurter loved, playing professor with very bright students.

By 1945 Black could identify the heart of his differences with Frankfurter, namely, the great discretion the Frankfurter-Cardozo approach vested in the Court. If judges can strike down state laws that fail to meet "civilized standards," then the courts had reverted to a "natural law concept whereby the supreme constitutional law becomes this Court's view of 'civilization' at a given moment." This philosophy, he declared, makes everything else in the Constitution "mere surplusage" and allows the Court to reject all of the provisions of the Bill of Rights and substitute its own idea of what legislatures can or cannot do.[59] But Black failed to explain what standards he would apply.

The answer came in *Adamson*. In conference Frankfurter convinced a majority of his colleagues that the issue had already been decided, and decided correctly. In *Twining* v. *New Jersey* (1908) the Court had ruled that a state law permitting comment on a defendant's refusal to testify did not violate procedural fairness.[60] Justice Reed, assigned the opinion, conceded that such behavior by the prosecutor in a federal proceeding would be unacceptable and a violation of the Fifth Amendment. But following *Palko*, he found no grounds for applying the self-incrimination privilege to the states. "For a state to require testimony from an accused," Reed concluded, "is not necessarily a breach of a state's obligation to give a fair trial."[61]

Black, joined by Douglas, dissented and set forth his belief in the "total incorporation" of the first eight amendments by the Fourteenth. In a lengthy appendix he presented the historical evidence he had assembled to support this position.[62] But what is most interesting is Black's rationale, which in many ways resembled Frankfurter's own views on limiting judicial power. Black rejected Cardozo's criteria as too vague, since phrases like "civilized decency" and "fundamental liberty and justice" can be interpreted by judges to mean many things. This "natural law" theory of the Constitution "degrade[s] the constitutional safeguards of the Bill of Rights and simultaneously appropriate[s] for this Court a broad power which we are not authorized by the Constitution to exercise." The only way to avoid this abuse of judicial power would be to carry out the original intent of the framers of the Fourteenth Amendment and apply all the protections of the Bill of Rights to the states.[63]

Frankfurter responded to Black in a separate concurrence that must surely rank as one of his most forceful and important opinions. In probably no other statement, either for the Court or in dissent, do we get such a clear exposition of Frankfurter's philosophy of judging, which his protégés at Harvard Law School later termed "process jurisprudence" (which some less than friendly critics have claimed was invented by Harvard for "our Felix").[64]

Relying on his own historical research, Frankfurter denied that the framers of the Fourteenth Amendment has intended to subsume all of the Bill of Rights. Frankfurter also responded to what he took as the most serious of Black's charges, that the vague criteria of *Palko* leaves judges too much discretion, and that protection of rights relies on the mercy of individual subjectivity. "The protection against search and seizure might have primacy for one judge, while trial by a jury of twelve for every claim above $20 might appear to another as an ultimate need in a free society."[65] But that is not how judges, certainly not members of the Supreme Court, approach their responsibilities. The real issue, he declared,

> is not whether an infraction of one of the specific provisions of the first eight Amendments is disclosed by the record. The relevant question is whether the criminal proceedings which resulted in conviction deprived the accused of the due process of law. Judicial review of that guaranty of the Fourteenth Amendment inescapably imposes upon this Court an exercise of judgment upon the whole course of the proceedings in order to ascertain whether they offend those canons of decency and fairness which express the notions of justice of English-speaking peoples even toward those charged with the most heinous offenses. These standards of justice are not authoritatively formulated anywhere as though they were prescriptions in a pharmacopoeia. But neither does the application of the Due Process Clause imply that judges are wholly at large. The judicial judgment in applying the Due Process Clause must move within the limits of accepted notions of justice and is not to be based upon the idiosyncrasies of a merely personal judgment. The fact that judges among themselves may differ whether in a particular case a trial offends accepted notions of justice is not disproof that general rather than idiosyncratic standards are applied. An important safeguard against such merely individual judgment is an alert deference to the judgment of the State court under review.[66]

Here one has the Frankfurter jurisprudence, its strengths and weaknesses, in a nutshell. Frankfurter portrays judging as a process removed from the fray of daily pressures. Protected in their sanctum, justices may engage in that process of discovery that will yield *the* right answer—not an objective, eternally fixed answer, but the right answer for the time. Judges thus reflect the advances that society has made; the due process clause does not prescribe the fairness of 1868, but today's fairness. Courts thus help keep the Constitution contemporary, but they must do so cautiously, always following strict intellectual processes and always deferring to those in the thick of the battle—the state courts and legislatures, which must be left free to reform their procedures according to their standards of fairness. As Frankfurter noted in another case: "Due process of law requires an evaluation based on a disinterested inquiry pursued in the spirit of science, on a balanced order of facts exactly and fairly stated, on the detached consideration of conflicting claims, on a judgment not ad hoc and episodic but duly mindful of reconciling the needs both of continuity and change in a progressive society."[67] Thus, if the judge adheres to certain methods and standards, it does not matter what the result is in a particular case, because the process will ensure ultimate fairness across the spectrum of cases. "Whatever shortcut to relief may be had in a particular case," Frankfurter wrote a year after *Adamson*, "it is calculated to beget misunderstanding and friction and to that extent detracts from those imponderables which are the ultimate reliance of a civilized system of law."[68] The *process*, not a particular *result*, is the desideratum of judging.

The great appeal of process jurisprudence is that it attempts to replace idiosyncrasy and individuality with objectivity and consistency. Public faith in the judicial process is enhanced if the public believes the judges are acting fairly and adhering to a common set of methods and principles in all cases, regardless of the results in specific instances.

Yet, can judging ever be quite as impersonal as Frankfurter suggested? Does scientific analysis really produce the right results? Did not Frankfurter's hero, Oliver Wendell Holmes, declare that the prejudices of judges have as much if not more to do with determining the law than the logic of the syllogism? As Black asked, how does one objectively determine the "canons of decency and fairness" that everyone accepts? Moreover, though due process is meaningful over a whole gamut of cases, individuals are on trial; individuals must cope with the criminal justice system; individuals must pay the penalties if found guilty; individuals suffer if deprived of their rights.

For Black, total incorporation provided at least a partial answer, in that judges would no longer subjectively determine what rights met the "canons of decency and fairness." There were still questions to answer. Even if the Fourth Amendment is applied to the states, what constitutes an "unreasonable search" still has to be determined. But the basic rights, the ones enshrined in the Constitution, would be in force and not dependent on a handful of judges determining that they met the canon.

Neither approach is without merit, and neither is without flaw. If Frankfurter refused to face up to the fact that process jurisprudence involved subjective evaluation, his approach did have the virtue of recognizing an acceptable diversity in a federal system and acknowledging that there could be more than one model of a fair and workable system. Its open-endedness about fairness also permitted judges, always exercising caution, to help keep basic constitutional guarantees current with the times.

Black's approach did do away with some but not all subjectivity, and debates over the reach of the exclusionary rule and expectations of privacy show that interpreting the "canons of decency and fairness" is an ongoing judicial function. Moreover, although on the face he appeared more "liberal" than Frankfurter, in many ways Black's rigid adherence to the text led to a cramped view of individual liberty. He took an uncompromising stand that the First Amendment permits no abridgment of speech. But since he could find no mention of privacy in the Constitution, he could not support the judicial claim that such a right exists.[69]

In the end the Court nominally embraced the Cardozo-Frankfurter approach of selective incorporation and then proceeded to adopt nearly all the guarantees of the first eight amendments. The Frankfurterian approach has not been without its defenders.[70] It might have had more if Frankfurter himself had not always taken the most restrictive view of what constitutes the "canons of decency and fairness." In many instances in the 1940s and 1950s, Frankfurter managed to hold the Court back from expanding the meaning or reach of a constitutional protection. The "due process revolution" of the Warren Court in the 1960s, however, reversed nearly every one of the Frankfurter positions.

Frankfurter's willingness to defer to state legislative wisdom (a trait that is not without value) led him to support the view that the Sixth Amendment right to counsel does not apply to the states, the position taken by the Court in *Betts v. Brady* (1942).[71] The historic meaning of that right, according to some scholars, involved no more than the right of an accused to employ counsel, not to have counsel furnished by the government.[72] The *Betts* holding accorded perfectly with Frankfurter's philosophy, in that the Court would not impose a blanket standard on all the states but would conduct a case-by-case review. Where "special circumstances" applied, such as mental retardation or illiteracy, then fairness would require assistance of counsel.

Black, Douglas, and Murphy dissented, with Black contending that denial of the right to counsel "is shocking to the universal sense of justice."[73] Over the next two decades, the Court found one special circumstance after another,[74] while state after state moved to guarantee counsel in at least all felony cases. Finally, one year after Frankfurter retired, Black spoke for a unanimous Court in reversing *Betts* and applying the Sixth Amendment guarantee to the states.[75]

The following year the Court extended the Fifth Amendment's privilege against self-incrimination to the states, noting in passing that "decisions of the Court since *Twining* and *Adamson* have departed from the contrary view expressed in those cases."[76] And in 1965 the Court explicitly overturned the *Adamson* holding and found the California law allowing comment on a defendant's failure to take the stand unconstitutional.[77]

One of Frankfurter's best-known criminal procedure opinions can be found in the 1949 case of *Wolf* v. *Colorado*, in which he tried to balance his sense of what constituted procedural fairness with a sensitivity to federalism.[78] In 1914 the Supreme Court had held that in federal prosecutions the Fourth Amendment bars the use of evidence seized through an illegal search and seizure, that is, by means that do not comport with the Fourth Amendment's strictures requiring an appropriate search warrant. The high court had explicitly rejected, however, the claim that the so-called exclusionary rule should apply to violations by state or local police.[79]

That decision predated the beginning of incorporation. Thirty-five years later *Wolf* brought the issue directly before the Court: Does the Fourteenth Amendment's due process clause apply the same standards to the states as the Fourth Amendment applies to the federal government? Frankfurter, speaking for a 6–3 majority, set forth the issue quite clearly:

> The security of one's privacy against arbitrary intrusion by the police—which is at the core of the Fourth Amendment—is basic to a free society. It is therefore implicit in "the concept of ordered liberty" and as such enforceable against the States through the Due Process Clause. . . .

Accordingly, we have no hesitation in saying that were a State affirmatively to sanction such police incursion into privacy it would run counter to the guaranty of the Fourteenth Amendment. But the ways of enforcing such a basic right raises questions of a different order. How such arbitrary conduct should be checked, what remedies against it should be afforded, the means by which the right should be made effective, are all questions that are not to be so dogmatically answered as to preclude the varying solutions which spring from an allowable range of judgment on issues not susceptible of quantitative solution. . . . Granted that in practice the exclusion of evidence may be an effective way of deterring unreasonable searches, it is not for this Court to condemn as falling below the minimal standards assured by the Due Process Clause a State's reliance upon other methods which, if consistently enforced, would be equally effective.[80]

Frankfurter appeared to be saying, according to one of his most ardent defenders, that while he personally as a legislator or police chief would want to apply the very highest standards, as a judge he had to defer to the wisdom of others. If the states take steps to ensure the reliability and integrity of their search procedures, then the federal courts should not interfere.[81] By this interpretation, the Fourteenth Amendment does not incorporate the criteria for enforcing the Fourth Amendment that govern the FBI, but the due process clause, by itself, has all the authority necessary to ensure procedural fairness. The remedies, therefore, should be left to the discretion of the states, which have to meet Fourteenth rather than Fourth Amendment standards. The values of federalism ought to prevail, provided the methods sanctioned by the states do not shock the conscience.

Justice Murphy, joined by Rutledge, dissented, complaining that he could not understand how Frankfurter could go as far as to admit that the Fourteenth Amendment, like the Fourth, prohibits illegal searches, and then refuse to apply the one remedy sure to prevent police abuse. For Murphy, the values of federalism took a backseat on the need for restraining the police from acting illegally.[82]

The problem, as quickly became clear, was that many states had no desire to rein in their police. As Justice Roger Traynor noted, the great right of the Fourth Amendment, the right to be secure in one's home against arbitrary police intrusion, although "wearing its rich constitutional cloak . . . went begging for recognition. Alone of the princely rights it often went begging in vain. It became a classic right without a remedy."[83]

In the years immediately following *Wolf*, the Court had two occasions on which to reconsider its ruling. In a 1952 case, *Rochin v. California*, in which Frankfurter delivered the opinion, one of the methods used by the police—pumping the defendant's stomach—so offended the Court's "sense of justice" that it excluded the evidence at trial—without, however, altering the *Wolf* decision.[84] Two years later a closely divided Court (this time with Frankfurter in the minority) reaffirmed the *Rochin* ruling and allowed use of the evidence since the police search, although "shocking," did not involve a physical assault on the suspect's person.[85]

By this time, Earl Warren had come on the Court, and Frankfurter's 6–3 majority in *Wolf* had eroded to 5–4; it would be just a matter of time before the Court rejected his views on the Fourth Amendment, as it would on other issues. Frankfurter's strength, his ability to win a majority during these years, stemmed from two sources. First, he did speak for a respectable tradition of constitutional interpretation, one that he had been vigorously preaching for more than 20 years. Aside from Black, Douglas, and Murphy, who had quickly espoused an advanced liberal position, the other Roosevelt appointees, as well as those named by Harry Truman, remembered all too well the judicial activism of the Four Horsemen and the constitutional crisis it had triggered. Frankfurter's call for judicial restraint, deference to other branches of government, and the maintenance of diversity within a federal system had a great deal of appeal, since it spoke directly to those issues that had troubled reformers for more than three decades.

Second, Frankfurter had been one of the most articulate critics of the old Court, and he brought formidable intellectual skills to bear in his effort to lead the Court along what he considered the proper path. Where Hugo Black had come to the Court with an unformed judicial philosophy, Frankfurter had been preaching the same doctrine ever since the early twenties. He claimed to build upon the legacy of Holmes, Brandeis, and Cardozo and easily overwhelmed colleagues such as Harold Burton and Sherman Minton. Frankfurter's opinions in cases such as *Colgrove* or *Wolf*, read in the light of the jurisprudential debates of the 1920s and 1930s, make a great deal of sense; but under the spotlight of the judicial philosophy of the 1960s, their weaknesses are exposed.

The cases that began to take more and more of the Court's attention after the war involved individual rights and liberties, not the protection of property. If one believes that there is no difference, jurisprudentially, in how these issues are treated, then the Frankfurterian approaches makes excellent sense. If, however, one distinguishes individual rights from property, then judicial restraint and institutional deference often appear to be little more than acquiescence in the deprivation of those rights. The weakness of the Frankfurterian approach can perhaps best be seen in his decisions in speech cases, especially those that arose during the Red Scare that followed World War II.

7

THE COLD WAR AND A FREE SOCIETY

In the spring of 1946 Winston Churchill stepped to the podium of Westminster College in Fulton, Missouri; in describing conditions in Europe, he declared that "from Stettin in the Baltic to Trieste in the Adriatic an iron curtain has descended upon the Continent." Within an amazingly short time the Soviet Union, our ally in the war against fascism, became our enemy. The United States would be engaged in a "cold war" against the Soviet Union for the next four decades.

The fear of communist expansion triggered a new Red Scare in the United States, one even worse than the hysteria following World War I. Then the bugaboo had been far more imaginary than real, and calm, rational people soon realized that the writings for which anarchists like Schenck and Abrams had been prosecuted posed no real threat to the body politic. False fears and the incitement of demagogues certainly fanned the flames of nativism and paranoia in the 1940s and 1950s; nevertheless, even the more level-headed person could find much to worry about. In a relatively short period of time Americans witnessed the Berlin blockade, the triumph of Mao Tse-tung and the Communists in China, the first Soviet atomic bomb, the discovery that British and American scientists had spied for the Soviets, the invasion of South Korea, and the exposure and subsequent conviction of the Rosenbergs.

In response to both real and imagined threats, federal and state governments established a number of so-called loyalty and security programs that affected nearly everyone who worked in government, from janitors on up; William O. Douglas called it "the most intensive search for ideological strays that we have ever known."[1] The various laws passed, the committees that attempted to ferret out "security risks," and the loyalty and security programs led to numerous court challenges, primarily under the First and to a lesser extent the Fifth Amendment, and required judges to balance the real or perceived needs of national security against the individual rights guaranteed in the Constitution.

Brandeis had warned, in the post–World War I cases, that in determining whether speech, no matter how seemingly inflammatory, actually posed a clear and present danger, courts "had to exercise good judgment; and to the exercise of good judgment, calmness is, in times of deep feeling and on subjects which excite passion, as essential as fearlessness and honesty."[2] But where Brandeis had seen the judiciary as fearlessly standing against the tide of mob emotion, Frankfurter saw danger in the courts becoming involved in any manner. "History teaches," he declared, "that the independence of the judiciary is jeopardized when courts become embroiled in the passions of the day."[3] Frankfurter privately deplored the excesses of McCarthyism and the witch-hunts conducted in the name of national security, and he risked personal opprobrium in his defense of some of the accused. On the bench, however, he continued to call for deference to the other agencies of government, since he approved of their nominal goal, repulsing communism.

Frankfurter, it should be noted, did not stand alone; until the mid-fifties only Black and Douglas protested the attacks on First Amendment rights, and their reputations as jurists suffered at the hands of Frankfurter's acolytes at Harvard, who attacked the Black-Douglas position while praising Frankfurter's "process jurisprudence" and devotion to judicial restraint and institutional deference.[4] If there is any group of cases that highlights the failure of Frankfurter's philosophy, it must be the First Amendment decisions that came out of this second Red Scare.

Unlike the earlier anarchists and socialists, communists during the 1930s seemed to have something to say to Americans. Members of the Communist party could be found on picket lines fighting for the rights of labor unions or protesting fascism in Europe. Between 1930 and 1935 the rolls of the party increased from 7,500 to around 30,000; that growth in turn generated legislative efforts both in Congress and in state houses to make membership in the party a crime. In March 1940 Congress reenacted the Espionage Act of 1917 and then in June passed the Alien Registration Act, or Smith Act, which drew together a variety of antialien and antiradical proposals. Although aimed primarily at the Communists, its broadly phrased terms could apply to anyone conspiring to overthrow the government, or even conspiring to advocate an overthrow. The measure required the registration of aliens, and within a short time the government had fingerprinted and registered over 5 million aliens.[5]

The Smith Act had little immediate impact because none of the men serving as attorney general during the war sympathized with its provisions.[6] Moreover, following the German invasion of Russia and American entry into the war, the United States found itself allied with the Soviet Union in a common war against fascism; no Americans, it seemed, supported that war with greater fervor than members of the Communist party.[7] The act came indirectly before the Court within a few months after its passage, when the justices invalidated a Pennsylvania alien registration act on the grounds that the federal law had preempted state legislation.[8] The Smith Act also figured in the efforts to deport Harry Bridges.[9]

After the war, however, anticommunist sentiment within the United States built as the iron curtain descended across Europe. Harry Truman established the Temporary Committee on Employee Loyalty in November 1946; following criticism that he had not gone far enough, he set up the full-scale Federal Loyalty and Security Program the next year. Under Executive Order 9835, the attorney general and the FBI launched a massive investigation of all federal employees. The attorney general compiled a list of allegedly subversive organizations; membership in any of these groups constituted "reasonable doubt" about a person's loyalty.[10]

The Court evaded the First Amendment issues involved in the blacklists when it granted a declaratory judgment removing three organizations from the attorney general's list. The Joint Anti-Fascist Refugee Committee claimed to be nothing more than a charity providing aid to Spanish Republicans, victims of the Spanish Civil War. It and two other groups denied that they were communist or engaged in any subversive activities and charged that their inclusion on the list had been an arbitrary act devoid of due process. The district and circuit courts had rejected their claim, but five members of the Supreme Court agreed with the petitioners, although the justices could not settle on a common rationale.[11]

Justice Burton, supported in part by Douglas, took the narrowest approach; he acknowledged that the case "bristled with constitutional issues" that he believed the Court should avoid, and he disposed of the case on procedural grounds. Frankfurter concurred in the result but did not avoid the constitutional questions. The arbitrariness of the attorney general had violated the Fifth Amendment's due process clause, which he lauded as "perhaps the most majestic concept in our whole constitutional system." Due process, Frankfurter claimed, does not operate as a mechanical yardstick, but as a process for evaluating facts and determining truth. "No better instrument has been devised for arriving at truth than to give a person in jeopardy of serious loss notice of the case against him, and opportunity to meet it." The attorney general had not given notice, established criteria for inclusion on the list, or held hearings at which the accused could respond, and thus had failed to meet the constitutional test.[12]

Where Frankfurter held that the attorney general could draw up such lists provided he followed certain procedures, Black, joined by Douglas, denied that the executive branch had any such authority, no matter what procedures it used. "Officially prepared and proclaimed governmental blacklists possess almost every quality of bills of attainder, the use of which was from the beginning forbidden to both national and state governments."[13] Although Black did not cast his opinion in First Amendment terms, he and Douglas seem to have been the only ones even to indirectly inquire into the right of the government to regulate ideas through proscriptive lists.

Despite the potential for abuse, the administration did move carefully in these early stages. By 1951 the Civil Service Commission had cleared more than 3 million federal employees. The FBI had initiated 14,000 full-scale investigations, which led to the resignation of some 2,000 persons, although it is unclear how many of them resigned solely because of the investigations. Only 212 persons were dismissed because of "reasonable doubt" as to their loyalty.[14] While actively seeking "security risks" inside the government, the Truman administration also went after the Communist party directly. On 20 July 1948 the Justice Department secured a grand jury indictment against 12 members of the party's national board, including Eugene Dennis and William Z. Foster, for conspiring with one another and with unknown persons to "organize as the Communist Party of the United States, a society, group, and assembly of persons who teach and advocate the overthrow and destruction of the Government of the United States by force and violence, and knowingly and willfully to advocate and teach the duty and necessity of overthrowing and destroying the Government of the United States by force, which said acts are prohibited by . . . the Smith Act."[15] It would take nearly three years from the initial indictment until the case reached the Supreme Court, following one of the most bombastic political trials in American history. During that time the Court and Felix Frankfurter had the opportunity to review several speech cases that would point the way to the fractured opinions in *Dennis v. United States* (1951).

The Supreme Court entered the postwar era with relatively little speech clause jurisprudence aside from the clear-and-present danger test developed by Holmes and Brandeis in the 1920s. But Holmes's famous aphorism about falsely shouting fire in a crowded theater is not a very useful analytical tool to determine when a danger is real, and if real, when it is proximate, and if proximate, when it is great enough to justify state intervention.

Justices Black and Douglas became increasingly unhappy with the test, especially as applied by the conservative majority after the war. Douglas believed that if Holmes and Brandeis had had the opportunity to develop their ideas more fully in additional speech cases, they would have eventually abandoned "clear and present danger" in favor of free and unrestricted speech except in the most dire emergencies. Douglas, in fact, claimed that the Holmes dissent in *Gitlow v. New York* (1925) "moved closer to the First Amendment idea."[16]

Black and Douglas, but especially Black, began to develop a new jurisprudence that put the First Amendment, particularly the speech clause, in a "preferred" position among constitutionally protected rights. They also argued for an "absolutist" interpretation of the First Amendment's prohibition against the abridgment of speech. The First Amendment, in their view, bars all forms of governmental restriction on speech; therefore, "there was no place in the regime of the First Amendment for any 'clear and present danger' test."[17] They came to this conclusion, as Black explained elsewhere, because the test "can be used to justify the punishment of advocacy." It can only function as a balancing test, and rights protected under the First Amendment cannot be balanced. The clear-and-present danger test had become "the most dangerous of the tests developed by the justices of the Court."[18]

For Frankfurter, on the other hand, the evaluation and balancing implicit in the clear-and-present danger test fit perfectly with his conception of the judicial function. By applying rigorous tools of analysis and clearheadedly evaluating the circumstances, judges would be able to say with reasonable certainty when a clear and present danger exists and warrants state action, and when it does not. But by this view, explicating First Amendment issues does not differ at all from explicating commerce clause questions. In a letter to Stanley Reed, Frankfurter asked, "When one talks about 'preferred,' or 'preferred position,' one means preference of one thing over another. Please tell me what kind of sense it makes that one provision of the Constitution is to be 'preferred' over another. . . . The correlative of 'preference' is 'subordination,' and I know of no calculus to determine when one provision of the Constitution must yield to another, nor do I know any reason for doing so."[19] Comments like this led Douglas to charge that Frankfurter saw the First Amendment not as a protection against state regulation of speech but in fact as an invitation to such regulation, with "the constitutional mandate being construed as only a constitutional admonition for moderation."[20] It is not so clear, however, that Frankfurter actually meant what he said, as evidenced in his opinions in the loudspeaker cases.

In 1948 and 1949 two cases reached the Court involving the use of loudspeakers on sound trucks. In the first case, *Saia v. New York* (1948), a 5–4 majority invalidated a local ordinance prohibiting the use of amplification devices without the consent of the police chief.[21] Speaking for the Court, Douglas found the restriction unconstitutional for establishing a standardless "prior restraint." While volume, time, and place regulations could be established, no public official should have the power to cut off speech at his uncontrolled discretion. Frankfurter, joined by Reed and Burton, dissented on the grounds that the city had made a reasonable decision; with amplification devices so easy to get, some sort of control had to be imposed to prevent unwanted "intrusion into cherished privacy."

The following year, in another 5–4 decision, the Court sustained a local ordinance; *Kovacs v. Cooper* (1949) involved subsequent punishment rather than prior restraint and, according to Justice Reed, only punished the emission of "loud and raucous noises."[22] In passing, however, Reed mentioned "the preferred position of freedom of speech." Frankfurter immediately recognized the danger to "correct analysis" of speech questions if he allowed this phrase to pass unchallenged,[23] so he entered a concurrence that is worth quoting at some length:

My brother Reed speaks of "the preferred position of freedom of speech." [This] is a phrase that has uncritically crept into some recent opinions of this Court. I deem it a mischievous phrase, if it carries the thought, which it may subtly imply, that any law touching communication is infected with presumptive invalidity. [I] say the phrase is mischievous because it radiates a constitutional doctrine without avowing it. . . .

The ideas now governing the constitutional protection of freedom of speech derive essentially from the opinions of Mr. Justice Holmes. The philosophy of his opinions on that subject arose from a deep awareness of the extent to which sociological conclusions are conditioned by time and circumstance. Because of this awareness Mr. Justice Holmes seldom felt justified in opposed his own opinion to economic views which the legislature embodied in law. But since he also realized that the progress of civilization is to a considerable extent the displacement of error which once held sway as official truth by beliefs which in turn have yielded to other beliefs, for him the right to search for truth was of a different order than some transient economic dogma. And without freedom of expression, thought becomes checked and atrophied. Therefore, in considering what interests are so fundamental as to be enshrined in the Due Process Clause, those liberties of the individual which history has attested as the indispensable conditions of an open as against a closed society come to this Court with a momentum for respect lacking when appeal is made to liberties which derive merely from shifting economic arrangements. Accordingly, Mr. Justice Holmes was far more ready to find legislative invasion where free inquiry was involved than in the debatable area of economics.

The objection to summarizing this line of thought by the phrase "the preferred position of freedom of speech" is that it expresses a complicated process of constitutional adjudication by a deceptive formula. And it was Mr. Justice Holmes who admonished us that "To rest upon a formula is a slumber that, prolonged, means death." Such a formula makes for mechanical jurisprudence.[24]

This is classic Frankfurter—the appeal to authority (Holmes), the cadence of the don before a somewhat slow-witted class, the lesson in history (an omitted section traces the history of speech cases), the implied criticism of judges who go beyond the tight bounds of judicial restraint—and yet there is something else here. A fair reading would lead one to conclude that Frankfurter did put speech on a higher plane—a preferred position—than other values. Judges would still balance, but perhaps the scales will be tipped. Perhaps there is a hierarchy of values that Frankfurter implicitly accepted, even as he tried to square the obvious importance of speech with the need for judicial deference.

What does seem clear, however, is that in the late 1940s and early 1950s Frankfurter's balancing more often than not tipped in favor of the state's restrictions rather than for speech. He joined Justice Jackson's dissent in the case of Father Terminiello, a defrocked priest arrested for disturbing the peace in a Chicago auditorium in 1946.[25] Terminiello specialized in attacking the Jews and the Roosevelt administration, and he went after both before 800 sympathizers in a Chicago auditorium in 1946. Outside over 1,000 protesters rioted, throwing rocks and stink bombs through the windows; police had all they could do to prevent the mob from storming the hall. After managing to get Terminiello and his party safely out of the building, the police arrested him on a disorderly conduct charge under an ordinance prohibiting "making any improper noise, riot, disturbance, breach of the peace, or diversion tending to a breach of the peace."

The case seemed custom-made for the Court to reexamine the question of whether "fighting" words, those that by their very offensiveness tended to disrupt the social order, qualified for protection under the First Amendment.[26] But the rather strange majority of Black, Reed, Douglas, Murphy, and Rutledge, speaking through Douglas, evaded the constitutional issue and voided the conviction on an allegedly improper charge by the judge, even though the attorneys for Terminiello had never raised this issue.

Jackson's dissent, joined by Frankfurter and Burton (Vinson dissented separately), accurately depicted the inflammatory situation and noted that the episode bore startling resemblance to the prewar struggle between totalitarian groups for what Hitler had called "the conquest of the streets . . . [as the] key to power in the state." Jackson asked whether the anti-Semitic garbage spewed out by Terminiello constituted the free discussion, the tool of democracy, that the First Amendment had been designed to protect. He doubted it, and believed the state has the right and the obligation to restrict speech of this sort.

Although Douglas's opinion received wide notice in the press as proof of the high level of tolerance in America, it provided the Court with no guidelines by which to decide future cases of a similar nature. On 15 January 1951 the Court handed down three decisions involving local restrictions on speech. In *Niemotke* v. *Maryland* it upheld the right of religious groups to speak in public parks,[27] and it upheld that right once again even when the speaker preached on street corners a doctrine

111

of hate against other religious groups.[28] But the Court upheld the conviction of Irving Feiner, a pro-Communist college student whose aggressive rhetoric before a hostile street-corner crowd raised the same issue as in *Terminiello*.[29] Feiner called President Truman a "bum" and condemned the American Legion as "a Nazi Gestapo." Since blacks did not have equal rights, he urged them to "rise up in arms." Two police officers, fearing the crowd would attack Feiner, asked him to stop. When he refused, they arrested him, and he was later convicted for disorderly conduct. Speaking for a 6–3 majority, Chief Justice Vinson upheld the conviction and, in a distortion of the clear-and-present danger test, held that Feiner had been arrested not for the content of his speech but "for the reaction which it actually engendered."[30]

In his concurrence, Frankfurter urged his colleagues not to second-guess the officials who had been on the scene; rather, the Court should defer to the state court's knowledge of local conditions rather than impose an "abstract or doctrinaire" interpretation of the Fourteenth Amendment. Beyond that, Frankfurter had a high opinion of the New York Court of Appeals and its sensitivity to civil liberties. It had ruled unanimously against Feiner, and he would not question that decision.[31]

The balancing in this case almost totally ignored the values of free speech. Vinson's ruling validated the so-called heckler's veto, by which evidence or fear of hostile audience reaction justifies silencing the speaker, and Frankfurter endorsed that position in his concurrence. "It is no constitutional principle," he declared, "that in acting to preserve order, the police must proceed against the crowd, whatever its size and temper, and not against the speaker."[32] By this formulation, it becomes exceedingly simple for police to suppress a speaker. Any group that does not like what it hears could create a disturbance in the audience, and rather than maintain order, the police could then stop the speaker. Aware of this danger, Vinson and Frankfurter suggested that the courts would not allow abuse of this practice, but they advanced no criteria to guide lower courts in their decisions.

The following term Frankfurter delivered the Court's opinion in a decision involving so-called group libel. Joseph Beauharnais, head of the White Circle League, distributed anti-Negro leaflets on Chicago street corners in the form of petitions to the mayor and city council asking them to use the police to halt the further encroachment of blacks into previously all-white neighborhoods. The pamphlets referred to the need "to prevent the white race from becoming mongrelized by the negro," and to the "rapes, robberies, knives, guns and marijuana of the negro."

Police arrested Beauharnais under an Illinois statute prohibiting the portrayal of "depravity, criminality, unchastity, or lack of virtue of a class of citizens, of any race, color, creed or religion." Following conviction and a $200 fine, he appealed on the grounds that the law violated liberty of speech and press. The Supreme Court upheld the conviction and the law by a 5–4 vote.[33]

Frankfurter noted that every state had laws protecting individuals from libel, and he saw no problem with attempting to protect groups as well. The question, then, was whether the due process clause of the Fourteenth Amendment prohibited such laws. (Frankfurter framed many of his speech opinions of this time in terms of due process rather than the First Amendment, since it provided an easier context in which to place his balancing test. As Black constantly pointed out, the First Amendment did not mandate a balance; it prohibited all abridgment of speech.)

Going into the state's past, Frankfurter noted a long history of racial tension, "from the murder of the abolitionist Lovejoy in 1837 to the Cicero riots of 1951." In the face of this history, "we would deny experience to say that the Illinois legislature was without reason in seeking ways to curb false or malicious defamation of racial and religious groups." The Court had to trust legislative judgment and allow the states some room for a "choice of policy," for the "trial-and-error inherent in legislative efforts to deal with obstinate social issues." And should the states abuse this discretion, "while this Court sits" it could "nullify action which encroaches on freedom of utterance under the guise of punishing libel."[34]

Here indeed Frankfurter's own words seem to confirm Douglas's charge that Frankfurter did not distinguish between First Amendment cases and commerce clause cases. Frankfurter's *Beauharnais* opinion echoes the rational basis test the Court had adopted to deal with economic policy questions: if the assembly has a rational basis for choosing as it did, the courts should not second-guess legislative wisdom. So here, too, it would seem that if the political branches had a reason for stifling speech, the courts would not interfere. In fact, Frankfurter wrote that "even when free speech is involved we attach great significance to the determination of the legislature." He wrote those words, however, not in *Beauharnais*, but in a case the Court had decided the previous term, *Dennis v. United States.*[35]

The *Dennis* case constituted the final judicial validation of the government's Loyalty and Security Program. Unions had been purged of known or admitted communists under Section 9(h) of the Taft-Hartley Act, sustained by the Court in *American Communications Association* v. *Douds* (1950),[36] and the government loyalty program had been upheld in *Bailey* v. *Richardson* (1951).[37] In *Dennis* the Court had to determine the constitutionality of the Smith Act as applied to leaders of the Communist party. They had been indicted for (1) conspiring to organize as an assembly of persons who teach and advocate the overthrow and destruction of the government of the United States by force and violence, and (2) advocating and teaching the duty and necessity of overthrowing the government by force and violence.

At no point in the indictment did the government allege that any revolutionary acts other than teaching and advocacy had taken place, and although "seditious conspiracy" remained a crime on the statute books, the Justice Department did not charge the 11 men with conspiring to overthrow the government. In essence, they were tried and convicted for a conspiracy to form a party to teach and advocate the overthrow of the government. By a vote of 6–2 (with former attorney general Tom Clark not participating), the Court confirmed the conviction.

The central issue involved reconciling the constitutional guarantee of free speech with a conviction for no more than speaking and teaching. The trial judge, Harold Medina, had solved the problem by the bridge of intent and had instructed the jury that it could find the defendants guilty if it believed the defendants intended to overthrow the government as soon as the opportunity arose. The highly respected Learned Hand had sustained the conviction on appeal, arguing that courts had to balance a number of factors in applying a version of the clear-and-present danger test. "In each case they must ask whether the gravity of the 'evil,' discounted by its improbability, justifies such invasion of free speech as to avoid the danger."[38] Given the recent events in Europe and Asia, it seemed evident that Russia intended to conquer the world, and that the American Communist party, as a highly disciplined arm of the international movement, stood ready to act at a moment's notice. The conspiracy existed, and the government could act to avert the evil.

Chief Justice Vinson closely followed Hand's reasoning in his plurality opinion for the Court, an opinion joined by Burton, Minton, and Reed. Although he paid lip service to the Holmes test, Vinson pointed out that communism posed a far different and more menacing danger than the anarchism and socialism Holmes and Brandeis had dealt with in the 1920s cases. Therefore, the clear-and-present danger test could not possibly mean that, before the government could act, it had to wait "until the *putsch* is about to be executed, the plans have been laid and the signal is awaited."[39] By this line of reasoning, the government not only could reach speech directly inciting unlawful action, conspiring to promote such action, or teaching that such action should occur, but it could act against those conspiring to organize a group that would teach that such action ought to occur.[40]

Michael Belknap claims that Frankfurter realized that the Hand-Vinson modification of the clear-and-present danger test "could produce harmful results in future cases which had nothing to do with communism."[41] He therefore refused to join in the plurality opinion, not because he objected to the results, but because he disagreed with Vinson's reasoning. Frankfurter's concurring opinion in *Dennis* clearly states his judicial philosophy regarding the First Amendment, and it stands in stark contrast to the powerful dissents filed by Black and Douglas.

Frankfurter began with the mandatory invocations of judicial restraint and deference. "History teaches," he declared, "that the independence of the judiciary is jeopardized when courts become embroiled in the passions of the day and assume primary responsibility in choosing between competing political, economic and social pressures." The primary responsibility for those decisions lies with the legislature, even in speech cases. Moreover, "there is ample justification for a legislative judgment that the conspiracy now before us is a substantial threat to national order and security."[42] A careful review of all the relevant decisions made it clear, he asserted, that the Court had reached the right results.

Frankfurter personally disagreed with the policy of the Smith Act and feared that its heavy-handedness would silence not only those who sought to overthrow the government but honest and loyal critics of its policies as well. Nevertheless, his devotion to judicial restraint and his refusal to accept a preferred-position status for speech or a special role for the courts in protecting civil liberties, left him limited room to maneuver. He tried to do so by reserving to the judiciary the right to review the application of laws that otherwise appear facially valid. He quoted from an essay by his former student Paul Freund, who asserted that the clear-and-present danger test becomes a simplistic and useless tool unless it takes into account numerous factors, including the relative seriousness of the danger, the availability of other forms of control, and the specific intent of the speaker.[43]

That is what the Court had done in this case, and Frankfurter emphasized that the seriousness of the communist danger far outweighed the "puny anonymities" that Holmes had defended in *Abrams* or the "futile" advocacies in *Gitlow*. The Communist party, with its extensive organization, membership, and discipline, constituted a serious threat to the nation. On the other hand, of course, freedom of speech must be respected. But not "every type of speech occupies the same position on the scale of values," and "it is not for us to decide how we would adjust [this] clash of interests. . . . Congress has determined that the danger created by advocacy of overthrow justifies the ensuing restriction of freedom of speech."[44]

If, in the judgment of the Court, Congress abuses its discretion, if it unreasonably tips the balance too far in favor of security at the expense of freedom, or if the executive applies the law in an arbitrary and unfair manner, the Court will intervene; otherwise, a reasonable judgment by Congress touching upon the security of the nation should not be overturned by the judiciary. Frankfurter's opinion in *Dennis*, read in the light of history, smacks more of judicial abdication of responsibility than measured deference and restraint.

It would be unfair to deride Frankfurter for failing to see then what others only saw later, but the evidence seems to suggest that while he privately opposed the Smith Act prosecutions, he truly did not believe the Court could interfere. Douglas's harsh judgment that Frankfurter saw no difference between the speech clause and the commerce clause seems borne out by Frankfurter's own words. Douglas and Black did see a difference, and their eloquent dissents in *Dennis*, derided at the time by the process theorists as unanalytical, hit the mark perfectly.

Douglas characterized the majority position, including Frankfurter's, as the product of fear and panic. He then quoted from Andre Vishinsky's *The Law of the Soviet State* (1938): there could be no freedom of speech for foes of socialism. Douglas warned his colleagues and the country that "our concern should be that we accept no such standard for the United States."[45] Eventually the country would recover from the Red Scare madness, and the Black-Douglas position would be hailed for its unflinching defense of free thought. Before that happened, however, many more cases came to the Court, and although Frankfurter could occasionally find procedural means to support free speech, his devotion to judicial restraint and deference put him more often than not in the antilibertarian camp.

The Dennis trial had been one of the most unruly in American history, thanks to nearly all of the participants. The defendants viewed the Smith Act charges as political persecution and wanted to use the opportunity to preach their gospel. Judge Harold Medina and the defense attorneys engaged in a constant and acrimonious interchange over procedure and the admissibility of certain types of evidence. Reporters covering the trial in New York began referring to the "battle of Foley Square." Immediately after the jurors returned their verdict of guilty, Medina avenged himself for what he believed to have been a deliberate effort to sabotage the judicial process. He called the defense lawyers before the bar and judged them guilty of contempt. He attributed 23 offenses to Harry Sacher, 18 to Richard Gladstein, 9 to George Crockett, 7 to Abraham Isserman, and 6 each to Eugene Dennis and Lewis McCabe; he then imposed sentences ranging from 30 days to 6 months in jail.[46]

The bar has a long tradition of defending unpopular defendants, and the American Bar Association's canon of professional responsibility notes that "history is replete with instances of distinguished and sacrificial services by lawyers who have represented unpopular clients and causes. Regardless of his personal feelings, a lawyer should not decline representation because a client or a cause is unpopular or community reaction is adverse."[47] Similarly, judges are expected to rise above political considerations and perform the duties of their office "unswayed by partisan interests, public clamor, or fear of criticism."[48]

By any fair reading of the trial, Harold Medina violated the canons of judicial propriety. The lawyers, certainly zealous in the defense of their clients, had matched Medina's abrasiveness, and while probably deserving of some rebuke, their conduct did not seem to warrant the heavy-handed vengeance Medina meted out. Moreover, in the anticommunist climate of the early 1950s, their persecution had only just begun. In addition to the contempt citations and jail terms, local bar associations moved to strip the Dennis attorneys of their right to practice law.[49] The attorneys appealed their contempt citations, and their case eventually reached the Supreme Court.[50]

Frankfurter probably would have liked to say, "a plague on all your houses," for he believed the defendants, their attorneys, and the judge had all made a mockery of the judicial process he held almost sacred. A larger issue faced the Court, however—the integrity of the legal system. If a judge as intemperate as Medina could provoke defense attorneys and afterward sentence them to prison for contempt, then unpopular defendants would be denied the constitutional protection of counsel because few lawyers would be willing to jeopardize career or freedom.[51] While the attorneys' behavior had been far from ideal, it seemed clear to Frankfurter that Medina, whom he had long disliked as a "most insufferable egotist," had to be reprimanded as well.[52]

The majority of the Court, however, did not share Frankfurter's agitation, and in May 1951 it voted to deny review. Only Black and Douglas had initially agreed with Frankfurter; but after considerable lobbying by Frankfurter, Robert Jackson changed his mind and agreed to a limited review. Upon reconsideration, he told his colleagues, he believed that the earlier refusal had had the undesired effect of making it difficult for unpopular defendants to secure adequate counsel. But unlike the others, Jackson wanted to examine the case on the narrowest possible basis: whether Medina, in passing judgment and punishing the lawyers himself, had violated Rule 42(a) of the Federal Rules of Criminal Procedure, which seemed to require a separate hearing in these circumstances.

The full-scale review did not change the outcome. Five members of the Court, speaking through Jackson, upheld Medina's ruling and noted that Rule 42(a) permits "summary disposition" by a judge if he hears or witnesses the conduct constituting the contempt, and that it gives the judge the discretion to deal with contempt either at the time it took place or at the end of the trial. Jackson avowed that the Court would "unhesitatingly" defend lawyers in the "fearless, vigorous and effective performance of every duty" pertaining to their responsibilities to their client, but not if they overstep these bounds and interfere with the orderly processes of justice. For Jackson, the leading trial lawyer on the Court, all other considerations seemed secondary to protecting the orderly process and the powers of the judge to maintain that order.[53]

Black, joined by Douglas, entered a short dissent that zeroed in on Medina's prejudicial behavior. Evidence throughout the trial indicated the judge's distrust of and hostility toward the attorneys. No lawyers who had been called "liar," "brazen," or "mealy-mouthed," as these men had, should then be tried for contempt before the very judge who had so denounced them. In Black's opinion, at the very least the petitioners were entitled to a jury trial on the contempt charges.[54]

Only Frankfurter, in his accompanying dissent, dealt with the substantive question of judicial misconduct and its potentially disruptive effect on securing counsel for unpopular defendants. In this case Frankfurter, for the first time since he had come on the bench, seemed like the Felix of old, the Harvard professor willing to stand up to public contumely for the sake of men he despised but who, no matter what their beliefs, were entitled to a fair trial under the American judicial system.

Although he initially asserted that the case involved only questions of procedural regularity, Frankfurter quickly went beyond that narrow issue. He appended 47 pages of excerpts from the trial transcript, consisting of exchanges between Medina and the attorneys, to show that "the contempt of the lawyers had its reflex in the judge." He then proceeded, chapter by verse, to detail Medina's misconduct. The trial judge had engaged in "dialectic, in repartee and banter, in talk so copious as [to] inevitably" weaken his own authority. Medina, Frankfurter charged, had so failed to exercise "moral authority" during the trial that for him to be the one to adjudicate the contempt did violence to the belief "that punishment is a vindication of impersonal law."[55]

The *Sacher* decision fortunately had few of the dire consequences that Frankfurter had feared, and in fact, three years later the Court in effect overruled the holding.[56] More importantly, the Red Scare soon reached its zenith, after which the country resumed some semblance of sanity in dealing with the threat of communist subversion. But before that happened, Frankfurter endured what he considered the most personally trying of any case he heard in his 23 years on the bench.

Without doubt the most controversial cold war cases to come before the Supreme Court involved the various appeals of Julius and Ethel Rosenberg, convicted in March 1951 under the Espionage Act of 1917 of passing atomic secrets to the Soviet Union in wartime. In April, Judge Irving Kaufman sentenced the two to death, and the court of appeals upheld the sentence in February 1952. Then began the convoluted series of petitions for review that did not end until the Rosenbergs died in the electric chair at Sing Sing Prison on the evening of 19 June 1953, the only persons ever executed for espionage in American history.

Between 7 June 1952 and 18 June 1953, the Court had the opportunity at least six times to accept the case for review on its merits, and in each case it declined to do so. Only Felix Frankfurter and Hugo Black, the two men who in the previous decade had so often opposed each other, voted in every instance for the Court to hear the case.

The Rosenbergs' attorneys attempted to raise a number of procedural and substantive issues; they claimed that their clients had been tried and sentenced to death for treason without the constitutional protections afforded persons accused of that crime. They also charged that the federal prosecutors had not met certain responsibilities under the federal criminal code, and that Judge Kaufman had been prejudiced against them. The Court of Appeals for the Second Circuit had upheld the trial court, but by a split vote. In effect, that court urged the Supreme Court to resolve the pending legal questions.[57]

Had the appeal come to the Court earlier, when Frank Murphy and Wiley Rutledge still sat, there is no question but that certiorari would have been granted. But both justices had died in 1949, and the Truman appointees proved to be politically cautious as well as conservative. With the Korean War and the Red Scare going on, the majority of the Vinson Court wanted nothing to do with so potentially explosive an issue.

In the first round of appeals, Frankfurter and Black expressed their concern about the imposition of the death sentence without Supreme Court review, as well as about the question of whether the Rosenbergs had in fact been tried for treason, not espionage, and thus been denied constitutional protection. Harold Burton voted with Black and Frankfurter the first two times because the two senior justices felt so strongly about the necessity of the Court reviewing the case; but thereafter he voted against granting certiorari.

As the months went by, Frankfurter grew increasingly concerned that the Rosenberg case would become another Sacco-Vanzetti case, and that the two convicted spies would become martyrs for the communists to hold up as examples of capitalist injustice. The country could not go through another such spasm; the Court, he believed, had to review the case and assure the nation that justice had been done. Whether the convictions stood or fell made no difference by itself; the Rosenbergs might be guilty, but they were entitled to all the protections the Constitution afforded to those accused of crimes, including review of the case when legitimate legal issues existed.

The attorneys for the Rosenbergs introduced new evidence in an appeal in April 1953, including claims that one witness had committed perjury and that the prosecutor had prejudiced the case by out-of-court statements. This time only Frankfurter and Black voted to grant certiorari; Burton did not consider the new arguments very pervasive and voted with the majority. This third refusal upset Frankfurter to the point that he took the unusual step for him of writing a dissenting opinion to the Court's denial of certiorari. But he reconsidered this step, worried that it might further embroil the Court in the growing national controversy over the case. After conferring with Black, the two issued a one-sentence statement that they still believed the Court should review the case.

He did, however, distribute a memorandum within the Court. He begged the pardon of his colleagues for bothering them again with this question, which he described as "the most anguishing situation since I have been on the Court," but then he literally pleaded with the brethren to reconsider their decision. He did not know whether the conviction itself should be overturned, but the only way to determine that would be by a full-scale review. The attorneys for the Rosenbergs had, he asserted, raised sufficient procedural questions for the Court to consider their validity.

Most important, Frankfurter declared, by not hearing the case the Court in effect abandoned the field to demagogues like Sen. Joseph McCarthy of Wisconsin. He had no fear of what he termed "the puny force of Communist influence in this country." But he did worry about the good men and women in the country "who feel as I do that it is a concession to Communism, not a safeguard against it, to retreat from reason and to compromise these cherished traditions which one likes to think of as the peculiar characteristics of an Anglo-American justice."[58]

Shortly afterward, on 22 May 1953, William O. Douglas circulated a memorandum in which he said that he had given further study to the allegations about prosecutorial conduct and had decided to vote for certiorari. This made three for review, still one shy, but Douglas upset the other members of the Court by indicating that he planned to issue a statement that he believed review necessary because "some of the conduct of the United States Attorney was 'wholly reprehensible' . . . [and] that it probably prejudiced the defendants seriously."[59]

Frankfurter immediately asked Chief Justice Vinson to reopen discussion, and he did so fuming inwardly at Douglas's turnabout. While he no doubt welcomed another vote, he believed it wholly unethical for Douglas to issue a statement in which he essentially prejudged the merits of the case. The Rosenberg attorneys wanted the review to decide just this issue—whether the U.S. attorney's conduct had prejudiced the trial. The Court's grant of certiorari in a case signifies no more than that four justices believe sufficient questions have been raised to warrant further study, not that a majority has been convinced that error exists. By threatening to go public in a way that might embarrass the Court, Douglas seemed to be blackmailing his colleagues into granting review. Justice

Jackson told Frankfurter that he considered the Douglas memorandum "the dirtiest, most shameful, most cynical performance that I have ever heard of in matters pertaining to law."[60]

Frankfurter immediately began lobbying both Jackson and Burton, who had voted with him and Black on the first two ballots. He quoted to Burton a short poem written by Eugene Wambaugh, who had taught constitutional law at Harvard when Frankfurter had been a student there:

> Let not the judgment that is just
>   Be judged too soon,
> But be reserved, if judge one must,
>   Till noon.
> Or yet till Evening, that the way
> Repentant may lie open all the day.

Frankfurter reminded Burton that Tom Mooney had been sentenced to death because of perjured testimony; he also talked to Burton about Sacco and Vanzetti, in whose case the courts had refused to look at the question of probable injustice. Douglas had "put the whole Court in a hole," but "we cannot ostrich-like bury our heads in the sand."[61]

Jackson reluctantly agreed to change his vote, providing the necessary fourth vote for certiorari; he did so, he told the Court, because of Douglas's proposed dissent. At a specially called conference the next day, Douglas stunned everyone by announcing that he wanted to withdraw his memorandum. It had been badly drawn, he conceded, and he had not realized it would embarrass anyone. Jackson, who had been prepared to vote for review to block Douglas, now changed his vote back, but Douglas said nothing. The conference dissolved with only Black, Frankfurter, and Douglas voting for review.

The last scenes of the tragedy played out in the middle of June. The Rosenberg attorneys made one last appeal, asking for a stay of execution and for oral argument before the Court on the stay.[62] Moreover, they brought in new evidence of perjury[63] and some new legal talent to assist them, including the legendary John Finerty, a longtime defender of civil liberties who had argued for Sacco and Vanzetti and had also played a role in the Mooney case. Unlike petitions for certiorari, petitions for a stay require a majority vote. Black, Frankfurter, and Jackson voted both to hear oral argument and to stay the execution. Douglas voted to stay the execution but not to hear the oral argument, whereas Burton was willing to hear oral argument but not stay the execution without the argument. As a result, the Rosenbergs lost both appeals by a 4–5 vote.

It seemed as if the Rosenbergs had run out their legal string, but then in a totally unexpected move, two lawyers, Fyke Farmer and Daniel Marshall, representing a coalition of civil libertarian and church groups, intervened with a claim that the Rosenbergs had been indicted, tried, and sentenced under the wrong law, that the Atomic Energy Act of 1946, not the Espionage Act of 1917, should have been applied.[64] They brought this evidence to Douglas on 15 June, two days after the last conference. He pored over the materials for the next two days, consulting, among others, Frankfurter and the chief justice. Vinson told him that Farmer had no standing to intervene, and that the Court had already disposed of the question of the applicability of the Atomic Energy Act. Frankfurter thought the issue worth looking into, but he refused to review Douglas's draft of a stay of execution.[65] Moreover, Frankfurter lectured Douglas, do what your conscience tells you, not what the chief justice says.

Frankfurter's coolness toward Douglas at this stage derived not from any desire to hasten the Rosenbergs to their doom but from his distrust of Douglas's motives. Douglas had had more than one opportunity to provide the crucial fourth vote for certiorari, or the fifth vote for a stay, and had flip-flopped from one side to another. Frankfurter and Jackson suspected that Douglas did not want the Court to review the case, that he just wanted to score points with the liberals and keep alive his political ambitions by writing militant but ineffective dissents.

On Wednesday morning, 17 June—two days before the scheduled execution—Douglas issued an order staying execution pending further proceedings in the district court on the question of the applicability of the Atomic Energy Act. Douglas assumed this would hold things up for a while; his order also provided for review of the district court's findings by the court of appeals. He signed and released the papers and immediately left by car for his summer vacation in the west.

Unknown to either Douglas or Frankfurter, Jackson had met on 16 June with the chief justice and Attorney General Herbert Brownell to discuss what to do should Douglas issue the stay. Vinson said that if Douglas issued a stay, he would immediately call the Court into special session to vacate it. Douglas issued the stay, Brownell immediately petitioned the Court to vacate the stay, and Vinson called a special session on 18 June. Douglas, although he had left his itinerary with the chief justice, only heard about the special session on his car radio near Pittsburgh. He immediately turned around and headed back to Washington.[66]

On 18 June, for the only time in this long and convoluted process, the justices heard argument in open court about the Rosenberg case, but arguments restricted to whether the Atomic Energy Act provision on the death penalty raised sufficient questions to support the stay or not. At different times five members of the Court had voted in one way or another to give the Rosenbergs their full day in court. But in the end only Black and Frankfurter voted to sustain Douglas's stay; the other six voted to vacate. The Court then announced that the order had been lifted; after a last-minute appeal for clemency to President Eisenhower had been denied, the Rosenbergs were executed shortly after eight o'clock that evening. Frankfurter, Jackson, and their clerks kept a somber death-watch in Jackson's chambers, awaiting the news that Ethel and Julius Rosenberg were dead.

At the conference earlier that day, an angry Frankfurter had questioned the Court's right to vacate, in such an unusual manner, a stay issued in chambers. He believed that everyone's mind had been made up even before the special session met, and that the justices had given in to the mob. In his dissent, issued a month later, he expressed these views and charged that the Court had rushed to judgment without adequate study or reflection. Can it be said, he asked, "that there was time to go through the process by which cases are customarily decided here?"[67] Certainly the judgment of history has been that, whatever the guilt or innocence of the Rosenbergs, their less than fair trial received inadequate review by the appellate courts.

One might question why Frankfurter even bothered to enter a dissent, and he himself noted that doing so after the deaths of the Rosenbergs "has the appearance of pathetic futility." But history also had its claims, and he proceeded to write a moving and eloquent essay on the dangers of allowing personal prejudice or political emotionalism to intrude on the legal process. Michael Parrish notes that Frankfurter's skepticism of absolutes yielded a philosophy of caution and restraint in most areas of the law, but that it also reflected his special sensitivity to human failings. In the Rosenberg case, as in the Sacco-Vanzetti case a generation earlier, he tried to warn against the "terrible possibility of judicially sanctioned death through error, bias or deceit."[68]

124

There is no question that Frankfurter realized the terrible dangers that antiradical hysteria could engender; he had seen them at work after World War I, and now he had witnessed a new and even more virulent strain in the McCarthy-era Red Scare. The very integrity of the legal order, the American system of impartial justice, had been debased, and without law there could be no liberty. He seemed to have reverted to his old libertarian stance, but his record on cold war cases the rest of the decade indicates that the reversion was only temporary.

He and Black continued to disagree on many issues, especially the reach of the First Amendment, but the bitter personal animosity that had prevailed between them in the 1940s gave way to a growing affection and respect. The rapprochement began at the time of Josephine Black's death in December 1951, when Frankfurter had spontaneously reached out to offer solace to Black in his time of grief.[69] The two men had then found themselves together in the Sacher and Rosenberg cases, and both men dissented in *Adler v. Board of Education,* a case testing New York's Feinberg law.[70] The state had authorized a list of subversive organizations, similar to the attorney general's list under the Smith Act, and then made membership by a public school teacher in any of these groups grounds for dismissal. The majority found no constitutional problem, since teachers could either obey the law or go work somewhere else.

Black immediately saw this as a violation of First Amendment guarantees of free speech and association. Frankfurter would not go that far and preferred to dissent on procedural grounds. No one had been fired yet, so no tangible case existed to justify the Court reaching a constitutional decision. As Black wrote on one of his former clerks, he and Felix had been traveling the same road regarding civil liberties, "although I continue to think (as I tell him) that he tries to go by the wrong route and stops so short as to defeat his own purpose."[71]

That "wrong route" often appeared in the internal security cases that reached the Court in the mid and late fifties. Although Frankfurter had described the communist menace as puny and deplored the witch-hunt atmosphere of the McCarthy years, he did not abandon the position he had taken in *Dennis,* that the evidence "would amply justify a legislature in concluding" that the Communist party constituted "a substantial danger to national security."[72] As late as 1961, according to notes in William O. Douglas's files, Frankfurter still defended the legitimacy of the Smith Act.[73]

More often than not, Frankfurter tried to get the Court to avoid deciding cases. Brandeis had once told him that sometimes the most important action the Court could take was to decide not to decide a case. Given the divisiveness of so many issues that came before the Court in these years, Frankfurter continually tried to persuade his colleagues that whenever an opportunity arose to avoid constitutional adjudication or to decide a case on narrower procedural grounds, they should do so. Frankfurter especially pushed this strategy in the various cases arising from the Subversive Activities Control Board (SACB).

Congress had enacted the Internal Security Act, also known as the McCarran Act, in the spring of 1950; through a number of highly complicated provisions, enforcers of the statute tried to force the Communist party to register as a subversive organization. To justify this admitted infringement on the First Amendment, Congress declared that an international communist conspiracy existed that constituted a clear and present danger to the United States. To enforce the law, Congress established the SACB, which enjoyed broad administrative discretion but remained answerable to the courts. Harry Truman vetoed the measure, calling it "the greatest danger to freedom of speech, press, and assembly since the Sedition Act of 1798."[74] Congress, however, fearful of being labeled soft on communism in an election year, promptly overrode the veto by large margins in both houses.

Frankfurter managed to deflect several challenges to the SACB, and Black later claimed that, in case after case affecting the so-called Communist front organizations, "the parties have been told that the crucial constitutional issue was not yet ripe."[75] Finally, and after much delay, the Court answered many of these questions in three related cases in early 1961. In the first case Frankfurter spoke for a 5–4 majority in upholding the registration provisions of the McCarran Act.[76] He denied that the First Amendment prevents Congress from requiring registration of members of "organizations substantially dominated or controlled by that foreign power controlling the world Communist movement." Congress had made such a determination, and the judiciary should defer to that finding.

That same day, the Court handed down two decisions on the Smith Act's membership clause. The majority drew a distinction between active and passive membership in an allegedly subversive group. In *Scales v. United States*,[77] it sustained a conviction for an activist member of the Communist party, while in the companion case it voided the conviction for someone who belonged to the party but had done little more than pay his dues.[78] In the conference discussion on these cases, Black and Douglas took their usual view that the Smith and McCarran acts impinged on First Amendment rights; Frankfurter stuck by his position that the Communist party had been adjudged a threat to national security and could be regulated.

A year later he would have allowed the state of Florida to commandeer the records of the state chapter of the National Association for the Advancement of Colored People (NAACP) under the guise of searching for communists; he stood with a 5–4 majority when the case was first discussed at conference.[79] But then he suffered a stroke and had to retire from the bench. His replacement, Arthur Goldberg, helped swing the decision the other way.

By then, the Court and the country had begun abandoning the madness of the McCarthy years. The Kennedy administration quietly ceased prosecutions under the Smith and McCarran acts, and in the remaining cases that reached the Court, a majority influenced by the earlier opinions of Black and Douglas reversed in fact if not in name many of the decisions Frankfurter had helped to craft.

Just as Frankfurter would be remembered for his courageous demand for justice in the Sacco-Vanzetti and Mooney cases in the first Red Scare, so Black and Douglas would be remembered for their eloquent defenses of free speech during the second. Although Frankfurter's continuing loyalty to procedural fairness could occasionally rally him to the cause, as in *Sacher* and *Rosenberg,* most of the time he remained a prisoner of his rigid adherence to judicial restraint and institutional deference. So long as he believed the courts have no special obligation to protect civil liberties, or that rules regulating expression do not differ in constitutional terms from those regulating commerce, or that courts have to defer to congressional findings without question, he could do little to fight the intolerance he saw and despised. His heroes, Holmes and Brandeis, had seen a similar challenge and laid the foundation for modern First Amendment jurisprudence. Frankfurter certainly had the courage to pursue a path similar to theirs, but he lacked the vision to do so.

8

CIVIL RIGHTS AND THE SUPER CHIEF

At the same time that the Supreme Court wrestled with the problems of free speech in the cold war, a new issue began percolating up through the federal judicial system. American blacks had begun their revolution against the tyranny of legal discrimination, especially the segregation by race prevalent throughout the South. Their struggle for equality posed a particularly difficult dilemma for Felix Frankfurter. As much as anyone then on the Court, he detested bigotry and had fought against it his entire life. Yet his philosophy of judicial restraint led him to question the Court's ability to reverse its previous validation of segregation and grant what American blacks demanded—equality under law.

Frankfurter's own life epitomized how talent and perseverance could be rewarded in a society that valued ability more than race or religion. In his America, all people deserved the opportunity to make the most of themselves, and he never hesitated to battle for that ideal. It is not surprising that as a Jew Frankfurter opposed a Jewish quota at Harvard.[1] But during his years as a professor he also provided legal advice to the NAACP. Moreover, at a time when the major law schools took few blacks, Frankfurter helped the careers of two black students at Harvard Law, not because they were black but because, like other Frankfurter protégés, they were talented.

Charles Huston stayed an extra year to do graduate work with Frankfurter and then went on to become one of the chief strategists in the NAACP's legal campaign against segregation. A few years later William Hastie entered Frankfurter's inner circle and, at his professor's recommendation, joined the NAACP legal staff after graduation. In 1948 Frankfurter took William Coleman, Jr. as his clerk for the term, the first black law clerk in the Court's history. When the selection committee at Harvard asked Frankfurter whether Coleman's appointment would cause him any difficulty, the justice shot back that he did not care what color a man was any more than he cared about his clerks' religious professions or lack of them.[2] Coleman also became a key strategist for the NAACP and then went on to a distinguished career that included a stint as secretary of transportation under Gerald Ford.

Yet Felix Frankfurter believed, and properly, that judges do not have the right to impose their own social views on the law, as economic conservatives had done in stymying liberal legislation in the Progressive and early New Deal eras. "Without strict adherence to reason," he wrote to Coleman, "and a refraining from permitting personal biases to enter adjudication, judges become covert little Hitlers."[3] Moreover, Frankfurter's philosophy of judicial restraint derived at least in part from his belief in the limited power of courts to change human frailty. In the 1925 article "Can the Supreme Court Guarantee Toleration?" he answered in the negative: the Court's responsibility lies in determining the constitutionality, not the liberality, of laws, and thus "the real battles of liberalism are not won in the Supreme Court . . . [but in] a persistent, positive translation of the liberal faith into the thoughts and acts of the community."[4]

When the NAACP began its challenge to legal segregation, no one could doubt that Frankfurter privately cheered on the campaign. But where in the Constitution could the Court find specific authority to strike down racial bigotry? Would the southern states even obey a Court decision invalidating segregation? If they resisted, the resulting damage to the Court would be incalculable; caution and strict attention to procedure, Frankfurter believed, should mark the Court's response to this challenge.

The three Civil War amendments, the Thirteenth through the Fifteenth, had been drafted primarily to free the slaves and to guarantee them the same rights and legal privileges enjoyed by whites. The southern states might have been expected to move immediately after their passage to create a system to segregate the races, but in fact, as C. Vann Woodward has shown, a full-scale pattern of enforced segregation did not take hold until the 1890s.[5] By then not only had northern liberals abandoned southern blacks, but the Supreme Court had given the process a green light. In the *Civil Rights Cases* (1883), the Court denied Congress any but the most limited remedial powers under the Fourteenth Amendment to combat racial prejudice.[6] In the 1890s the Court decided several cases involving state statutes that established formal segregation of the races. In the most famous of these, *Plessy v. Ferguson* (1896), Justice Billings Brown asserted that the Fourteenth Amendment had never been intended to abolish "distinctions based upon color."[7] Although nowhere in the opinion can the phrase "separate but equal" be found, the Court's ruling approved legal segregation, provided the law did not make facilities for blacks inferior to those for whites. Within a short time, "Jim Crow" had become dominant throughout the southern and border states.

In the 1930s the NAACP began its campaign to eliminate segregation and made a deliberate decision that the only way it could be successful would be by attacking racial prejudice in the courts.[8] In *Missouri ex rel. Gaines v. Canada* (1938), the first major case to reach the Court, Chief Justice Hughes startled the South by insisting that if it wanted to keep segregated schools, then it would have to make them equal as well.[9] World War II temporarily prevented the NAACP from aggressively pursuing its goals, but the Hughes decision had given the organization its first real tactical victory. In dozens of cases initiated immediately after the war, NAACP lawyers charged that southern states had segregated blacks while not providing equal facilities, thus denying blacks the Fourteenth Amendment's guarantee of equal protection under the law.[10]

Frankfurter had not been on the Court when it decided *Gaines,* but he did participate in one of the few important civil rights cases decided by the Court during the war, *Smith v. Allwright* (1944), in which the Court, by an 8–1 vote, struck down the all-white primary.[11] The Court had sustained the white primary scheme as recently as 1936,[12] but then had partially restricted that ruling in 1941 in the *Classic* case.[13] The NAACP recognized that *Classic* had been decided on narrow grounds; it involved a claim by registered white members of the Democratic party in Louisiana that their votes in the 1940 primary had not been counted. *Classic* may have looked more like a voting fraud case than a civil rights decision. But Thurgood Marshall had gambled that with the liberal makeup of the Court in the 1943 term, he might be able to use *Classic* as a way to get at the all-white primary itself; his gamble paid off.

At conference on 15 January 1944, all the justices except Roberts voted to overrule *Grovey*, and on 17 March Chief Justice Stone assigned the decision to Frankfurter. That afternoon a troubled Robert Jackson came to Frankfurter's chambers and said that he had something delicate to discuss, but that he would talk with the "customary feeling of freedom" the two friends enjoyed. He urged Frankfurter not to write the decision in *Allwright*, since the decision, unpalatable to the South in any event, would be even more so if it came from the pen of a member who, in light of southern prejudices, had three disqualifications.

"You are a New Englander, you are a Jew, and you are not a Democrat—at least not recognized as such."

Frankfurter replied that all three accusations were true and asked Jackson what he thought should be done. Jackson said that unless Frankfurter had objections, he would go see Stone and suggest that the chief reassign the case.

"Of course, I am primarily interested in this matter for the Court's sake," Jackson added, "but I am also concerned about you. A lot of people are [set] on exploiting Anti-Semitism, as you well know, and I do not think they ought to be given needless materials."

Frankfurter recognized the force of Jackson's argument and agreed that he would do whatever would be best for the Court. Jackson immediately went to see Stone, and the next day the chief justice saw Frankfurter. Stone was evidently embarrassed over the whole matter and understandably did not like the idea of having to make assignments out of fear of arousing prejudice. Frankfurter apparently let him stew in this for a while before offering to return the case to him for reassignment.

The case went to Stanley Reed, whose opinion appalled Frankfurter. At conference Frankfurter had argued that the Court ought to overrule *Grovey*, "without any pussyfooting," and admit forthrightly that it had changed its mind regarding the policy considerations. Reed, in Frankfurter's view, took exactly the wrong approach, and Frankfurter prepared a concurring opinion that he suppressed only at Jackson's strong insistence. The incident left a sour taste in Frankfurter's mouth and no doubt shaped his views in subsequent civil rights cases.[14]

After the war, in every one of the antisegregation suits to reach the high court, Frankfurter voted to support the NAACP's campaign against legalized discrimination. The first of the major postwar cases involved not education but housing. In 1917 the Supreme Court had struck down local ordinances enforcing racial segregation as a deprivation of property rights in violation of the Fourteenth Amendment.[15] To get around this ruling, property owners turned to restrictive covenants that, as private agreements between buyers and sellers, presumably did not come within the reach of the due process or equal protection clauses.

In *Shelley v. Kraemer* (1948) Chief Justice Vinson ruled for all six sitting justices that so long as the discriminatory intent of the covenants could be enforced in state courts, the states were sanctioning racial discrimination in violation of the Fourteenth Amendment.[16] The justices did not rule the covenants themselves illegal, since private discrimination remained constitutionally permissible, but they did make the covenants unenforceable. In *Hurd v. Hodge,* a companion case, the Court also voided enforcement of restrictive covenants in the District of Columbia. Although the Fourteenth Amendment did not apply to the national government, the chief justice held that such agreements violated the 1866 Civil Rights Act, and that it went against public policy to allow a federal court to enforce an agreement that was unenforceable in state courts.[17] Frankfurter entered a separate concurrence in *Hurd.* The expert on jurisdiction preferred that the Court base its decision on the traditional discretion allowed to equity courts, because "equity is rooted in conscience. . . . In good conscience, it cannot be 'the exercise of sound judicial discretion' by a federal court to grant the relief here asked for when the authorization of such an injunction by the States of the Union violates the Constitution."[18] Privately, however, as he explained to Chief Justice Vinson, the reliance on Fourteenth Amendment grounds would support the argument Black had made in *Adamson,* which Frankfurter rejected "both as scholarship and as law."[19]

Following *Shelley,* the Court began to hear more and more cases involving claims of racial segregation. Some cases involved restrictive covenants,[20] some involved labor unions,[21] but everyone recognized that the most explosive issue would be segregation in public schools.

In 1948, a few months before *Shelley,* the Court ordered the state of Oklahoma to provide Ada Sipuel, a black woman it had excluded from the University of Oklahoma Law School, with a legal education "in conformity with the equal protection clause of the Fourteenth Amendment and to provide it as soon as it does for applicants of any other group." The state Board of Regents angrily created a law school overnight, roping off a small section of the state capitol in Oklahoma City and assigning three teachers to attend to the instruction of Ms. Sipuel and "others similarly situated." When the NAACP appealed back to the Supreme Court, a majority of the justices, including Frankfurter, refused to consider whether the state had in fact established an equal facility.[22]

Then in 1950, on one day, the Court handed the NAACP three major victories. It slapped down the University of Oklahoma, which, after having been forced to admit a black man to its graduate education program, made him sit outside the door of the classroom, eat in a separate facility, and use a restricted section of the library.[23] In *Henderson v. United States* the Court unanimously ruled that segregated tables on interstate dining cars violated the Interstate Commerce Act, which prohibited subjecting any person to "any undue or unreasonable prejudice or disadvantage."[24]

The most important decision that day involved efforts to keep Negroes out of the University of Texas Law School.[25] To keep its law school lily-white, Texas had established in 1946 a makeshift school for blacks at Prairie View University. In *Sweatt v. Painter* (1950) the state contended that it had provided equal facilities; but the justices certainly knew what made a good law school and unanimously rejected the state's claim that its separate law school for blacks was equal to that at Austin. Although Thurgood Marshall invited the Court to reexamine the *Plessy* doctrine, the justices were not ready. In a memo to Vinson, Frankfurter urged that the Court "now not go a jot or tittle beyond the Gaines test. The shorter the opinion, the more there is an appearance of unexcitement and inevitability about it."[26]

Vinson tried to do that, but the *Gaines* test involved a showing that the separate black facilities did not compare in quality to those used by whites. In listing the differences between the University of Texas and Prairie View, the chief justice spoke not only about physical characteristics but about intangibles such as "reputation of the faculty, experience of the administration, [and] position and influence of the alumni." In doing so he opened up the way for the NAACP to launch its long-awaited frontal assault on *Plessy* by showing, through the use of sociological materials, that separate by nature could never be equal.[27]

Some members of the Court had anticipated that a direct attack on "separate but equal" would soon be on their doorstep, and they were not disappointed. At the beginning of the 1952 term the Court accepted cases challenging the school segregation laws in Delaware, Virginia, South Carolina, and Kansas, as well as the District of Columbia. The justices heard initial arguments in the combined cases in the fall of 1952 but could not reach agreement. Frankfurter and his law clerk that term, Alexander Bickel, prepared a series of questions on the legislative history of the Fourteenth Amendment, the authority of the Court in the area, and potential remedies. He then presented these questions to the other justices and suggested that the cases be assigned for reargument in the October 1953 term, a suggestion of his that for once his colleagues quickly accepted. Specifically, the Court asked counsel on both sides to discuss whether Congress in proposing the Fourteenth Amendment, and the states in adopting it, had intended to ban racial segregation in schools. Further, if the Court ruled segregation invalid, how should the decision be put into effect?

Frankfurter's caution on segregation has occasionally been misinterpreted as hostility to civil rights or support for the separate-but-equal doctrine. Neither charge is true, and in fact Frankfurter's strategy of caution and delay played a key role in making it possible for Earl Warren to mass the Court unanimously in *Brown v. Board of Education*. In the late forties Frankfurter began a file on school segregation for his personal use; he understood how sensitive and volatile a departure from separate-but-equal would be. This sensitivity, combined with his already cautious approach to decision-making, kept him warning his colleagues in the pre-*Brown* cases to write as narrowly as possible. Instead of charging up to the central question—and to Frankfurter, the inescapable one—of whether segregation violated the Constitution, he preferred a more conservative approach, taking cases as they came and deciding them on the narrowest possible grounds. The Court did not have to "go out and meet problems," he told his colleagues.[28]

According to Richard Kluger's account, the main problem seemed to be that at best only five members of the Court were willing to reverse *Plessy*. William O. Douglas evidently stood ready to strike down any form of racial discrimination, as did Hugo Black; the Alabaman, probably more than anyone on the bench at that time, knew that tampering with racial relations in the South would be a highly volatile issue. Harold Burton and Sherman Minton, both Truman appointees, also appeared ready to abandon the separate-but-equal doctrine. But, according to Kluger, Chief Justice Vinson, Stanley Reed, and Tom Clark, all from southern or border states, had no problem viewing segregation as distinct from discrimination.[29]

More recent research by Mark Tushnet, however, casts doubt on the Kluger interpretation, and thus on the role Felix Frankfurter played in the *Brown* deliberations. According to Tushnet, nearly all the members of the Court in 1953, including Vinson, Reed and Clark, were ready to overturn *Plessy* if a way could be found to do so. The problem, then, was not, as Kluger described it, of winning over a minority so that the vote could be unanimous, but of devising a strategy that would carry out the wishes of the justices. The issue, as Tushnet points out, was not new; the Court had been moving in this direction for at least a decade. In 1953 they had reached a point of no return; in *Brown* they had to face the issue of segregation directly.[30]

Frankfurter privately opposed separate-but-equal, as did Robert Jackson, but the two leading advocates of judicial restraint did not know how the Court could reach out and summarily overturn a half-century of precedent. Jackson did not share the prejudices of Vinson, Reed, and Clark, but the evidence indicates that he did not believe the Court had the power to invalidate segregation. Frankfurter hoped that history might shed some light on what the framers of the Fourteenth Amendment had intended, and he set Bickel to work researching that topic. Bickel's labors yielded a lengthy memorandum that, at best, indicated an ambiguity on the part of those who drafted and then voted to ratify the amendment. While it certainly did not provide the support he wanted, to Frankfurter's credit he circulated the memorandum so that his colleagues, whatever their views, might be able to consult it.[31]

Frankfurter correctly understood that if the Court decided to reverse *Plessy*, it could not do so by a 5–4 or even a 6–3 vote; it would have to be unanimous. According to Bickel, the justice worried that a decision striking down segregation would be disobeyed, "which would be the beginning rather than the end of a controversy."[32] Therefore, all the justices, with the exception of Douglas and Black, had good reason to want the cases delayed. Some merely wanted to avoid a hard decision; for Frankfurter, procrastination might have seemed the only way to eventually bring the Court around to a position acceptable to all of its members. During that spring of 1953 Frankfurter described himself as a *Kochleffel,* a cooking spoon stirring things up and keeping them simmering until the right time came for the Court to act.[33]

Then on 8 September 1953 Fred Vinson died of a heart attack in his Washington hotel apartment at the age of 63. All the members of the Court came to his funeral in Louisa, Kentucky, but at the graveside at least one of them quietly rejoiced in his passing. To Felix Frankfurter, Vinson, despite his opinions in *Sipuel, Shelley,* and *Sweatt,* had been the chief obstacle to the Court reaching a workable and judicially defensible settlement of the segregation cases. With the five consolidated

135

cases due for reargument that fall, Frankfurter viewed Vinson's death as almost providential. "This is the first indication I have ever had," he told a former clerk, "that there is a God."[34] Three weeks later Dwight Eisenhower named Earl Warren as chief justice of the United States.

When Warren arrived in Washington, he found among the pile of papers on his desk a memorandum Frankfurter had circulated to the justices that, on first reading, might have led the new chief justice to believe that Frankfurter opposed overturning *Plessy*. "It is not our duty," he lectured, "to give a Constitutional stamp to our merely personal attitudes toward these issues. . . . However passionately any of us may feel . . . he travels outside his judicial authority if on the basis of his private feelings he declares unconstitutional the policy of segregation."[35]

Richard Kluger, in his magisterial history of the *Brown* case, wrote that Frankfurter "was reportedly outraged that Eisenhower would name a mere politician to lead the Court."[36] But to a friend Frankfurter apparently rejoiced in the nomination. Warren, he said, "brings to his work that largeness of experience and breadth of outlook which may well make him a very good Chief Justice provided he has some other qualities which, from what I have seen, I believe he has."[37]

For Frankfurter, who never seemed to learn, Warren's appointment provided still another "student," one more opportunity to teach someone the "right" way to be a judge. He began preparing memoranda and reading lists for Warren, attempting to overwhelm him with both his learning and his helpfulness. Gerald Gunther, whom Frankfurter had indirectly arranged to be Warren's clerk, recalls that the chief once asked Frankfurter if he could recommend some reference he could consult on a relatively minor point of jurisdiction. A half-hour later Frankfurter's clerk wheeled a library cart into Warren's chambers loaded with volumes that could clear up the point.[38]

Frankfurter and Warren got off to a good start, however, because they both agreed on the proper strategy for dealing with the segregation cases. According to one Warren biographer, Frankfurter may have suggested the strategy and then relied on Warren's political skills to pull it off.[39] Essentially, the chief justice would avoid having the Court decide any of the issues in the cases until he could be sure of unanimity. He would allow the justices to talk themselves out and, he hoped, into agreement in the process.

The Court had heard oral argument in October 1953, but Warren delayed putting *Brown* on the conference agenda until December. He then began discussion by stating that in his view *Plessy* could only be sustained if one believed that blacks were inherently inferior to whites. Warren did not accept that premise, and therefore he would be ready, at the right time, to vote to invalidate segregation. Although the chief justice had no doubts about the principle, he had a number of questions about how to implement the decision. So he suggested that no formal vote be taken until the justices had had ample opportunity to talk about it among themselves, informally, "from week to week, dealing with different aspects of it—in groups, over lunches, in conference. It was too important to hurry it."[40]

In one stroke, as Frankfurter silently cheered, Warren had shifted the debate away from the validity of segregation to the question of how best to implement a decision abolishing segregation. Between December and the following May, Warren, with behind-the-scenes help from Frankfurter, gradually forged a consensus among the justices. Frankfurter worked closely with the chief justice and on 15 January 1954 circulated a five-page memorandum containing some ideas that he hoped "might stimulate good thoughts in others." The memorandum is crucial because in it Frankfurter suggested what became a key element in the Court's resolution of the cases.

Normally, the beneficiaries of a Supreme Court decision are the winning appellants and those who will be "similarly situated" in the future. All but a handful of decisions are thus prospective, because it would be bad law as well as bad policy to make them retrospective. While this procedure may work hardships on some people whose cases had been decided under the old and now invalid rule, to apply it retrospectively in their benefit would only result in administrative chaos.

A decision striking down segregation, Frankfurter pointed out, "would be drastically different from decrees enforcing merely individual rights before the Court." Earlier cases, such as *Sipuel* and *Sweatt*, had involved individual claimants; here the Court would be ordering a total transformation of statewide school systems in nearly 20 states. Even in the unlikely circumstance that such a decision was met with all the goodwill in the world, merely announcing the unconstitutionality of segregation would not be enough to transform the school systems into "integrated schools." Frankfurter then went on to discuss the difficulties that the courts and the states would face and suggested that, initially at least, the Court wanted above all to get the process of desegregation started:

Surely we can take as a starting point that in enforcing the Four-teenth Amendment the Court is, broadly speaking, promoting a pro-cess of social betterment and not contributing to social deterioration. Not even a court can in a day change a deplorable situation into the ideal. It does its duty if it gets effectively under way the righting of a wrong. When the wrong is a deeply rooted state policy, the court does its duty if it decrees measures that reverse the direction of the constitutional policy so as to uproot it "with all deliberate speed" (*Virginia v. West Virginia,* 222 U.S. 17, 20 [1911]).

It did not really matter what solution the states took, and in fact different school systems could adopt different measures depending upon their local circumstances. It was important, Frankfurter declared, that the Court not get involved in the day-to-day details but restrict itself to the an-nouncement of the great principle.[41]

The memo and its moderate tone had a far greater effect on the deliberations than Frankfurter's normal pedantic abrasiveness. He offered several possible methods by which the federal court system might oversee desegregation, and he recognized that the long-entrenched system would not disappear overnight. Tom Clark appears to have changed his mind following the memo, and by early February, unanimity had become a distinct possibility, Warren began the difficult task of writing an opinion that would attract all of the justices; he wanted no dissents and no concurrences.

Unbeknownst to Warren or any of his colleagues, Frankfurter at this time spoke almost every day with Philip Elman of the Solicitor General's office; Frankfurter's former law clerk from the 1942 term, Elman was responsible for preparing the government's brief in the desegregation cases. That brief advocated exactly the strategy that Frankfurter was si-multaneously urging within the Court, namely, separating the announce-ment of the principle from the implementing decree. The justice kept Elman apprised of the views of the other members of the Court and of deliberations within the conference and evidently made suggestions that Elman incorporated into the brief in support of Frankfurter's strategy, including use of the "all deliberate speed" formula.

Elman rationalized Frankfurter's obvious breach of judicial ethics by saying that "he didn't regard me as a lawyer for any party; I was still his law clerk. He needed help, lots of help, and there were things I could do in the Department of Justice that he couldn't do." Normally, Elman and Frankfurter would not discuss cases that Elman had argued before the Court, but *Brown* was an extraordinary case, and the ordinary rules didn't apply.[42]

Frankfurter also credited Elman with helping to block the misguided and, according to Elman, incompetent efforts of the "leaders of the colored people who proposed a remedy which not only would not have succeeded with the Court [immediate integration] but, what is even worse, would have had disastrous consequences to the National interest."[43]

Justices are certainly free to talk to whomever they want and perhaps even need someone off the Court they can confidentially discuss their work with, as Brandeis did with Frankfurter. But one can just imagine Frankfurter's righteous indignation if he had learned that Hugo Black or Bill Douglas had been discussing a case then before the Court with one of the lawyers involved, and laying out strategy with that person.

While Frankfurter plotted with Elman, the chief justice wrote a bit of the opinion here, talked about other pieces there, and occasionally circulated a partial draft. By early May only Stanley Reed still supported *Plessy*. Warren, with eight votes, confronted Reed directly and told him that he now had to decide whether to stand alone in defense of racial segregation or join the others. Reed capitulated, and on 17 May 1954 Earl Warren handed down the most important decision of the century, declaring that racial segregation in the nation's public schools violates the constitutional guarantee of equal protection under the law.[44] In the euphoria following the announcement, Frankfurter wrote to Warren: "*This* is a day that will live in glory. It is also a great day in the history of the Court and not in the least for the course of deliberation which brought about the result. I congratulate you."[45]

Both Black and Frankfurter believed that the success of implementing *Brown* depended upon southern moderates, and in the first few months following the decision it appeared that the Court's decision would be accepted in the South. Gov. Thomas Stanley of Virginia called for "cool heads, calm study, and sound judgment." The respected *Louisville Courier-Journal* assured its readers that "the end of the world has not come for the South or for the nation."[46] Even before the Court heard argument on how to implement *Brown*, Baltimore adopted a freedom-of-choice plan, enabling 3,000 blacks to attend previously all-white schools. Louisville, Kentucky, changed over its school system within a semester.

Frankfurter believed that the Court would have to play to these moderate elements if desegregation would ever succeed peacefully. During the summer of 1954 he interrupted his vacation in Charlemont, Massachusetts, to write Earl Warren suggesting that the Court needed to do a great deal of research before framing its implementation decree. On the one hand, the South should not be allowed to resort to gerrymandering devices to thwart desegregation. On the other, nothing should be done to alienate the many southern lawyers he knew who pleaded for a solution that would allow moderates to move the South into the new era. "The Southern States are fever patients," he wrote. "Let us find out, if we can, what healthy bodies do about such things."[47]

Throughout this time Frankfurter kept referring over and over again to the many southern lawyers he knew, presumably former students of his at Harvard Law School. Because he claimed to know them and claimed that they all urged a moderate course, his proved to be a strong voice in determining the Court's conduct. In fact, Frankfurter knew very few southern lawyers and had very little correspondence with lawyers practicing below the Mason-Dixon line.[48]

Had he really had good contacts in the South, Frankfurter would have realized that the initial moderation had quickly given way to a determination to resist the Court's ruling. This could not have been any clearer than at the oral argument on the implementation decree. Because of the death of Justice Jackson and delays by some southern senators in confirming his successor, John Marshall Harlan, oral argument on implementation, known as *Brown II*, did not begin until 11 April 1955. The NAACP wanted full compliance immediately; the southern states wanted a gradualism with no end date at all. The hostility of the lawyers representing six former Confederate states could not be missed, nor the crudeness of some of their argument. Negroes constituted 22 percent of Virginia's population, claimed Archibald Robertson, but they constituted "78 percent of all cases of syphilis and 83 percent of all cases of gonorrhea. . . . Of course the incidence of disease and illegitimacy is just a drop in the bucket compared to the promiscuity."[49]

The Court had absolutely no intention of allowing the South to ignore the decree or to drag its feet forever; but the justices did recognize how ingrained segregation had become in the South and how it could not be wiped away overnight merely because the Court had declared it unconstitutional. Even before he received Frankfurter's suggestion, Earl Warren had put several clerks to work researching the problem, and they had come up with three general propositions: the Supreme Court should formulate a simple decree; the cases should then be remanded to the district courts for execution and supervision; and the high court should frame some guidelines for the lower courts to follow.[50]

Frankfurter had been thinking about the implementation decree ever since he realized that Warren would be able to get the justices to agree in *Brown I*. At one point he suggested a special master to oversee desegregation. But he abandoned that idea in favor of having local federal district courts—whose judges would be familiar with local customs—ride herd on the school districts. He had also considered various deadlines but in the end decided that any fixed date might be arbitrary and unrealistic.[51]

On 14 April 1955, shortly after the justices heard the last of the oral argument, Frankfurter circulated another memorandum, one that immediately caught Hugo Black's attention. The Supreme Court must not function as a "super school board." He saw the Court as having two alternatives: issuing either a very limited decree permanently enjoining the segregation of the plaintiffs and other black children in the school districts of the states involved in the suit, or a more loosely worded decree allowing district courts to take local conditions into account. Frankfurter also advised against a fixed date for compliance, which the NAACP had strongly urged, because it might be perceived as arbitrary.

At the conference on 16 April, Warren listened carefully to the discussion and soon realized that all the justices shared Frankfurter's cautious approach. They wanted the South to get on with the business of desegregation but did not want to do anything to play into the hands of the growing opposition. All agreed that the decree should be universal and that all segregation in schools by race would henceforth be barred by the Constitution. They also agreed that the cases should be returned to district courts for oversight. That left the question of guidelines, and here a phrase that Frankfurter had used in a memorandum a year earlier, "all deliberate speed," appealed to Warren.[52]

On 31 May 1955 Chief Justice Warren, again speaking for a unanimous Court, issued the implementing decree that had been anticipated and dreaded for over a year. In seven brief paragraphs, the Court held that segregation had to be ended everywhere, but that varying local conditions required different solutions. Local school districts had to make a "prompt and reasonable start toward full compliance," and oversight would be lodged in the district courts. Federal judges should exercise the "practical flexibility" traditionally associated with equity, but delay and noncompliance should not be contemplated. The Court set no deadline;

nor did it require that preliminary plans be filed within 90 days, as the Justice Department had urged. Instead, desegregation should proceed "with all deliberate speed."[53]

There is general agreement that *Brown II* was a disaster, and that the Court seriously miscalculated both the degree of southern intransigence and the power of so-called moderates.[54] Although the caution at the heart of the decree is typical of Frankfurter, and the ill-conceived idea of "all deliberate speed" was suggested by him, he cannot and should not bear the blame for the massive resistance that marked southern attitudes and policies for the next decade. He may have been more cautious than the other members of the Court, but they all worried about how the decree would be received and how it could be enforced. The Court, as Alexander Hamilton pointed out long ago, has neither the sword nor the purse at its disposal. Given the emotionalism and complexity of the situation, it is impossible to say whether a more forthright directive from the Court would have been more effective, or would have sparked even greater resistance. In 1955 the Warren Court decided that, with the decree, it ought to step back and give the states, guided by the district judges, a chance to comply.

Frankfurter had played an extremely effective if somewhat uncharacteristic role in the drama of the two Brown cases.[55] He believed that his strategy of delay had allowed Earl Warren to utilize his great political skills to "mass the Court" and to emphasize the importance of the decree by having all nine justices endorse it. Shortly after the decision he wrote to Learned Hand that unanimity in the case could not have occurred without the "wise and skillful ways" by which Warren had managed affairs.[56]

A few years later, however, Frankfurter dismissed as "hogwash" much of the credit given to Warren and implied that success had resulted from the new chief following Frankfurter's advice.[57] "If the 'great libertarians' had had their way," he wrote to Hand, "we would have been in the soup."[58] These two letters, just three years apart, illustrate the familiar pattern of Frankfurter patronizing a new member of the Court and then turning against him when he refused to accept Frankfurter's guidance.

Warren, at first, seemed a most promising prospect, but Frankfurter misinterpreted the Californian's caution in taking over the chief's role as eagerness to be tutored by the former professor. When Warren asked

Frankfurter a due process question, Frankfurter quickly sent along a copy of every opinion he had written in the previous 15 years on the subject and rejoiced when Warren wrote later that summer saying that he was reading through them, "endeavoring to orient myself in that field."[59] In the next two terms Warren sought Frankfurter's advice on a number of subjects, and Frankfurter responded not only with what had been asked but with offers of further assistance, as well as effusive praise for some of Warren's opinions and speeches before bar groups.

But as Warren began to feel more comfortable in his role, he not only found that he needed Frankfurter's advice less but also began to resent the patronizing tone.[60] Here again, comparison with Black is instructive. Warren had had little time to prepare for his new role when named to the Court; but he was urged by the attorney general to hasten to Washington in time for the new session because the Court faced many difficult questions. Not wishing to embarrass either himself or the Court, Warren asked Black, as the senior justice, to preside at the conference until he could acclimate himself. Black accepted the invitation and, during the few months he led the conference discussions, never once tried to "teach" Warren what had to be done. When Warren felt ready, he took over the reins and Black just as easily slid back into his old role, confident that in time he and Warren would work well together.

By the summer of 1955 Warren could no longer be considered a neophyte, and he chafed under the constant barrage of suggestions and reading material that came down from Frankfurter's chambers. More important, Warren had begun to enunciate his own activist view of the Court; an analysis of his voting patterns indicates a definite shift toward Black and Douglas, a shift soon accentuated by the arrival of William Brennan in 1956.[61] By the end of the 1956 term Frankfurter had lumped the chief justice with the "hard-core liberal wing" of the Court, whose "common denominator is a self-willed self-righteous power-lust." Warren, Black, and Douglas, he told Learned Hand, desired "to join Thomas Paine and T. Jefferson in the Valhalla of 'liberty' and in the meantime to have the avant-garde of the Yale Law School . . . praise them!"[62] Conditions deteriorated during the late fifties as the Court took on a more activist coloration, and Warren's patience with Frankfurter, if he had had any left, snapped with the Little Rock decision.

Compliance with the *Brown* decree in the midfifties had ranged from minimal to none. Dwight Eisenhower thought the decision a disaster and provided absolutely no moral leadership in support of the Court. There can be little doubt that his attitude stiffened southern resolve to resist desegregation.[63] The president would have liked to serve out his two terms without getting involved in the controversy. But Gov. Orville Faubus of Arkansas went too far when he defied a federal court and sent in the National Guard to prevent the local school board from desegregating the Little Rock schools. With this affront to federal authority, Eisenhower had no choice but to act; he sent federal troops to the city to escort black students to class.

The school board, which had defied the governor in the first place by agreeing to a desegregation plan, now asked for a delay in implementing court-ordered desegregation. District Judge Harry Lemley agreed that time for the parties to cool down would be in order and granted a 30-month delay, only to have that ruling reversed by the court of appeals only two weeks before school was scheduled to open for the 1958–59 school year. The appeals court gave the school board a 30-day stay so that it could appeal to the Supreme Court. In that time, however, Governor Faubus called a special session of the legislature and asked for authorization to close public schools rather than allow integration and to transfer state funds to private schools.[64]

The justices all cut short their summer recess to return to Washington in late August for a special session to hear the school board's appeal, which constituted the first real test of judicial authority to enforce *Brown*. At oral argument, an infuriated Earl Warren could hardly believe his ears when the school board's attorney, Richard C. Butler, argued in effect that if a governor of a state believed a Supreme Court decision wrong, he need not obey it. Before the Court could announce its decision, the Arkansas legislature passed the measures Faubus had requested. But the Little Rock school board, still wanting to keep its schools open, refused to bow to the pressure and returned to the Supreme Court hoping for a ruling that would allow it, as Butler said, to get out from between the millstones of a conflict between the state and federal governments.

Frankfurter's response to the Little Rock case in some ways mirrored perfectly his colleagues' sense of outrage at Faubus's defiance; in other ways it absolutely infuriated them. Shortly before the Court heard the second oral argument on 11 September 1958, Frankfurter suggested to Warren that, before counsel began, he acknowledge the courage of the school board in standing up to the governor, and that he also praise Butler. The ultimate hope for peaceful resolution of school desegregation, Frankfurter lectured Warren, "largely depends on winning the support of lawyers of the South for the overriding issue of obedience to the Court's decision." Therefore, the Court ought "to encourage every manifestation of fine conduct by a lawyer like Butler."[65]

Warren, still incensed by Butler's earlier claim, refused to even consider such a suggestion, and Frankfurter complained to John M. Harlan, who had become his closest ally on the Court, that the chief justice did not understand the situation. His attitude, Frankfurter charged, "is more like that of a fighting politician than that of a judicial statesman," a far cry from the praise Frankfurter had heaped on Warren only four years earlier.[66]

In conference immediately following oral argument, the justices quickly and unanimously agreed to affirm the court of appeals at once; Frankfurter and Harlan would draft a brief, unsigned order to that effect. Warren then asked Brennan to write the opinion supporting the Court's decision. Brennan went to work immediately and within a week had a draft ready for the justices to discuss. At that meeting, Warren recalled, Frankfurter pointed out that there had been some changes on the Court since *Brown*; to show that the Court in 1958 still maintained the same view as that of 1954, he suggested that every member of the Court sign the opinion. This had never been done before, and some of the justices must have raised their eyebrows over such a nontraditional proposal coming from Frankfurter. But they all agreed.[67]

Brennan's original draft had been meticulous to the point of dullness, but his second draft, thanks to a suggestion from Hugo Black, had a sense of urgency. Brennan adopted, without a single change, Black's description of the case as one involving "questions of the highest importance to the maintenance of our federal system of government. . . . We conclude that these contentions call for clear answers here and now."[68] Brennan went back to John Marshall's opinion in the *Marbury* case to reassert the Court's authority: "It is emphatically the province and duty of the judicial department to say what the law is." When Frankfurter received the revised draft of Brennan's opinion, he scribbled back: "Dear Bill, You have now made me content. Yours, FF."[69]

At noon on 29 September 1958 the Court convened to announce its decision, and the unprecedented signing of the opinion by all nine justices had exactly the effect that Frankfurter had intended—it dramatically signaled to Faubus and to all southerners that the Court remained united in its determination to desegregate the nation's schools. Frankfurter signed the opinion along with the other eight members of the Court and then completely shocked them by announcing that he would enter a concurrence, since he disagreed with some of the language in the opinion!

Earl Warren could hardly believe Frankfurter would do this. After all, Frankfurter had been his chief ally in the drive for unanimity in the *Brown* decisions and had also proposed that all the justices sign the Little Rock decision to reinforce the public perception of a united court. In his memoirs Warren implicitly accused Frankfurter of duplicity and betrayal. This event, claimed the chief justice, constituted the only "event that greatly disturbed us during my tenure," since the justices "were all of one mind in that case."[70]

Frankfurter explained his decision to concur separately in terms of his special relationship with southern lawyers and law professors:

> That is an audience which I was in a peculiarly qualified position to address in view of my rather extensive association, by virtue of my twenty-five years at the Harvard Law School, with a good many Southern lawyers and law professors. I myself am of the strong conviction that it is to the legal profession of the South on which our greatest reliance must be placed for a gradual thawing of the ice, not because they may not dislike termination of segregation but because the lawyers of the South will gradually realize that there is a transcending issue, namely, respect for law as determined so impressively by a unanimous Court in construing the Constitution of the United States."[71]

The gist of Frankfurter's concurrence did not significantly differ from Brennan's opinion in its condemnation of resistance to lawful authority by force. "The Constitutional rights of respondents," Brennan had written, "are not to be sacrificed or yielded to the violence and disorder which have followed upon the actions of the Governor and Legislature."[72] On this point Frankfurter added his own gloss. The request of the school board for postponement implied that: "law should bow to force. To yield to such a claim would be to enthrone official lawlessness, and lawlessness if not checked is the precursor of anarchy. On the few tragic occasions in the history of the Nation, North and South, when law was forcibly resisted or systematically evaded, it has signalled the breakdown of constitutional processes of government on which ultimately rest the liberties of all."[73]

Brennan and Black drafted a separate opinion to distance themselves from Frankfurter's concurrence but withheld it at Justice Harlan's suggestion. "It is always a mistake," Harlan counseled, "to make a mountain out of a molehill." They withdrew the separate opinion, but as Brennan later told James Simon, "Felix was a pariah around here for days." Most of his colleagues, accustomed to his outbursts, eventually made their peace with him, but not Earl Warren. The former governor had been a politician all his life, and it was his political skills that ultimately earned him the nickname of "Super Chief." For better or for worse, throughout his career Warren broke with people he considered to have betrayed his trust. Once on that list, Warren never forgave a person. Relations between the chief justice and Felix Frankfurter had been cool before *Cooper;* they turned frigid in the four years that remained of Frankfurter's service on the high court.[74] And aside from the contretemps in the Little Rock case, Frankfurter's efforts to keep the Court on the straight and narrow of judicial restraint ran into a force that overwhelmed it, the so-called due process revolution of the Warren Court.

9

DUE PROCESS AS
FUNDAMENTAL FAIRNESS

There is a certain irony in the frequent description of the judicial activism of the Warren Court as a "due process revolution,"[1] since Felix Frankfurter's jurisprudence revolved around the due process clause of the Fourteenth Amendment, albeit in a far more restricted manner.[2] It is also ironic that, although Hugo Black's campaign for total incorporation of the Bill of Rights did push the Court to extend many constitutional guarantees, Frankfurter's flexible approach actually provided a far more useful tool to judicial activists. Only Frankfurter's strong commitment to judicial restraint prevented him from traveling the path that his own philosophy rationalized.

We have already discussed the differences between Frankfurter and Hugo Black over the incorporation doctrine, and their opposing views in *Adamson v. California* (1947) (see chapter 6). The debate over the meaning of due process is different; the key question is not whether the framers of the Fourteenth Amendment intended to apply the Bill of Rights to the states, but what the phrase itself, used in both the Fifth and the Fourteenth amendments, means. Both Frankfurter and Black had rebelled against the conservative use of so-called substantive due process to protect property rights and defeat reform legislation. But in regard to *procedural* due process, most often associated with criminal prosecutions, the two men differed; like their *Adamson* opinions, their views in this area have shaped the modern debate.

Frankfurter, as Mark Silverstein has pointed out, boxed himself into a jurisprudential contradiction almost from the time he went onto the Court. On the one hand, he continued to oppose judicial subjectivity, by which judges can interpret statute or constitution in the light of their own prejudices. But he also opposed absolute standards as a means of controlling subjectivity because he believed that judges need some flexibility in interpreting the law. As we have seen before, Frankfurter adopted the paradigm of the scientific expert, one who reaches a proper conclusion through correct reasoning. Theoretically, such an enlightened judge would be free from overt subjectivity as well as from rigid dogma. Judges could enforce principles, but they would discover those principles in a disintegrated, scientific manner. Although nominally not a legal Realist, Frankfurter had shared the Realists' perception that individual traits predispose judges toward particular, subjective ends. He knew that cannot be changed, yet he resisted imposing external standards to limit judicial discretion. Judges have to choose, Frankfurter believed, but they have to choose in an enlightened manner.[3]

Black not only opposed judicial subjectivity, he also opposed leaving judges free to choose from among competing alternatives. He distrusted so-called experts; leaving constitutional choices in their hands smacked too much of an elitism—the few choosing the right course for the many—that offended his populist sensibilities. His answer was the imposition of absolutes through a literal reading of the Constitution. But in narrowing the scope of judicial discretion, Black made the Court the prime vehicle for guaranteeing the values of those absolutes, thus increasing the power of judges.[4]

Throughout his career Black searched the text of the Constitution for guidance; he understood that he could not always read the document literally, but he sought the meaning that he believed had been intended by the framers. In many ways, his was an extremely conservative approach, and indeed, Black saw himself as a strict constructionist. Due process required some discretion in cases where the facts do not fit into a framework easily governed by the clear meaning of the text. His distrust of judicial subjectivity, however, always made him insist on as narrow a discretion as possible. Hugo Black's absolutism could be very supportive of an expanded meaning of some civil rights and liberties; it could also be very restrictive.

Frankfurter, on the other hand, recognized that judges have to make decisions, and that at the Supreme Court level there are rarely any easy cases. In making those decisions, in choosing from competing alternatives, judges do make law. This cannot be helped, but in doing so they have to pay "due deference to the presuppositions of the legal system. . . . Of course I know these are not mechanical devices, and therefore not susceptible of producing automatic results." At best, those presuppositions provide parameters within which judges operate.[5]

In the 1920s and 1930s Frankfurter had castigated judges for their abuse of judicial review, but once on the Court he seemed to accept its inevitability. Judges should not, of course, impose their own prejudices; they have to restrain themselves and follow certain rules, and above all they have to be deferential to the political branches. They have to be "judicial statesmen," and for Frankfurter this meant a very limited role for the courts, especially in the area of protecting civil liberties.[6] Strict fidelity to proper standards overrides all other considerations, including a judge's personal views.[7]

The question of due process is crucial in criminal procedure because if the police are not restrained by procedural safeguards, then persons suspected or accused of crimes are totally at the mercy of the state. Frankfurter once pointed out that "ours is the accusatorial as opposed to the inquisitorial system. Society carries the burden of proving its charge against the accused . . . by evidence independently secured through skillful investigation."[8] To protect against police abuse, the Bill of Rights spells out restrictions on the national police; those protections do not have to be incorporated because the due process clause by itself governs state police practices.

Frankfurter, unlike Black, did not believe in a static and absolute interpretation of due process. The meaning of due process, Professor Frankfurter had declared in 1930, is not found in the Constitution. "It is the Justices who make the meaning. They read into the neutral language of the Constitution their own economic and social views. . . . Let us face the fact that five Justices of the Supreme Court are the molders of policy rather than the impersonal vehicles of revealed truth."[9] Once on the bench, Justice Frankfurter attempted to develop guidelines for lower court judges. Relying on Cardozo's *Palko* opinion, he spoke often of "those canons of decency and fairness which express the notions of justice of English-speaking peoples even toward those charged with the most heinous offenses."[10] The courts should tolerate neither police tactics that "offend the community's sense of fair play and decency" nor conduct that "shocks the conscience."[11] Frankfurter thus equated due process with fundamental fairness. But one can argue that fairness, like beauty, may be in the eye of the beholder, and that possibility upset Hugo Black. If judges have the discretion to determine fairness on the basis of what shocks them, then due process will vary from judge to judge and court to court. The guarantees of the Constitution have to be absolute, not dependent upon any one judge's notions of fairness.

Problems of due process had intrigued Frankfurter through much of his academic career; as we have seen, he and Black began their debate over its meaning soon after Frankfurter came onto the bench. At first Black seemed to take a fairly flexible approach to due process, but by 1942 his view had solidified. "Due Process for me," Frankfurter recorded Black as saying, "means the first nine amendments and nothing else."[12] Frankfurter could not accept so rigid a view. In the conference debate over an appeal of the murder conviction of the notorious Louis "Lepke" Buchalter,[13] he explained how he saw the judicial role in determining due process:

I said I hear a great deal of talk about granting freedom of utterance to opinions that we loathe. I thought it was no less important to vindicate people we despise. People like Lepke who for me are human vermin, should receive from us the same consideration as others—if not it simply means that we do not care for law as such and we are in the same position as those in Russia and Germany where it is enough that people are wicked in the eyes of the authorities, and it does not matter that appropriate procedure is followed to establish wickedness. . . . It cannot be that a physically extorted confession would upset a conviction but a subtler way of framing a conviction by having the prosecution collaborate with the chief witness for the state in the giving of dishonest answers in a vital issue in a case, does not offend our fundamental sense of decency which is the essence of due process. This could only be on the assumption that we cannot trust five members of the highest court of the land to exercise a judgment of whether or not a thing does offend fundamental decency because forsooth they would vest too much discretionary power in a majority of the Court who, one would suppose, are disciplined by the responsibility of their office and the great tradition of the history of this Court. Are we really prepared . . . to say we are morally impotent to apply due process as historically it has been applied and instead twist and contort in all sorts of funny ways other provisions of the Constitution to accomplish the same result, or at least results that sometimes are desired to be accomplished?[14]

Here, in a nutshell, is Frankfurter on due process: one need not incorporate other provisions; the due process clause by itself is a sufficient limit on state abuse; judges "know" what is fundamentally fair and what is not; judges have the power and the duty to pronounce what is fair and what offends that fairness.

But not everyone, not even all judges, define "fairness" in precisely the same way, and so, within fairly broad parameters, Frankfurter stood ready to defer to state legislatures in their determination of proper procedure. The Fourteenth Amendment, he argued, should not be applied "so as to turn this Court into a tribunal for revision of criminal convictions in the State courts." Due process does not restrict the states "beyond the narrow limits of imposing upon them standards of decency deeply felt and widely recognized in Anglo-American jurisdictions."[15]

The problem with this approach is that it has few if any objective standards; for Frankfurter, those practices that shocked his conscience violated due process. It did not shock his conscience, for example, if states chose not to provide counsel to defendants in noncapital felony cases. Although in the famous Scottsboro case Justice Sutherland had come close to holding a right to counsel as an essential of due process, the Court had grounded its opinion in that case on fundamental fairness.[16] The Court did not even recognize a right to counsel for federal defendants until 1938,[17] and so a majority of the Court did not see any necessity to extend this right to the states in *Betts v. Brady* (1942). Frankfurter joined Justice Roberts's opinion for the Court holding that denial of counsel does not violate standards of fundamental fairness in every instance; the courts should therefore evaluate the circumstances on a case-by-case basis.

Black, it should be noted, did find the situation offensive. As noted in chapter 6, he had learned from his practice that few nonlawyers understand the law, and they could hardly know how to plan and carry out an adequate defense. The Court continued to hear one case after another in which defendants had been denied counsel, and in each circumstance a majority found that "special circumstances" had existed so that "fundamental fairness" required a new trial with the assistance of counsel.[18] Although Frankfurter would vote to provide counsel in specific cases, he steadfastly refused to abandon the *Betts* rule. One year after his retirement from the bench, the Court unanimously reversed *Betts* and with Justice Black speaking for the Court, extended the Sixth Amendment right to counsel to the states.[19]

The debate over the meaning of due process almost came to a head in a 1945 confession case, *Malinski v. New York*.[20] Morris Malinski and two accomplices had been arrested on suspicion of the murder of a police officer. The police took Malinski not to a station house but to a hotel room, where they stripped him naked and subjected him to intense questioning until he confessed. A few days later, he confessed a second time. Five members of the Court considered the first confession coerced, thus tainting the conviction. One of the codefendants, however, a man named Sidney Rudish, had been convicted of murder at least in part on the basis of the coerced confession. Douglas, Black, and Frankfurter all voted to void Malinski's conviction but then voted to affirm Rudish's.

Douglas had initially been willing to affirm both convictions, but Black and Frankfurter indicated they would dissent—Black on the grounds that the forced confession violated the Fifth Amendment's ban against self-incrimination, and Frankfurter because the police behavior appalled him. "I think the requirements of 'due process,'" he told Douglas, "are an independent constitutional demand and not merely the compendium of some of the specific 'ten amendments.' Therefore, for me, the prosecutor's performance and general conduct of a trial may offend, for me, 'due process' even without my considering that such incidents help establish self-incrimination."[21] Frankfurter elaborated in a concurring opinion. His predecessors on the Court, he noted, had been correct in refusing to hem in the meaning of due process by limiting it to the first eight amendments. Due process possesses a "potency different from and independent of the specific provisions contained in the Bill of Rights." Due process is "not a stagnant formulation of what had been achieved in the past but a standard for judgment in the progressive evolution of the institutions of a free society." Within its scope it includes steadily evolving "notions of justice of English-speaking people" and "a demand for civilized standards of law."[22] According to Tinsley Yarbrough, this concurrence provoked Black to promise that he would soon answer Frankfurter's "natural law" exposition, a promise he kept in his *Adamson* dissent.[23]

A fair reading of Frankfurter's concurrence in *Malinski* would endow courts with the enormous power and responsibility of keeping the constitutional guarantees such as due process up to date and determining

what constitutes current "civilized standards of law." It means, as Frankfurter once acknowledged, that the Court has the moral duty of ascer-
taining the conscience of society.[24] For Black, this function properly
belonged to the legislatures, not to the courts. Frankfurter, on the other
hand, saw it as the peculiar province of judges acting, of course, as judicial statesmen and adhering to the highest standards of impartial analysis. But rigorous analysis requires some objective criteria, and as
Frankfurter admitted, "these standards of decency are not authoritatively
formulated anywhere."[25]

But is there a scientific means of determining what society, or even
a large part of it, considers civilized behavior? Looking at the not-too-
distant past, we cannot but be shocked at the large number of what we
consider petty crimes that could be punished by death in England, or the
tortures routinely applied to suspected "enemies of the state," or the in-
anity of imprisonment for debt. At what point did society determine that
such punishment violated civilized standards? Most people today would
condemn police use of the third degree or the exaction of confessions by
torture, yet there are persons who believe the police should do anything
necessary in apprehending criminals and should not be "shackled" by
overly precise judicial interpretations of the Fourth, Fifth, and Sixth
amendments. How will history judge, one wonders, the debate over capital punishment carried on in the Supreme Court in the 1970s and
1980s? Will society eventually agree with Justices Brennan and Marshall
that the death penalty violates civilized behavior?

Frankfurter also opposed the death penalty,[26] and yet in a 1947 case
he exercised the restraint he considered an essential limit on judicial
interpretation of due process. Willie Francis, a young black man, was
convicted of murder and sentenced to death in Louisiana. He had been
strapped into the electric chair, the switch had been closed, and the
device malfunctioned. Francis then sued to block Louisiana from trying
again, on the grounds that a second attempt would violate due process.[27]

Frankfurter cast the fifth vote to send Francis back to the electric
chair. In conference he told his colleagues that the state's action, while
hardly defensible, did not shock his conscience. To Harold Burton, who
prepared a powerful dissent in the case, Frankfurter wrote an anguished
letter noting his opposition to the death penalty and explaining his
vote:

> I have to hold on to myself not to reach your result. I am prevented
> from doing so only by the disciplined thinking of a lifetime regarding

the duty of this Court. . . . Holmes used to express it by saying he would not strike down state action unless the action of the state made him "puke." . . . And that being so, I cannot say it so shocks the accepted, prevailing standards of fairness not to allow the state to electrocute . . . that we, as this Court, must enforce that standard by invocation of the Due Process Clause. . . . And when I have that much doubt I must, according to my view of the Court's duty give the state the benefit of the doubt and let the state action prevail.[28]

A year later he told Learned Hand that he was personally shocked that the state would insist on a "second go for a pound of flesh." But while he considered it "barbaric," he knew that the community, either in Louisiana or in the country at large, did not share his view, and "therefore, I had no right to find a violation of the Due Process Clause."[29]

Frankfurter, it should be noted, joined in the result in *Francis* but wrote separately after Reed made several concessions to Black regarding the implied applicability of Fifth and Eighth amendment standards to the state. In his concurrence, Frankfurter again declared that if he had voted to deny Louisiana a second chance at executing Francis on due process grounds, "I would be enforcing my private view rather than the consensus of society's opinion, which for purposes of due process, is the standard enjoined by the Court."[30]

Herman Pritchett finds Frankfurter's entire due process rationale in this case untenable. Frankfurter claimed to rely on society's consensus. "But how did he know what the consensus of opinion was on a subject that had never risen before?" Pritchett asks. "Instead of the result at which he arrived, could he not have assumed with equal validity that his own personal aversion at sending this man on a second trip to the electric chair was what any normally sensitive human being would have felt?"[31]

The *Francis* opinion came down about two months after *Adamson*, in which Frankfurter and Black had spelled out their differing views on incorporation and, to a lesser extent, the meaning of due process (see chapter 6). A few weeks later Frankfurter again cast the fifth and deciding vote in a capital punishment case, but this time to overturn the conviction.[32] A 15-year-old black youth had confessed to murder after police subjected him to hours of intense interrogation without allowing him to see a lawyer, friends, or even his family. Frankfurter's separate opinion was almost sanctimonious in its tone of congratulatory self-righteousness:

155

Humility in this context means an alert self-scrutiny so as to avoid infusing into the vagueness of a Constitutional command one's merely private notions. Like other mortals, judges, though unaware, may be in the grip of prepossessions. The only way to relax such a grip, the only way to avoid finding in the Constitution the personal bias one has placed in it, is to explore the influences that have shaped one's unanalyzed views in order to lay bare prepossessions.

It would hardly be a justifiable exercise of judicial power to dispose of this case by finding in the Due Process Clause Constitutional outlawry of the admissibility of all private statements made by an accused to a police officer, however much legislation to that effect might seem to me wise. . . . But whether a confession of a lad of fifteen is "voluntary" . . . or "coerced" . . . is not a matter of mathematical determination. Essentially it invites psychological judgment—a psychological judgment that reflects deep, even if inarticulate, feelings of our society. Judges must divine that feeling as best they can from all the relevant evidence . . . and with every endeavor to detach themselves from their merely private views.[33]

One seeks in vain in these two concurrences for any hint of an objective standard by which to make the appropriate judgment. Frankfurter believed these cases, especially *Francis*, epitomized his ability to reach a detached judgment in emotion-ridden situations. Yet one cannot help wondering if Frankfurter's efforts to discern community standards were anything more than a bow to majoritarian sentiment. As in the speech cases discussed earlier, Frankfurter stood willing to allow the states great leeway in delimiting individual liberties, provided they did not go so far as to shock his conscience.

Wallace Mendelson, in a book defending Frankfurter and belittling Black, makes an interesting comment. For Black, "plainly the essence of law is Justice—as he sees it." In contrast, "the essence of law for Mr. Justice Frankfurter is regularity and uniformity. To emphasize these—along with neutrality as the crux of the judicial function—and to leave the other elements of Justice largely to the lawmaking branches of government is to emphasize the Separation of Powers."[34]

But Frankfurter himself claimed that it is the judge's obligation, through constant reinterpretation of the due process clause, to ensure fundamental fairness in the criminal justice system, to ensure that police procedures do not shock the conscience, to ensure that the state lives up to society's consensus on civilized behavior—to ensure, in other words, justice. Mendelson asserts, although not using these words, that Frankfurter abandoned justice to the elective branches, where it properly belonged. If this is true, then Frankfurter's pride in judicial restraint, in reining in his own biases in favor of community standards, was not judicial statesmanship but judicial abdication; Frankfurter himself at one point came close to admitting this. In 1953 he conceded that "the duty of deference cannot be allowed imperceptibly to slide into an abdication by this Court."[35]

Frankfurter always considered himself something of an expert on the Fourth Amendment. In a letter to Frank Murphy he suggested that Fourth Amendment rights need greater protection by the Court than do First Amendment guarantees. Freedom of speech, he noted, would always attract powerful defenders against encroachment. "But the prohibitions against unreasonable search and seizure is normally invoked by those accused of crime and criminals notoriously have few friends."[36] *Unreasonable*, whose meaning is very subjective, is the key word in the Fourth Amendment in attempting to understand Frankfurter's views on search-and-seizure cases. Its vague meaning requires judges to "strik[e] a balance between competing interests," namely, the individual's right of privacy and security in the home against the need of society to investigate crimes and bring wrongdoers to justice.[37]

It is unlikely that had he still been on the Court in 1965 Frankfurter would have gone along with William O. Douglas's discovery of a constitutional right to privacy in the penumbras of the Bill of Rights.[38] Frankfurter did believe strongly in privacy but grounded that belief entirely in the Fourth Amendment, which he claimed should be viewed in the light of the colonists' grievances against British behavior.[39] No one on the Court, he once told Zechariah Chafee, felt as strongly as he did about unreasonable searches and seizures. In the 15 "pure" Fourth Amendment cases decided during his tenure on the Court—that is, those involving federal agents—Frankfurter voted in 14 to exclude evidence he considered to have been illegally seized.[40] Frankfurter, in fact, led a campaign during the Vinson years to require a high standard of behavior by agents of the federal government, against whom the Fourth Amendment operated directly.

The law has always held that in connection with a proper arrest, a search without a warrant can include only those objects "in plain sight" of the arresting officers. In *Harris* v. *United States* (1947) the Federal

Bureau of Investigation (FBI) agents conducted a five-hour search of the four-bedroom apartment in which they arrested George Harris, looking for evidence related to his alleged check-forging operation.[41] They did find some Selective Service classification cards unlawfully in his possession, and on this charge they secured his conviction. Justice Vinson wrote for the 5–4 majority that upheld the conviction on a "totality of the circumstances" rationale. Frankfurter entered a passionate dissent, claiming that the protection of the Fourth Amendment "is not an outworn bit of Eighteenth Century romantic rationalism but an indispensable need for a democratic society."[42]

Although the Court seemed to have adopted at least part of Frankfurter's *Harris* argument in subsequent cases,[43] the conservative Truman appointees swung the pendulum back. In *United States* v. *Rabinowitz* (1950) Justice Minton essentially allowed an extensive warrantless search at the time of a proper arrest.[44] Frankfurter entered a strong dissent, calling on the Court to establish the highest standards of conduct for federal agents. Two years later he dissented again, in a case in which a Chinese laundry operator had been convicted of smuggling opium on the basis of conversation recorded by a supposed friend wired for sound. Frankfurter, like Brandeis and Holmes before him, considered wiretapping a "dirty business," especially when conducted without an appropriate warrant.[45]

But severe as he might have been about federal agents violating the Fourth Amendment, Frankfurter took a completely different tack when it came to the states, where, as Fred Graham notes, as late as the 1960s "search warrants have been oddities."[46] With state officers Frankfurter applied the "shock the conscience" test. While values of federalism are certainly important, one wonders if widely disparate standards of police conduct are either indispensible or valuable to a pluralist system.

The Supreme Court had begun to hold federal agents to a strict accountability under the Fourth Amendment when it imposed the exclusionary rule in the 1914 case of *Weeks* v. *United States*.[47] The exclusionary rule prohibits the use of evidence seized illegally and provides a simple prophylactic standard. As a result, the government, especially the FBI, trained its officers well in the proper procedures required by the Constitution. The Fourth Amendment, however, does not mention an exclusionary rule; in fact, it does not mention any means by which to enforce its ban against unreasonable search and seizure. There has been considerable debate about the wisdom of the judge-made exclusionary rule, but there is also general agreement that it is the only rule that makes the Fourth Amendment effective. Exclude the evidence, and police will have to be more careful; allow illegally seized evidence into court, and there is no incentive for police to obey the search-and-seizure clause.

Justice William Day, the author of the *Weeks* opinion, explicitly noted that the exclusionary rule applies only to federal agents, not to state or local police. In the next 30 years not only did officials in some states ignore the warrant clause but an active collusion developed between state and federal officials under the so-called silver platter doctrine. Dicta in two 1927 cases held that evidence seized in an illegal state search is admissible in federal court provided there has been no "federal participation."[48] As a result, in circumstances where federal agents could not meet the warrant requirement, a quiet word to state friends could result in a state raid, with the evidence then turned over to federal prosecutors.

This anomalous situation came to the Court's attention in *Wolf* v. *Colorado* (1949), and Frankfurter's opinion for the Court highlighted his devotion to the idea of privacy as well as his willingness to tolerate state invasions of that privacy.[49] The case is significant because it is one in which Frankfurter, applying his and Cardozo's standards, incorporated part of the Bill of Rights and applied it to the states through the Fourteenth Amendment. The security of one's privacy, he wrote,

> against arbitrary intrusion by the police—which is at the core of the Fourth Amendment—is basic to a free society. It is therefore implicit in "the concept of ordered liberty" and as such enforceable against the States by the Due Process Clause. The knock at the door, whether by day or by night, as a prelude to a search, without authority of law but solely on the authority of the police, did not need the commentary of recent history to be condemned as inconsistent with the conception of human rights enshrined in the history and the basic constitutional documents of English-speaking peoples.[50]

But if the Fourth Amendment now applied to the states, that did not mean that the methods used to enforce that right also applied. The exclusionary rule, effective as it might be, remained judge-made law and not part of the Fourth Amendment. States could therefore develop their own minimal standards to ensure compliance with due process requirements. Nevertheless, "in a prosecution in a State court for a State crime the Fourteenth Amendment does not forbid the admission of evidence obtained by an unreasonable search and seizure."[51] In other words, states could ignore the Fourth Amendment, even though it now applied to them, provided they did not act so unreasonably as to shock the conscience.

Wallace Mendelson suggests a functional explanation for the *Wolf* opinion. The Court has a direct supervisory duty over lower federal courts to see that meticulous attention is paid in enforcing constitutionally directed rights, but it has a lesser responsibility toward state courts in a federal system. It thus appropriately sets a lower level of enforcement, the "shock the conscience" standard. In *Wolf*, Professor Mendelson claims, Frankfurter

> struck a balance somewhere between the two extremes. Characteristically, the balance struck was predicated not on the high standards which the Justice would doubtless require if he were acting as a legislator or police chief but upon an objective, outside norm—the practice of a majority of state (indeed a majority of all Anglo-American supreme) courts. Surely such a pedigree warrants as within the realm of reason state convictions based on improperly obtained, but *incontestably reliable*, evidence.[52]

If this is what Frankfurter had in mind, and there is some evidence to support this assumption, then a fair reading of his *Wolf* opinion is that Frankfurter would have liked the states to maintain the same high standards as federal criminal procedure; that he hoped applying the Fourth Amendment to the states would get them to establish high standards; and that he believed that their failure to do so would still be acceptable because a federal system allows diversity, and that almost any practice that does not "shock the conscience" is permissible under this double standard.

Totally missing is a sense that rights without enforcement are not rights at all. Justice Douglas, in his dissent in *Wolf*, argued that even without judicial articulation of the exclusionary rule it exists implicitly in the Fourth Amendment by a simple commonsense reading: if the amendment protects against search and seizure without an appropriate warrant, than it can only do so by making any evidence seized—even "incontestably reliable evidence"—inadmissible. The exclusionary rule serves primarily as a prophylactic caution to the police, namely, obey the rules or you cannot use what you find.

Using a later parlance, Frankfurter advocated a "totality of the circumstances" approach: a court recognizes the constitutional ideal but does not impose it in a rigidly absolute manner. Judges balance all the factors, and if they believe the police acted reasonably, then they will admit the evidence; if the police exceeded the bounds of reason, if their actions "shock" the judicial conscience, the evidence is excluded.

In the next decade the Court heard two more cases in which it reaffirmed the Frankfurterian approach. Antonio Rochin and his wife were in bed on the second floor of their home when police burst into the room without a warrant. Rochin quickly swallowed two cellophane-wrapped capsules on the nightstand; after police failed in trying to man-ually force him to regurgitate, they took him to a hospital and had his stomach pumped against his will. The remains of the capsules proved to be controlled substances that Rochin had illegally, and the trial court sentenced him to two months in jail. The Court found the police con-duct so shocking that the evidence had to be excluded from a state trial.[53] In the second case, police made repeated illegal entries into the defen-dant's house to install a listening device. A bare majority of the Court found this behavior abhorrent but, since there had been no physical as-sault on the defendant, upheld the conviction. Frankfurter found the whole episode outrageous and voted with the dissenters.[54]

Justice Black had concurred in *Wolf*. He believed that the Fourth Amendment applies fully to the states, but his strict reading of the Con-stitution did not reveal any exclusionary rule. In the decade following *Wolf*, Black came to agree with Douglas that without such a rule the Fourth Amendment is a dead letter. After Earl Warren, William Bren-nan, and Potter Stewart joined the Court, all three tended toward a strict objective standard for the Fourth Amendment as opposed to Frank-furter's more subjective approach.

In 1960, over Frankfurter's dissent, the Court did away with the silver platter doctrine by which evidence seized by state and local police in violation of the Fourth Amendment could then be handed over to federal officials for use in federal prosecutions. Potter Stewart caught the meaning of the exclusionary rule perfectly: "Its purpose is to deter—to compel respect for the constitutional guaranty in the only effective avail-able way—by removing the incentive to disregard it."[55] That decision set the stage for one of the Warren Court's major criminal procedure rulings, *Mapp v. Ohio*, in 1961.[56]

The case that came to the high court initially appeared to be a First Amendment problem. Police officers attempted to gain entrance to the home of Dollree Mapp because they had information that a person wanted in connection with a bombing was hiding there. She refused to let the officers in without a warrant; three hours later they returned waving a piece of paper they claimed was a warrant but refused to let her read. When Mapp tried to grab the paper, police manhandled and handcuffed her, then proceeded to search the house. In a trunk in the basement the police found a cache of pornographic items; they arrested her for possession of obscene materials. The state courts conceded that there had probably never been a warrant, but the prosecution correctly claimed that, under *Wolf*, it could use evidence obtained by a warrantless, unreasonable search. On appeal, Ms. Mapp's lawyer urged overturning the conviction, not because the police conduct shocked the conscience, but on the First Amendment grounds that the material seized was not obscene. Neither in the briefs nor in oral argument did either side even mention the exclusionary rule.

Although Frankfurter found the police conduct egregious, the majority of the Court refused to even apply the shock the conscience test. Rather, the Court overruled *Wolf* and adopted a strict standard approach akin to the one Frankfurter had been urging for more than 15 years in relation to federal searches and seizures. In *Wolf* the Court had applied the Fourth Amendment but not the exclusionary rule and had warned the states that flexibility requires acceptable standards of conduct. By 1961 it had become apparent that the states had made little or no effort to establish minimal standards. Black had come to accept Douglas's view that Fourth Amendment guarantees, to be effective, require the exclusionary rule, and Warren, Brennan, and Stewart agreed with that view. Thus a majority now existed to shift the standard of police conduct away from Frankfurter's flexible and essentially standardless approach to a strict adherence to constitutional requirements.[57]

Frankfurter, along with Whittaker, joined John Marshall Harlan's dissent and appeal to the Court to continue to allow the states greater flexibility in their procedures. Harlan believed that the rationale in *Wolf*, that the exclusionary rule had been created by judges and was not an essential part of the Fourth Amendment, remained valid.

Mapp may be seen as the demise of the fundamental fairness approach to due process questions. The record of states in meeting even minimal procedural standards regarding Bill of Rights protections, such as counsel, the exclusionary rule, and confessions, had proven disappointing. Many states, according to California judge Roger Traynor, never even reviewed their evidentiary rules in light of *Wolf,* and this "indifferent response must have been disheartening to a Court that had expressed its reluctance to invoke federal power to upset state convictions based on unconstitutionally obtained evidence."[58] The Frankfurterian view asserted that these rights exist, but establishing a two-tiered system of standards fails to protect those rights at the state level. The opposing view, that Bill of Rights guarantees should be strictly enforced in both state and federal courts, meant that a person's rights do not depend upon what court he or she is tried in, or upon what police conduct a particular judge finds shocking. But it did break down some of the traditional distinctions of the federal system, distinctions Frankfurter held dear, and it also gave enormous supervisory power to the Supreme Court, a power Frankfurter believed should be exercised by the legislatures.

Events moved quickly in the next few years and accelerated after Frankfurter left the bench in 1962. The case-by-case analysis of *Betts* gave way to the incorporation of the Sixth Amendment right to counsel in *Gideon.* Similarly, in confession cases decided under the Fifth Amendment's protection against self-incrimination, the Court during Frankfurter's tenure had adopted a fundamental-fairness, totality-of-circumstances approach that it applied on a case-by-case method.[59] By 1959, however, at least four members of the Court—Black, Douglas, Brennan, and Stewart—had adopted a strict standard approach and had also accepted Justice Black's view of the interconnection between the Fifth Amendment ban against self-incrimination and the Sixth Amendment right to counsel. That view triumphed in the 1964 case of *Massiah* v. *United States.*[60]

Implementing the strict standard approach and applying it rigorously to both state and federal courts comprised the Warren Court's due process revolution.[61] By the time Earl Warren retired as chief justice in 1969, nearly every one of the cases decided according to the old fundamental fairness approach to due process had been overruled. Although snippets of Frankfurter opinions were occasionally quoted, the post-Frankfurter Court ignored the rulings he had delivered and the dual standard he had espoused.

Not everyone rejoiced at this development; conservatives claimed, for instance, that the high standards required by the Warren Court hampered effective police work. In the 1970s and 1980s, as more conservative justices replaced Hugo Black, William Douglas, Potter Stewart, and

Abe Fortas, the Court resurrected fundamental fairness in the guise of totality of circumstances, but with some significant differences: the basic standards would apply equally to both state and federal law enforcement officers; and the Court, not the legislature, would determine what constitutes due process.

10

THEME AND CODA

As James Simon has pointed out, efforts to label Hugo Black and Felix Frankfurter as "liberal" or "conservative" in the postwar years are fruitless. On the Fourth Amendment, for example, despite his willingness to set a different standard for the states, Frankfurter took a far broader view than Black did of the privacy that the amendment protected. And although Black took a far more libertarian approach to the speech clause of the First Amendment, Frankfurter proved to be the champion of a Jeffersonian notion of the separation of church and state.[1]

The first of the modern establishment clause cases reached the Court in 1947 and involved a challenge to a New Jersey law allowing townships to reimburse parents for bus fare for their children attending private or parochial schools. A local taxpayer challenged the payments as a form of establishment of religion, and the Supreme Court had to deal with the question of just what constitutes an establishment of religion.[2]

The Court had earlier incorporated the free-exercise clause of the First Amendment; at the time it assumed that the establishment clause also applied against the states.[3] In *Everson*, Justice Black made that incorporation clear and also set down what still remains basic jurisprudence for establishment clause cases:

The "establishment of religion" clause of the First Amendment means at least this: Neither a state nor the Federal Government can set up a church. Neither can pass laws which aid one religion, aid all religions, or prefer one religion over another. Neither can force nor influence a person to go to or to remain away from church against his will or force him to profess a belief or disbelief in any religion. No person can be punished for entertaining or professing religious beliefs, for church attendance or nonattendance. No tax in any amount, large or small, can be levied to support any religious activities or institutions, whatever they may be called, or whatever form they may adopt to teach or practice religion. Neither a state nor the Federal Government can, openly or secretly, participate in the affairs of any religious organizations or groups and vice versa. In the words of Jefferson, the clause against establishment of religion by law was intended to erect a "wall of separation between Church and State."[4]

Black continued with a brilliant exposition of the historical forces that had led to the adoption of the First Amendment; anyone reading his opinion fully expects that he will hold the New Jersey statute unconstitutional. Instead, he affirmed it, leading to one of the great judicial epigrams, Justice Jackson's comment comparing Black's reasoning to Byron's Julia who, "whispering 'I will ne'er consent,'—consented."[5]

It is surprising to find Black, famous for his absolutist position, in this case taking a balancing approach and finding the state's subsidy of bus fare a "reasonable" means of promoting the welfare of the children. He evidently believed from the start that the New Jersey law did not violate the Constitution and never changed his mind about his *Everson* opinion.[6]

Felix Frankfurter, who had found no problem with the state forcing Jehovah's Witnesses to violate their conscience by saluting the flag, who had preached deference to state legislative authority and reasonableness in constitutional interpretation, in *Everson* took an absolutist approach that separation means just that—separation, full and complete. Frankfurter fought Black's conclusion vociferously but, at least in this case, not publicly.

Four justices dissented, Frankfurter, Jackson, Rutledge, and Burton. Frankfurter joined in Jackson's dissent as well as in the one filed by Rutledge. A possible reason for his declining to write one himself is suggested by a letter he had written a friend a decade earlier explaining his silence during the Court-packing fight in 1937. "I am the symbol of the Jew, the 'red,' the 'alien,'" he told Grenville Clark. "Instead of bringing light and calm and reason . . . [I] would only fan the flames of ignorance, of misrepresentation, and of passion."[7] In the conference room, however, as Black later recalled, Frankfurter "fought long, hard, and loud."[8]

Initially only Frankfurter and Rutledge voted against the New Jersey law, then Jackson and Burton joined them. Frankfurter now went after Frank Murphy, the only Catholic member of the Court, who had passed when the conference discussed *Everson*. And, as happened so often, Frankfurter overplayed his hand. You have "false friends," he told Murphy, who flattered him for their own purposes. "What follows is written by one who cares about your place in history, not in tomorrow's columns." Follow your conscience, Frankfurter urged, and uphold the great American doctrine of separation of church and state. "You have a chance to do for your country and your Church such as never came to you before—and may never again. . . . No one knows better than you what *Everson* is about. Tell the world—and shame the devil."[9] When Murphy refused to join, Frankfurter lambasted him for failing to live up to his responsibilities as a judge and declared that Murphy's biographers would have to explain why Murphy had allowed his Catholicism to take precedence over his responsibilities as an American and as a justice of the high court.[10]

Thwarted in his efforts to convert Murphy, Frankfurter urged Jackson and Rutledge to strengthen their dissents. Rutledge, under constant pressure from Frankfurter, wrote and rewrote his opinion six times to take account of all the suggestions. Black, aware of Frankfurter's campaign, kept revising his opinion as well, bolstering the basic theme that the First Amendment requires a high wall of separation—but still approving the reimbursement law. An angry Frankfurter later called the decision "characteristic of Black[,] to utter noble sentiments and depart from them in practice."[11]

The next term the Court decided another establishment clause case, and Frankfurter tried to undo what he considered the damage of *Everson*. The Champaign, Illinois, school system had, like many systems across the country, put aside one hour a week when clergymen from all denominations could come into the schools and provide religious instruction to adherents of their sects; only Reed thought the plan constitutional. Vinson assigned Black the opinion for the Court.[12] Although both Black and Frankfurter agreed that the released-time program violated the First Amendment, Frankfurter wanted the Court's decision in *McCollum* to avoid any reliance on *Everson*.

He called the four dissenters from *Everson* together in his chambers, and they all agreed that "it would be stultification for us" to join in Black's draft and its approving references to the earlier case.[13] Frankfurter then circulated a memorandum stating that he would not agree to any opinion that mentioned *Everson*. Black shot back that he would not agree to one that did not.[14] But where Frankfurter at this point dug in and refused to compromise, Black agreed to omit certain references to *Everson* that offended Burton and Rutledge, and they signed on to his opinion. A furious Frankfurter decided that, much as he preferred to remain silent on this issue and let others make his case, he had to write his own concurrence.

Frankfurter began by noting that he had dissented in *Everson* because he believed that "separation means separation, not something less." In his initial draft Frankfurter painted such broad strokes that Reed and Burton questioned whether he also opposed released-time programs that met off school property. Frankfurter said he did not and made explicit that he was discussing only religious education that occurred in public school buildings, a central consideration in the justices' vote on the Illinois plan.

One key to Frankfurter's decision to write in *McCollum* was his view of the public school as an Americanizing and unifying force, a place where children from all backgrounds develop a common American outlook. He always remembered the effect that Miss Hogan had on him at P.S. 25 in New York,[15] and he feared that religious education in the schools would destroy that "most powerful agency for promoting cohesion among a heterogeneous democratic people. The public school must keep scrupulously free from entanglement in the strife of sects."[16]

The *McCollum* decision stirred up a nationwide furor among religious groups, nearly all of which operated some form of released-time program. One indication of the emotion involved was the charge of Edward S. Corwin, the eminent constitutional scholar, and normally a voice of reason, that the Court was trying to set itself up as a national school board. Hugo Black somewhat laconically commented that "few opinions from this Court in recent years have attracted more attention or stirred wider debate."[17]

That reaction is often pointed to as the reason behind the Court's 6–3 vote in 1952 to uphold a New York released-time program that took place off school grounds.[18] Justice Douglas, writing for the majority, seemed to go out of his way to note that the First Amendment does not require a total separation (a reasonableness argument not unlike that used by Frankfurter in due process cases). Such a separation, he believed, would be impossible, for "we are a religious people whose institutions presuppose a Supreme Being." Total separation of church and state in such an environment could only lead to antagonism between the two, a result obviously not contemplated by the framers.[19]

Black and Jackson dissented in *Zorach*, and Frankfurter, while concurring in Jackson's opinion, submitted a separate dissent in which he charged that the school system did not "close its doors" when some of its pupils went off to religious instruction.[20] Those who remained were being deprived of their opportunity for instruction, since teachers did not plan substantive work for the time when they knew a significant portion of their classes would be absent.[21]

Although disconcerted by the vote in *Zorach*, Frankfurter took great pleasure in the fact that both he and Black had dissented, one more step down their road to reconciliation. Frankfurter dropped Black a note proudly reporting that they were both being attacked by religious groups for their dissents. "And for good measure," he added, there is "some rancid Billy Graham stuff whereby we shall be reviled as atheists. But then, it wouldn't be the first time that you and I are reviled."[22]

Almost a decade later, in his last full term on the Court, Frankfurter took part in the four companion cases involving Sunday closing laws. A strict reading of the First Amendment would have required striking down these laws, but Chief Justice Warren wrote the opinions for the Court sustaining them. He acknowledged that their origins had been religious; at one time they were a means to enforce the sabbath, but that time had long since passed. The blue laws now served the secular purpose of ensuring all citizens of at least one day's rest in seven. The laws, therefore, bore "no relationship to establishment of religion as those words are used in the Constitution."[23]

Only Justice Douglas, who had come to repent his vote in *Everson* and from these cases forward would espouse a strict separationist philosophy, dissented in all four cases; he pointed out that no matter how you explained it, blue laws derived from the Fourth Commandment, not the Constitution.[24] Frankfurter, given the vehemence of his views in the earlier cases, might have been expected to dissent as well, but instead he submitted an extensive concurrence, joined by Harlan, in which he substantially agreed with Warren in all four cases.[25] He went on for 90 pages with a historical dissertation on the origin and development of Sunday closing laws, concluding with a table listing the laws in each state as well as the exceptions each state granted. Frankfurter made this whole effort because Warren had relied a great deal on Black's opinion in *Everson;* Frankfurter still wanted to negate the influence of that decision. By building up what he considered an irrefutable historical record, the Court could approve the laws as a bow to a secular tradition.

One wonders how Frankfurter would have voted in the school prayer case, in which the Warren Court finally adopted the strict view of separation he had urged 15 years earlier at the time of *Everson.*[26] But he fell sick that term and did not participate in the case.

In 1957, to celebrate Frankfurter's seventy-fifth birthday, the *Yale Law Journal* dedicated its December issue to him. No other law journal took notice of the event, not even Harvard's. Such milestones had long been an occasion for this type of homage; Frankfurter himself had helped arrange a number of such celebrations to honor Holmes, Brandeis, and Cardozo. While Frankfurter no doubt took satisfaction in his capture of Yale, the lack of recognition elsewhere only underscored the fact that he had never been able to exercise the leadership over the Court that he and his supporters had expected. Although he had managed to keep the Court's activist wing hemmed in over the past dozen years, that limited hegemony would soon pass. He and Hugo Black were no longer the bitter enemies they had once been, but he still worried over the growing influence of Black's constitutional views, especially after the arrival of Warren and Brennan on the Court. The *Mapp* case in 1961 had shown Frankfurter that a majority of the Court would no longer pay heed to his calls for restraint and deference. The following year the Court handed Frankfurter an even more stunning defeat, eliciting from him his last major dissent.

Frankfurter thought he had erected in *Colgrove v. Green* (1946) a high and impenetrable wall to block judicial challenges to malapportioned state legislatures (see chapter 6). Then the civil rights movement burst on the national scene, and the NAACP went to court to challenge various southern devices to deprive blacks of their votes. In *Gomillion v. Lightfoot* (1960) blacks challenged a gerrymandering scheme in Tuskegee, Alabama, that redrew city boundaries from a square into "an uncouth twenty-eight-sided figure" and had the effect of disenfranchising all but four or five of Tuskegee's registered black voters without depriving a single white of the franchise.[27] In briefs and in oral argument, Alabama had argued that the doctrine of *Colgrove* barred jurisdiction.

Frankfurter rejected this claim completely. The facts in *Colgrove* had affected all citizens; in Tuskegee "the inescapable human effect of this essay in geometry and geography is to despoil colored citizens, and only colored citizens, of their theretofore enjoyed voting rights. That was not *Colgrove v. Green.*"[28] The Fifteenth Amendment spoke directly to the issue of black suffrage, and that fact removed the case from the realm of political questions into direct constitutional litigation.

Despite Frankfurter's best efforts to distinguish *Gomillion* from *Colgrove*, the inherent contradiction could not be hidden. If black citizens could secure judicial redress because their votes had been diluted, then why should not white citizens, suffering from a different form of the same ailment, be able to seek similar relief? Justice Douglas in his concurrence hammered this point home, repeating the points he had made in his dissent in *Colgrove*. One week later the Court noted probable jurisdiction in a case challenging Tennessee's apportionment scheme.[29]

The Tennessee legislature had not been reapportioned since 1901, even though the state constitution allocated representation on a population basis. The challengers claimed that because of this malapportionment, they could not secure redress through the traditionally preferred manner of legislative reform; the malapportionment foreclosed that option. They asked the Court to block any further elections under the 1901 apportionment and either direct at-large elections or decree a reapportionment based on the latest census figures.

Before the Court could decide whether to grant or deny relief in *Baker*, it had to decide whether it had the power to do so. Frankfurter in *Colgrove* had argued that the Court lacked jurisdiction in so-called political questions; before the Court could act it had to determine if it had jurisdiction. If it followed *Colgrove*, as Frankfurter urged his colleagues to do, then the petitioners would have to find some other way to break out of their trap. To affirm jurisdiction required overruling *Colgrove*.

The Court heard oral argument on *Baker* on 19 and 20 April 1961, then ordered reargument for 9 October 1961.[30] On 26 March 1962 the Court announced its decision. Justice Brennan held that jurisdiction existed, that the complaint stated a justiciable cause of action, and that the claimants had standing to pursue the case and seek relief. Brennan did not specifically overrule *Colgrove*; he noted accurately that four of the seven justices who participated in that case had held that jurisdiction existed, but also that one of them had believed that a remedy could not be provided before the next election and had therefore voted to sustain

Frankfurter's ruling. Frankfurter's former student did his teacher proud, although it is doubtful that Frankfurter appreciated it. Brennan knew what the objections would be and prepared a careful and lengthy opinion developing all of the salient points, each of which led to the inevitable conclusion that the Court could, in fact, take jurisdiction.

Six justices either joined in or concurred with Brennan; Whittaker did not participate, and Harlan and Frankfurter entered lengthy dissents. An obviously angry Frankfurter prefaced the delivery of his dissent with the comment, "Today the Court begins a process of litigation that it requires no prophet to say—and Cassandra was sometimes right—will outlast the life of the youngest member of this Court."[31]

The majority decision would plunge the Court into a task for which it had neither the experience nor the ability to handle—devising "what should constitute the proper composition of the legislatures of the fifty states." Frankfurter retraced the history of the political question, explaining why previous courts in their wisdom had refused to entertain such claims. One could hardly fail to note that the states had "widely varying principles and practices that control state legislative apportionment"; about the only common feature he could discern was "geographic inequality in relation to the population standard."[32]

The Court, he predicted direly, had plunged itself into a morass from which it would be impossible to emerge, a quagmire lacking judicially discoverable or administrable standards, an area infected by partisan politics. The federal system itself would be endangered by a new and "virulent source of friction and tension" as the judiciary became embroiled in political matters. The Court had taken a terrible step.

One wishes that Frankfurter had gone out on a better note, perhaps a decision in which he could have reinforced his concern for Fourth Amendment rights or the separation of church and state. His prophecies of a judicial nightmare never materialized; although the entrenched legislatures fought to prevent reapportionment, once it had happened and a majority of the population controlled a majority of the legislative seats, all opposition ceased. Justice Douglas provided a judicially manageable standard, "one man, one vote,"[33] which Chief Justice Warren then applied in *Reynolds* v. *Sims* (1964), a suit against the Alabama apportionment scheme.[34] The obvious justness of the decision, and the equally obvious facility with which it could be implemented, made Frankfurter's opinion seem, in subsequent readings, more and more paranoid and unrealistic. Compared to the democratic majesty of Warren's opinion in *Reynolds*, Frankfurter's claim that "there is not under our constitution a judicial remedy for every political mischief" sounds crabbed and vision-less.[35] Warren spoke to the possibilities of democracy, Frankfurter appar-ently could see only its limits.

Frankfurter had been in poor health through most of the 1961 term and in *Baker* had relied more than usual on his clerk, Anthony Amster-dam. Then in April 1962 his longtime secretary, Elsie Douglas, found him sprawled on the floor of his chambers, the victim of a stroke that left him paralyzed on his left side. He hoped to recover sufficiently to take his seat on the Court at the beginning of the 1962 term, but by August he realized that he had to retire from the institution he had faith-fully served, in one way or another, for most of his adult life.

Although confined to a wheelchair, he remained an animated con-versationalist, always eager to hear the latest political or legal gossip. Dean Acheson arranged for him to receive John F. Kennedy, a meeting strikingly parallel to one Frankfurter himself had arranged 30 years ear-lier, when he brought Franklin Roosevelt to meet Oliver Wendell Holmes. And like Holmes, Frankfurter found himself enamored of the new occupant of the White House; that young man, he told Acheson, has grace.

Acheson came frequently, as did many of his former clerks, who heard him complain about the shoddy work of the Warren Court and especially about the shortcomings of the chief justice and, of course, William O. Douglas. Frankfurter did not, however, criticize his old ne-mesis Hugo Black, who in the sixties found himself unable to go as far along the path of judicial activism as some of his colleagues. Frankfurter particularly liked Black's opinion in the sit-in cases: he argued that nei-ther history nor law supported civil rights activists' claims that the First and Fourteenth amendments protect their trespass on private property to protest segregation.[36] Black periodically visited Frankfurter and would often say afterwards that Felix had helped him to see something or the other in a new light. As James Simon points out, the two men never reconciled all their jurisprudential differences—and given their philoso-phies, never could—but they came to appreciate each other as persons and to recognize that each brought out the best in the other. Their mon-umental struggle, despite its often rancorous moments, had benefited both the Court and the country.[37]

Frankfurter worked on his papers with Max Freedman, and not sur-prisingly for a man who would never leave anything to chance that he could arrange, he planned his funeral. He wanted the memorial service in his apartment, as Brandeis's had been. He did not want a rabbi, he told playwright Garson Kanin, but he did want his former clerk Louis Henkin to be the last to speak. Why? Kanin asked.

"Because he is my only close personal friend who is also a practicing, orthodox Jew. He knows Hebrew perfectly and will know exactly what to say. I came into this world a Jew and although I did not live my life entirely as a Jew, I think it is fitting that I should leave as a Jew."[38]

The last few years saw his strength gradually decline, and he and Marion, who had herself been ill for years, spent nearly all of their time together, going out for an occasional ride holding hands. On 21 February 1965 he suffered another stroke and died quietly a few minutes after 5:00 P.M. on Washington's birthday. Hugo Black, then on vacation in Florida, picked up the morning newspaper the next day and gasped at the headline. "Oh!" he exclaimed, "Felix is dead!" And then he cried.[39]

About 100 people attended the service in his apartment, including President Lyndon Johnson and all the members of the Supreme Court except William O. Douglas. Paul Freund, Brandeis's law clerk and Frankfurter's pupil, protégé, and friend, spoke about what they would all remember about "F.F."—his patriotism, his infectious good humor, his love of the law and of his friends, his courage—"not least in later years when he exercised the courage of judicial restraint and risked the misunderstanding and alienation of friends outside the law." Most of all they would miss the person; who of us, Freund asked, "will not continue to feel that iron grip on the arm, to hear the full-throated greeting, to be rocked with explosive laughter, and to be moved by the solicitous inquiries about ourselves and our dear ones."

Freund then read the same passage from Bunyan's *Pilgrim's Progress* that Frankfurter had read at Brandeis's service nearly a quarter-century earlier, the section on the death of Mr. Valiant-for-Truth: "My sword I give to him that shall succeed me in my pilgrimage, and my courage and skill to him that can get it. My marks and scars I carry with me, to be a witness for me that I have fought his battles who now will be my rewarder."

Louis Henkin then rose and recited the kaddish, the age-old mourners' prayer, which is not a lamentation, as he explained, "but a *magnificat* which has bound generations of Jews to each other." It begins, "May His great Name be blessed forever and to all eternity." The prayer is not about death but is an affirmation of life.

One can appreciate Felix Frankfurter's contribution to American jurisprudence even if one believes that he misgauged some basic trends in the nation's life or disagrees with his views about the role of courts in protecting individual liberties. The values that he cherished are not inconsequential and in fact are essential in any scheme of ordered liberty. He matured intellectually at a time when conservative judges used their power to invalidate the reforms enacted by the legislature, that branch of the government most reflective of the will of the people. For him judicial restraint meant that the popular will should not be thwarted by the courts unless a specific constitutional prohibition existed. The ideal of popular democracy is a powerful notion, and all but the most elitist among us would agree that the will of the people should be the dominant force in a free government.[40]

But the voice of the people is not necessarily the voice of God. Whatever their other virtues, majorities are rarely tolerant of dissident beliefs and dissenting voices. Although Americans may pay lip service to the protection of minority views or the rights of accused persons, American history shows few instances of the majority, on its own volition, behaving in such an ideal manner.

The Constitution is a unique document that empowers the will of the majority while at the same time limiting that power. Resolving the inherent tension of these two aims is the unique function of the Supreme Court. Frankfurter put it quite well when he wrote: "The Founders knew that Law alone saves a society from being rent by internecine strife or ruled by mere brute power however disguised. . . . To that end they set apart a body of men, who were to be the depositories of law, who by their disciplined training and character and by withdrawal from the usual temptations of private interest may reasonably be expected to be 'as free, impartial, and independent as the lot of humanity will admit.'"[41]

Frankfurter had studied the Court too long and too well not to recognize that judging could not be a mechanical exercise by which one follows rigid rules to "discover" the law. He knew, even if he could not bring himself to admit it openly, that the emotions and biases of judges, as well as their learning and discipline, play a role in judicial decision-making. In his philosophy of selective incorporation, judges definitely made value decisions as to the greater importance of certain provisions of the Bill of Rights over other parts. Felix Frankfurter, not the founders, expounded a moral relativism; the rational balancing he expounded as the heart of his jurisprudence required that judges identify some values as more important than others.

Hugo Black tried to negate this balancing by tying the judges to an absolutist interpretation of the Constitution. Although this view may be a more attractive option in certain areas—such as the protection of individual liberties—it lacks the flexibility that Frankfurter saw, and rightly so, as one of the essential attributes of judging. Frankfurter understood that not all questions, not even all legal questions, are amenable to simple answers. Situations beyond the wildest imaginings of the framers require judges to search long and hard in the Constitution and its history to determine what part of the document, if any, applies. In difficult cases judges must look to history, experience, and precedent and then through disciplined reasoning reach the best result they can. Because this process is not infallible, judges must have humility; they must be willing to recognize that the other arms of government have as legitimate a claim to being right in these instances as the courts. The obvious solution is, therefore, judicial restraint and deference to the coordinate branches.

There is much to commend in a judiciary that is cautious in exercising its authority and aware that in a federal system the Constitution distributes power between the states and the national government as well as between the branches of government. A Supreme Court that has its own political agenda and pursues it actively violates the republican philosophy of a scheme of separated powers. All this Felix Frankfurter preached for almost a half-century, first at Harvard Law School and then on the Supreme Court. Following the activism of the Four Horsemen and the constitutional crisis they triggered, judicial restraint constituted a powerful and appealing message in the 1940s and early 1950s; Frankfurter's ideas have also been taken up in recent years by conservatives, such as Robert Bork and Edwin Meese, who charge the Court with exceeding its proper responsibilities.

The problem, as Frankfurter once acknowledged, is that judicial restraint can quickly become judicial abdication. While the courts should certainly respect the judgments of the other branches of government, they have a responsibility to measure those actions against constitutional standards. The argument can be made that in hard and complex questions courts should defer to the judgments of the elective branches; Frankfurter often made that argument. It can also be argued that in such situations the wisdom of the judiciary is as compelling as that of legislatures, and that it is sometimes the unique responsibility of the courts—not the legislatures—to make those judgments.

There is a consistency between the academic writings of Professor

Frankfurter and the judicial opinions of Justice Frankfurter. As mentioned earlier, Frankfurter's judicial philosophy matured in the late 1920s and early 1930s and, with one or two minor exceptions, did not change after he went onto the bench. The challenges coming before the Court, however, did change radically at just about the time Frankfurter donned the black robe. Prior to World War II, nearly all the major questions confronting the Court involved economic policy; although the Constitution places certain limits on the national government in this area, for the most part the constitutional grants of power in regard to interstate commerce and taxation are broadly defined. Under John Marshall and Roger Taney, as Frankfurter demonstrated, the Court took an expansive view of the constitutionally granted powers, so that between 1880 and 1937, the use of so-called freedom of contract and substantive due process to cripple these powers obviously represented an effort by judges to substitute their policy preferences for those of the legislatures.[42] In calling for judicial restraint and deference, Frankfurter was calling for a return to an older tradition.

Following the war, economic issues practically disappeared from the Court's docket; they were replaced by questions of civil liberties and civil rights. Here again Frankfurter's views appear to have been solidified well before he went on the Court, and they ran counter not only to the views of his colleagues but to the general sentiment among the population that the Court had a particular role to play in safeguarding individual rights and liberties. It was not just a question of "selective incorporation" as against "total incorporation," or "preferred" values as against "nonpreferment." Frankfurter did not believe that the Court had a special role to play in protesting rights. As has been shown at numerous points in this book, Frankfurter treated questions of free speech the same as questions of economic regulation—in both, the courts should defer to the legislatures.

There is no question that Frankfurter played an important role in the segregation cases. Yet, if the courts had deferred to the state legislatures, can one honestly believe that Alabama and Mississippi and the other southern states would have voluntarily abandoned Jim Crow? During the 1950s Frankfurter urged his colleagues not to second-guess Congress, while congressional committees ran roughshod over civil liberties and abridged freedom of speech and association. He warned the justices not to touch apportionment, even if that meant the continued denial of effective suffrage for majorities in state after state.

Frankfurter claimed that he modeled himself after Holmes and

Brandeis, yet one looks in vain in his opinions for the type of concern they showed in regard to free speech. What can one compare in Frankfurter's career to Holmes's dissent in *Abrams* or the Brandeis opinion in *Whitney?* Frankfurter pointed with pride to his dissent in *Barnette,* the second flag salute case, and even suggested that Roosevelt include a copy of it in the presidential library. In it, he deferred to the wisdom of a state legislature in forcing young children to violate their religious beliefs by saluting the flag. His last major opinion, his dissent in the apportionment case, called for continuing the dilution of voting rights in the name of judicial restraint.

It is not that Frankfurter lacked a vision, but rather that time outran his vision; he would have been the perfect judge a generation earlier. Once on the bench he seemed ignorant of the tides of history, of the country's changing social and political climate—the same sins for which he, as an academic commentator, had lambasted the conservative judges of the 1920s and 1930s. He remained consistent, but consistency is not always a virtue.

Frankfurter's failure to gain the leadership on the Court was due not just to his abrasive personality. Black, Douglas, Murphy, Brennan, Warren, and other strong-minded justices resented his patronizing tone and schoolmasterish lecturing. They also believed that the Court had a special obligation to do justice in protecting the rights of racial minorities and of those with dissident points of view. They believed that a person's rights should not depend on whether he or she comes to trial in one state rather than another. In the long run the Warren Court may be judged as too activist, as having gone too far in its judicial revolution. But in the 1950s and 1960s Warren, Brennan, Douglas, and Black reflected the general sentiment that the Court ought to be the guardian of the Bill of Rights.

Is that the job of the Court? Frankfurter on numerous occasions seemed to indicate that it is, that the Court has the responsibility and the authority to interpret constitutional protections in the light of modern conditions, thus keeping the Bill of Rights up to date. But when it came time to put that theory into practice, he could not overcome his stronger belief in a court of exceedingly limited powers.

Fortunately for the Court and the nation, during most of our history the Supreme Court has been composed of justices with varying judicial philosophies. While there have been periods when one or another particular jurisprudence was in the ascendant, for the most part justices with differing viewpoints have reached commonsense conclusions that have met with the approval of the American people. Reaching these conclusions in times of rapid social and political change is difficult, and there will be some who cannot make the transition from one era to another. Felix Frankfurter did not make the transition, and in that sense his story is a tragic one.

But by adhering to his beliefs in judicial restraint, in deference to the coordinate branches of government, in respect for precedent, Frankfurter held up a clear standard that forced the advocates of change such as Hugo Black to rethink their assumptions. Black did not always agree with Frankfurter, but that did not matter. In the 23 years Felix Frankfurter sat on the U.S. Supreme Court he forced his more activist colleagues to slow down and think about what they were doing. If he could not get them to adopt his vision of a time past, he did help them to hone their own vision of the times to come.

CHRONOLOGY

1882   Felix Frankfurter born 15 November in Vienna, Austria.

1894   Frankfurter family emigrates to United States.

1901   Graduates from City College of New York in June.

1902   Enters Harvard Law School.

1905   On 4 May hears Louis D. Brandeis deliver address urging students to become the "people's attorney." Graduates from Harvard Law first in his class; joins New York firm of Hornblower, Byrne, Miller & Potter.

1906   Joins Henry Stimson in U.S. Attorney's office.

1909–1910   Follows Stimson into private practice and works for him in unsuccessful New York gubernatorial campaign.

1911   Joins War Department in May as counsel for Bureau of Insular Affairs.

1914   Joins faculty of Harvard Law School in the summer. War breaks out in Europe in August; Frankfurter joins American Zionist movement at Brandeis's request.

1915   Publishes first book, *Cases under the Interstate Commerce Act.*

1916   Brandeis nominated to Supreme Court in January. Brandeis begins subsidy of Frankfurter's reform work.

1917   On 19 March defends Oregon minimum wage law before Supreme Court. United States enters World War I in April; Frankfurter rejoins War Department as assistant to Secretary Newton D. Baker. Goes on ill-fated Morgenthau mission to Gibraltar in the summer; meets Chaim Weizmann. In the fall, sent west with Mediation Commission in attempt to settle copper strikes.

1918   Reports on Mooney case to President Woodrow Wilson. Sent to Europe in March to explore attitudes of labor groups toward Wilson "Fourteen Points" peace proposal. Wilson establishes War Labor Policies Board in May, with Frankfurter as chairman. Confrontation in July with Judge Gary over 12-hour day in steel mills. Armistice 11 November ends hostilities.

1919   Goes to Paris in February to represent American Zionists at the peace conference. Meets with Prince Faisal in March to discuss Arab cooperation with establishment of Jewish homeland in Palestine. Returns to Harvard Law School in the fall. On 11 November presides over Boston rally protesting American intervention in Russia. Marries Marion A. Denman 20 December.

1920   Palmer raids begin 2 January. Sacco and Vanzetti arrested in May for payroll robbery in South Braintree, Massachusetts. Frankfurter named Byrne Professor of Administrative Law.

1921   Conservative Harvard alumni attack Zechariah Chafee, Jr., in the spring. Frankfurter resigns from Zionist Organization in June with other members of the Brandeis faction. Sacco and Vanzetti convicted of murder 14 July; appeals process starts.

1921–1922   Works on Cleveland Crime Survey.

1923   Argues Washington, D.C., minimum wage law before Supreme Court (*Adkins v. Children's Hospital*) 14 March.

1927   Publishes article on Sacco and Vanzetti in *Atlantic* (March) and *The Business of the Supreme Court* (with James Landis) and *Mr. Justice Holmes and the Constitution*. Sacco and Vanzetti executed 24 August.

1929   Stock market crashes in October; depression begins.

1930   Publishes *The Labor Injunction* (with Nathan Greene) and *The Public and Its Government*.

1931   Publishes *Cases . . . on Federal Jurisdiction* (with Wilbur G. Katz).

1932   Declines on 29 June appointment to Supreme Judicial Court of Massachusetts. Franklin D. Roosevelt elected president.

1933   Publishes *Cases . . . on Administrative Law* (with J. Forrester Davison) and *Mr. Justice Brandeis*. Declines in March Roosevelt's offer of U.S. solicitor-generalship. Helps draft Securities Act in the spring.

1933–1934   Serves as Eastman Professor at Oxford University.

1937   Roosevelt unveils Court-packing plan in February. Frankfurter publishes *The Commerce Clause under Marshall, Taney and Waite.*

1939   Nominated associate justice of the U.S. Supreme Court on 5 January. Confirmed by the Senate 17 January. Takes seat on bench 30 January. Delivers first opinion, in *Hale* v. *Bimco Trading Co.*, on 27 February.

1940   Arranges in April for Henry Stimson and Robert Patterson to head War Department. Delivers opinion in first flag salute case (*Minersville School District* v. *Gobitis*) 3 June. Helps draft lend-lease bill in the fall.

1942   On 19 February Roosevelt authorizes deportation of those of Japanese descent from West Coast.

1943   Delivers dissent in second flag salute case (*West Virginia Board of Education* v. *Barnette*) 14 June. On 21 June Court approves Japanese relocation in *Hirabayashi* case.

1945   Dispute in the summer over retirement letter for Owen Roberts.

1946   Chief Justice Harlan Stone dies 22 April; dispute between Black and Jackson begins. Delivers opinion in *Colgrove* v. *Green* 10 June.

1947   Delivers opinion in *Adamson* v. *California* 23 June.

1948   Concurs in *McCollum* v. *Board of Education* 8 March.

1949   Delivers opinion in *Wolf* v. *Colorado* 27 June.

1951   Delivers concurrence in *Dennis* v. *United States* 4 June.

1952   Delivers dissent in *Sacher* v. *United States* 10 March. Delivers opinion in *Beauharnais* v. *Illinois* 28 April.

1953   Court hears arguments on Rosenberg case on 18 June; Rosenbergs executed that evening. Fred Vinson dies 8 September; succeeded by Earl Warren as chief justice.

1954   Court hands down decision in desegregation cases 17 May.

1955   Court issues implementation decree (*Brown II*) 31 May.

1958   Delivers opinion in *Perez* v. *Brownell* 31 March. On 29 September, all members of Court sign decree in *Cooper* v. *Aaron,* The Little Rock desegregation case; Frankfurter also enters lone concurrence.

1960   Delivers opinion in *Gomillion* v. *Lightfoot* 14 November.

1961   Concurs in Sunday closing cases 29 May.

1962   Dissents in *Baker* v. *Carr* 26 March. Suffers stroke 5 April. Retires from the Court 28 August.

1965   Dies in Washington, D.C., 22 February.

1975   Marion Frankfurter dies.

NOTES AND REFERENCES

INTRODUCTION

1. Harold L. Ickes, *The Secret Diary of Harold L. Ickes,* 3 vols. (New York: Simon & Schuster, 1954), 2:552.

2. "Justice Frankfurter," *The Nation* 148 (14 January 1939): 52.

3. Archibald MacLeish, "Foreword," in Archibald MacLeish and E. F. Pritchard, Jr., eds., *Law and Politics: Occasional Papers of Felix Frankfurter, 1913–1938* (New York: Harcourt Brace, 1939), xiii.

4. Stone had lobbied the President to name Frankfurter on the grounds that only Frankfurter was capable of holding his own with Chief Justice Charles Evans Hughes; Alpheus Thomas Mason, *Harlan Fiske Stone: Pillar of the Law* (New York: Viking, 1956), 482. For the extensive lobbying efforts on Frankfurter's behalf, see Michael E. Parrish, *Felix Frankfurter and His Times: The Reform Years* (New York: Free Press, 1982), 275–78.

5. Editorial, *New York Times,* 6 January 1939. Irving Brant, who would later be disillusioned with Frankfurter, recalled that at the time of the nomination, "I was astonished when I read that Boston conservatives were advising their fellow travelers around the country . . . to lay off him. How right they were." Quoted in Gerald T. Dunne, *Hugo L. Black and the Judicial Revolution* (New York: Simon & Schuster, 1977), 195.

6. Felix Frankfurter and James M. Landis, *The Business of the Supreme Court: A Study in the Federal Judicial System* (New York: Macmillan, 1927).

7. Felix Frankfurter, oral history interview with Gerald Gunther, 15 September 1960 Washington, D.C., in microfilm, Felix Frankfurter Papers, Harvard Law School Library (hereafter cited as FF-HLS).

8. In a poll conducted among legal scholars in 1970, Frankfurter ranked among the 12 "great" justices, but even by then, as the authors of the study conceded, the ranking seemed to result more from his intellectual ability than from his influence. One of the participants considered Frankfurter "consistently overrated" and charged that he had used his brilliance to restrict the development of the law. Albert P. Blaustein and Roy M. Mersky, *The First One Hundred Justices* (Hamden, Conn.: Archon Books, 1978), 37, 44.

9. Oliver Wendell Holmes, Jr., *The Common Law* (Boston: Little, Brown, 1881), 5.

10. G. Edward White, *The American Judicial Tradition*, exp. ed. (New York: Oxford, 1988), ch. 8.

11. Felix Frankfurter, "Rigid Outlook in a Dynamic World," *Survey Graphic* 27 (1938): 5.

12. Felix Frankfurter, "United States Supreme Court," *Encyclopedia of the Social Sciences* 14 (1930): 480.

CHAPTER 1

1. Harlan B. Phillips, eds., *Felix Frankfurter Reminisces* (New York: Reynal, 1960), 17–33.

2. Holmes, *The Common Law*; Arthur E. Sutherland, *The Law at Harvard: A History of Ideas and Men, 1817–1967* (Cambridge, Mass.: Harvard University Press, 1967), 202.

3. Louis D. Brandeis, "The Opportunity in the Law," *American Law Review* 30 (1905): 555; see also David W. Levy, "The Lawyer as Judge: Brandeis' View of the Legal Profession," *Oklahoma Law Review* 22 (1969): 374.

4. For Stimson, see Henry L. Stimson and McGeorge Bundy, *On Active Service in Peace and War* (New York: Harper & Brothers, 1947) and Godfrey Hodgson, *The Colonel: The Life and Wars of Henry L. Stimson, 1867–1950* (New York: Knopf, 1990).

5. Phillips, *Frankfurter Reminisces*, 38.

6. Ibid., 42; see also Frankfurter interview, 15 September 1960, FF-HLS.

7. Phillips, *Frankfurter Reminisces*, 42–43.

8. The psychological relationship of "mentor-mentee," as developed in Daniel J. Levinson et al., *The Seasons of a Man's Life* (New York: Knopf, 1978), is applied to Frankfurter in H. N. Hirsch, *The Enigma of Felix Frankfurter* (New York: Basic Books, 1981); on Stimson and Frankfurter, see pp. 27–29. Hirsch's psychological analysis of Frankfurter's career has caused some controversy and must be used with caution, but it does offer some useful insights.

9. Phillips, *Frankfurter Reminisces*, 48.

10. Hirsch, *Enigma*, 30.

11. For example, Stimson's office managed to secure contempt convictions against railroad magnate E. H. Harriman and banker Otto Kahn for refusing to answer questions about their alleged stock manipulation. But a battery of high-priced lawyers convinced a bare majority of the Supreme Court to reverse on the grounds that the Interstate Commerce Commission (ICC) had exceeded its investigative authority. *Harriman v. Interstate Commerce Commission*, 211 U.S. 407 (1908).

12. Phillips, *Frankfurter Reminisces*, 46–49; Parrish, *Frankfurter*, 30–31.

13. Ibid., 14.

14. Joseph P. Lash, ed., *From the Diaries of Felix Frankfurter* (New York: Norton, 1975), 104, entry for 22 October 1911. It is impossible to know how consistently Frankfurter kept his diary, for there are large gaps in the manuscript. Following some entries for 1911, the next remnants deal with 1928, then 1933, and then some of the Court years.

15. Phillips, *Frankfurter Reminisces*, 56.

16. *Porto Rico v. Rosaly y Castillo*, 277 U.S. 270 (1913).

17. His tenure there is well described in Parrish, *Frankfurter*, 39–50.

18. *Phillips, Frankfurter Reminisces*, 58; Holmes to Frankfurter, 8 March 1912, quoted in Hirsch, *Enigma*, 33.

19. Stimson to Frankfurter, 19 September 1912, Felix Frankfurter Papers, Manuscript Division, Library of Congress (hereafter cited as FF-LC).

20. Melvin I. Urofsky, "Wilson, Brandeis and the Trust Issue, 1912–1914," *Mid-America* 49 (1967): 3–28.

21. Brandeis to Frankfurter, 12 July 1912, FF-HLS.

22. Frankfurter to Buckner, 6 January 1912, FF-LC; Parrish, *Frankfurter*, 58.

23. Frankfurter to Buckner, 11 March 1913, FF-LC. In his memoirs Frankfurter declared that he had "very high respect" for Garrison as "a character and as a man"; Phillips, *Frankfurter Reminisces*, 69. The particular area that Garrison wanted Frankfurter to work on was development of water power on land owned by the government.

24. Denison to Warren, 12 June 1913, and Warren to Denison, 16 June 1913, FF-LC.

25. Felix Frankfurter, "The Zeitgeist and the Judiciary," reprinted in MacLeish and Pritchard, *Law and Politics*, 6, 9.

26. For Pound, see David Wigder, *Roscoe Pound: Philosopher of Law* (Westport, Conn.: Greenwood, 1974).

27. Parrish, *Frankfurter*, 60–61; Hirsch, *Enigma*, 38–39.

28. Brandeis to Denison, 12 July 1913, in Melvin I. Urofsky and David W. Levy, eds., *Letters of Louis D. Brandeis*, 5 vols. (Albany: State University of New York Press, 1971–78), 3:134. In the end, a good portion of the money came from Jacob Schiff, who disagreed with most of Frankfurter's ideas but wanted to open the door for Jews to join the Harvard Law faculty.

29. Phillips, *Frankfurter Reminisces*, 78.

30. Charles Forcey, *The Crossroads of Liberalism: Croly, Weyl, Lippman and the Progressive Era, 1900–1925* (New York: Oxford, 1961), 181–82.

31. Phillips, *Frankfurter Reminisces*, 289–91. Frankfurter often referred to himself as a "believing unbeliever" or a "reverent agnostic," but he left specific instructions that the kaddish, the traditional Jewish mourners' prayer, be read at his memorial service (see chapter 10).

32. For the Brandeis era in the Zionist movement, see Melvin I. Urofsky, *American Zionism from Herzl to the Holocaust* (Garden City, N.Y.: Doubleday/Anchor, 1975), chs. 4–7.

33. A. L. Todd, *Justice on Trial: The Case of Louis D. Brandeis* (New York: McGraw-Hill, 1964), passim; see also Urofsky and Levy, *Brandeis Letters*, 4:25–209, passim.

34. 208 U.S. 412 (1908); for the background of the case and the development of the "Brandeis brief," see Alpheus Thomas Mason, *Brandeis: A Free Man's Life* (New York: Viking, 1946), 245–52, and Josephine Goldmark, *Impatient Crusader: Florence Kelley's Life Story* (Urbana: University of Illinois Press, 1953), ch. 13.

35. "Tattler," *Nation* 104 (15 March 1917): 320.

36. *Bunting v. Oregon*, 243 U.S. 426 (1917), and *Stettler v. Oregon*, 243 U.S. 629 (1917); Brandeis recused himself in both cases.

37. Laski to Holmes, 7 November 1916, in Mark DeWolfe Howe, ed., *The Holmes-Laski Letters*, 2 vols. (Cambridge, Mass.: Harvard University Press, 1953), 1:35.

38. Hirsch, *Enigma*, 48–51.

39. The bizarre nature of the Morgenthau mission is detailed in William Yale, "Am-

bassador Henry Morgenthau's Special Mission of 1917," *World Politics* 1 (1949): 308–20; see also Phillips, *Frankfurter Reminisces,* 145–53. Brandeis, who worried that the anti-Zionist Morgenthau might do something to endanger either the Zionist program or the Palestinian settlements, was delighted to have Frankfurter on the scene to make sure no rash decisions or statements were made.

40. Lowenthal, a former student of Frankfurter at Harvard and then clerk to Judge Julian Mack, had protested that he had very little knowledge of economics, mining, or labor relations. "Neither does anybody else," said Frankfurter, "so come along" (Parrish, *Frankfurter,* 92).

41. James W. Byrkit, *Forging the Copper Collar: Arizona's Labor-Management War of 1901–1921* (Tucson: University of Arizona Press, 1982).

42. Phillips, *Frankfurter Reminisces,* ch. 13.

43. For full details, see Richard Frost, *The Mooney Case* (Stanford, Calif.: Stanford University Press, 1968).

44. Wilson released the report to the public at the end of January 1918; see *New York Times,* 27 January 1918. Following the California Supreme Court's affirmation of the conviction, Wilson did urge Gov. William D. Stephens to commute the sentence. The reluctant Stephens did not act until after further revelations of tainted evidence were made; he then commuted the sentence to life imprisonment. Despite repeated efforts by liberals in the 1920s and 1930s to free Mooney, he remained in prison until pardoned by Gov. Floyd Olson in 1939.

45. Roosevelt to Frankfurter, 19 December 1917, FF-LC. Frankfurter responded firmly, but in a tone more of sorrow than anger. Frankfurter to Roosevelt, 7 January 1918, FF-LC.

46. James M. Beck, "The Mooney Case," with a reply by Felix Frankfurter, *New Republic* 29 (18 January 1922): 212–21.

47. On this point see Robert D. Cuff, *The War Industries Board: Business-Government Relations during World War I* (Baltimore: Johns Hopkins University Press, 1973), chs. 1–4.

48. Frankfurter to Brandeis, probably December 1917, FF-LC.

49. Felix Frankfurter, "Memorandum for the Secretary of War," 7 January 1918, FF-LC; Brandeis to E. M. House, 9 January 1918, in Urofsky and Levy, *Brandeis Letters,* 4:332–34.

50. Quoted in Bernard M. Baruch, *American Industry in the War, Report of the War Industries Board* (Washington, D.C.: Government Printing Office, 1921); 288.

51. Parrish, *Frankfurter,* 108–10.

52. Melvin I. Urofsky, *Big Steel and the Wilson Administration* (Columbus: Ohio State University Press, 1969), 269–71.

53. Many industries still paid workers by the day rather than the hour, so reduction of hours worked would have to include an upward adjustment of wages to maintain the workers' incomes. See, in general, Marion C. Cahill, *Shorter Hours: A Study of the Movement since the Civil War* (New York: Columbia University Press, 1932).

54. Frankfurter to Gary, 9 July 1918, Records of the War Labor Policies Board, record group 1, box 16, "8-hour day" folder, National Archives, Washington, D.C. (hereafter cited as WLPB Records).

55. Phillips, *Frankfurter Reminisces,* 141.

56. Minutes of Frankfurter-Gary Meeting, 20 September 1918, 9:15 A.M., WLPB Records.

57. For details of the strike and the events leading up to it, see David Brody, *Labor in Crisis: The Steel Strike of 1919* (Philadelphia: Lippincott, 1965). U.S. Steel did not end the 12-hour day until 1922.

58. Cuff, *War Industries Board,* 259.

59. Frankfurter to Hand, 21 January 1919, quoted in Parrish, *Frankfurter,* 116–17.

60. Parrish, *Frankfurter,* 114–15.

61. Frankfurter to Stephen S. Wise, 20 September 1917, Frankfurter Papers, Central Zionist Archives, Jerusalem, Israel (hereafter cited as FF-CZA). For full details on the negotiations leading to Wilson's endorsement, see Urofsky, *American Zionism,* 207–20.

62. William L. Westermann to William C. Bullitt, 27 March 1919, quoted in Urofsky, *American Zionism,* 232.

63. Phillips, *Frankfurter Reminisces,* 155. Although Liva Baker claims that "at the Peace Conference [Frankfurter] was Brandeis' eyes, ears, and spokesman" (Liva Baker, *Felix Frankfurter* [New York: Coward-McCann, 1969], 83), in fact Frankfurter received almost no advice or instructions from Brandeis at the time. The jurist had enough faith in Frankfurter that it was unnecessary to "instruct" him: "Events shift so constantly that I have felt it impossible to advise in any respect and have confidence in your own good judgment." Brandeis to Frankfurter, 16 May 1919, FF-LC.

64. Phillips, *Frankfurter Reminisces,* 155–56; *New York Times,* 5 March 1919.

65. Frankfurter to Thomas Reed Powell, 5 October 1954, Thomas Reed Powell Papers, Harvard Law School Library (hereafter cited as Powell Papers). The letter was written when Frankfurter heard about Westermann's death.

66. Brandeis to Frankfurter, 5 and 9 June 1919, and Frankfurter to Brandeis, two cables, 6 June 1919, FF-LC.

67. Harry N. Howard, "An American Experiment in Peace-Making: The King-Crane Commission," *Moslem World* 32 (1942): 122–46.

68. Michael Parrish's description of Frankfurter at Paris (*Frankfurter,* ch. 8) makes him out to be a far more crucial figure and gives him far greater credit for some of the Zionist accomplishments than I would. There is no doubt, though, that Frankfurter was at the very center of Zionist activity in Paris, and that he acted not only as Brandeis's lieutenant but independently as well.

69. Frankfurter to Wilson, 8 and 14 May 1919, and Wilson to Frankfurter, 16 May 1919, FF-HLS.

70. Brandeis believed Frankfurter was "the closest [American] friend of Dr. Weizmann," and Weizmann on more than one occasion tried to entice and/or bully Frankfurter into becoming more active in the movement. "Brandeis could have been a prophet in Israel," Weizmann claimed, "and you have the makings of a Lasalle. Instead you are choosing to be only a professor at Harvard and Brandeis only a judge in the Supreme Court." Weizmann to Frankfurter, 27 August 1919, FF-CZA.

CHAPTER 2

1. Brandeis to Laski, 29 November 1928, in Urofsky and Levy, *Brandeis Letters,* 5:364.

2. The best account of this period remains Robert K. Murray, *The Red Scare: A Study in National Hysteria* (New York: McGraw-Hill, 1955).

3. Brandeis to Alice Brandeis, 14 June 1919, in Urofsky and Levy, *Brandeis Letters*, 4:400.

4. Conservative Harvard alumni saw red and inundated the school with letters of protest. Thomas Nelson Perkins, a member of the highly respected Boston law firm of Ropes, Gray & Gorham and counsel to the Harvard Corporation, met with Frankfurter and tried to get him to act more moderately. "In normal times it may well be that the world needs the stimulus that comes from real disagreement," Perkins said. "At the present time it seems to me that it is important not to rock the boat." Moreover, Frankfurter's outspokenness would make it difficult to raise money for the law school. Some of his friends, including Holmes and Learned Hand, also advised him to avoid confrontation, but Frankfurter believed that in academia speech could not be fettered. Parrish, *Frankfurter*, 121–22.

5. Phillips, *Frankfurter Reminisces*, 171–73.

6. *Colyer v. Skeffington*, 265 Fed. Rep. 17 (1920).

7. The most notorious of these cases was *Schenck v. United States*, 249 U.S. 47 (1919), in which Holmes upheld the Espionage Act and put forth his "clear-and-present danger" test. The criticism stung Holmes, and he agreed to meet with Chafee, who convinced him that the First Amendment required a far more generous reading. The story is told in Fred D. Ragan, "Justice Oliver Wendell Holmes, Jr., Zechariah Chafee, Jr., and the Clear and Present Danger Test for Free Speech: The First Year, 1919," *Journal of American History* 58 (1971): 24.

8. For details of the Chafee incident, see Sutherland, *The Law at Harvard*, 250–58, and Jerold S. Auerbach, "The Patrician as Civil Libertarian: Zechariah Chafee, Jr. and Freedom of Speech," *New England Quarterly* 42 (1969): 511. See also Donald L. Smith, *Zechariah Chafee, Jr.: Defender of Liberty and Law* (Cambridge, Mass.: Harvard University Press, 1986).

9. Brandeis to Chafee, 19 May 1921, and Brandeis to Frankfurter, 20 May 1921, in Urofsky and Levy, *Brandeis Letters*, 4:558, 559.

10. There have been a number of books on the case. See Roberta S. Feuerlicht, *Justice Crucified: The Story of Sacco and Vanzetti* (New York: Farrar, Straus & Giroux, 1977); Herbert B. Ehrmann, *The Case That Will Not Die: Commonwealth v. Sacco and Vanzetti* (Boston: Little, Brown, 1969); and Francis Russell, *Tragedy in Dedham: The Story of Sacco and Vanzetti* (New York: Harper & Row, 1962). Frankfurter's role in the case is detailed at length in Parrish, *Frankfurter*, ch. 10.

11. Parrish, *Frankfurter*, 179.

12. Phillips, *Frankfurter Reminisces*, 209–13.

13. David W. Levy, *Herbert Croly of the New Republic* (Princeton, N.J.: Princeton University Press, 1985), 285–88.

14. Phillips, *Frankfurter Reminisces*, 214–15.

15. Felix Frankfurter, "The Case of Sacco and Vanzetti," *Atlantic Monthly* 139 (1927): 409, republished in book form as *The Case of Sacco and Vanzetti: A Critical Analysis for Lawyers and Laymen* (Boston: Little, Brown, 1927).

16. Parrish, *Frankfurter*, 185.

17. Phillips, *Frankfurter Reminisces*, 215–17.

18. Ibid., 217.

19. Following the execution in August 1927, she helped a young newspaper reporter, Gardner Jackson, edit the deathhouse letters of the two men, *The Letters of Sacco and Vanzetti* (New York: Viking, 1928). The work provided only a brief respite, and her depression increased as soon as she finished the book.

20. Four years earlier Holmes had written the Court's opinion in *Moore* v. *Dempsey*, 261 U.S. 86 (1923), overturning the murder conviction of a Negro by an all-white jury in a trial that had been dominated from start to finish by a mob. But as Holmes told Harold Laski, "I thought that the line must be drawn between external force, and prejudice—which could be alleged in every case." Moreover, Holmes had little sympathy for the defendants and thought the whole affair had been blown out of proportion to give "the extremists a chance to yell." Howe, *Holmes-Laski Letters*, 2:971, 974–75.

21. Philippa Strum, *Louis D. Brandeis: Justice for the People* (Cambridge, Mass.: Harvard University Press, 1984), 403.

22. Frankfurter started out concerned only with the irregularities of the trial but, like most of their defenders, eventually came to believe in the innocence of Sacco and Vanzetti. The controversy over their guilt or innocence has not died, and one can still find well-reasoned articles on both sides of this issue.

23. Brandeis to Frankfurter, 2 June 1927, FF-HLS; Bruce Allen Murphy, *The Brandeis/Frankfurter Connection* (New York: Oxford, 1982), 79.

24. Brandeis to Frankfurter, 19 and 25 November 1916, FF-HLS, published in Urofsky and Levy, *Brandeis Letters*, 4:266–67.

25. Although I have criticized both the author and Oxford University Press for the manner in which I believe they exploited the information, and although there are some factual as well as interpretive errors in the work, Murphy presents new and useful information about an important subject. Unfortunately, the uproar over his style has precluded serious debate on substantive issues.

26. Brandeis to Frankfurter, 19 November 1916, FF-HLS.

27. Brandeis to Frankfurter, 25 November 1916, FF-HLS.

28. The *New York Times* (18 February 1982), which ran a front-page story on the Murphy revelations, editorialized that the "Brandeis-Frankfurter relationship was wrong . . . [and] violates ethical standards." Frankfurter's old friend Archibald MacLeish confessed that "reading about these activities, with their undertones of the dubious, has been one of the most disturbing experiences of my life"; *New York Times*, 21 February 1982. Reporter Bob Woodward declared that "a payoff is a payoff—secret money for secret lobbying and other efforts. . . . A whore may like and believe in his or her work, but prostitution is just that, despite the passions one might bring to it"; review of *The Brandeis/Frankfurter Connection, Washington Post*, 11 April 1982. Although some scholars have challenged Murphy's facts and interpretations, the fact remains that Frankfurter, for a period of 20 years, secretly accepted money in connection with his reform work.

29. Brandeis did in fact send a constant stream of suggestions to Frankfurter, and the breadth of these proposals is amazing. See Melvin I. Urofsky and David W. Levy, eds., *"Half-Son, Half-Brother": The Letters of Louis D. Brandeis to Felix Frankfurter* (Norman: University of Oklahoma Press, 1991). Some of these letters are also available in *Brandeis Letters*, vols. 4 and 5.

30. After a series of irregular payments, Brandeis arranged for the payment of $3,500

yearly between 1926 and 1938, which, according to Murphy, was worth in 1981 dollars between $19,150 and $26,150, depending on the year involved (Murphy, *The Brandeis/ Frankfurter Connection,* 42).

31. Frankfurter to Brandeis, undated, quoted in Hirsch, *Enigma,* 225, n. 69.

32. *Adkins v. Children's Hospital,* 261 U.S. 525 (1923); Frankfurter had prepared the brief and argued the case before the Supreme Court.

33. To take but one example from many, Brandeis wrote to Frankfurter on 4 September 1922, during nationwide strikes by coal and rail workers, outlining a number of steps that he believed would improve relations between labor and management. The substance of the letter, with the wording unchanged, appeared a few weeks later as the unsigned article, "What to Do," *New Republic* 32 (4 October 1922): 136.

34. See Brandeis to Frankfurter, 3 June 1924, FF-LC, and Felix Frankfurter, "Corollaries of the Immigration Law," *New Republic* 39 (11 June 1924): 61.

35. For example, four days after Charles A. Lindbergh flew solo across the Atlantic, Brandeis suggested that the *New Republic* "should draw the lesson of his heritage." Brandeis to Frankfurter, 25 May 1927, FF-HLS. Frankfurter, of course, had little time at that moment to spare for anything other than his efforts to save Sacco and Vanzetti.

36. Frankfurter kept notes of these conversations in law school exam booklets. They have been transcribed and annotated in Melvin I. Urofsky, "The Brandeis-Frankfurter Conversations," *Supreme Court Review* 299 (1985).

37. Brandeis to Frankfurter, 24 September 1925, FF-HLS.

38. The best known of these research efforts helped to make Frankfurter's reputation as an authority on the Supreme Court. James M. Landis enjoyed the first "fellowship," and he and Frankfurter published a pioneering article, "The Business of the Supreme Court," *Harvard Law Review* 38 (1925): 1005. Seven other articles followed in this series, and they nearly always benefited from advice made by Brandeis to Frankfurter. Eventually the two men published all the pieces in book form as *The Business of the Supreme Court: A Study in the Federal Judicial System* (New York: Macmillan, 1927). Brandeis made numerous suggestions on whom Frankfurter should send the book to so that it might accomplish some good.

39. Landis and Frankfurter cowrote the seven "Business" articles published in book form in 1927; they began a review of the Court's current work in "Business of the Supreme Court at October Term 1928," *Harvard Law Review* 43 (1929): 33. During the 1930s Henry M. Hart, Jr. and Adrian S. Fisher worked on what eventually became an annual review of the Court's work. This review still appears each November in the *Harvard Law Review* as a team project of the student editorial board, with a foreword written by a distinguished scholar.

40. Brandeis to Frankfurter, 14 July 1928, FF-LC.

41. See, for example, Brandeis to Frankfurter, 19 October 1929, FF-LC. Among the articles that grew out of the Frankfurter seminars were Lloyd W. Pogue, "State Determination of State Law and the Judicial Code," *Harvard Law Review* 41 (1928): 623; Erwin Griswold and William Mitchell, "The Narrative Record in Federal Equity Appeals," ibid., 43 (1928–29): 483; and John E. Lockwood, Carlyle E. Maw, and Samuel Rosenberry, "The Use of Federal Injunction in Constitutional Litigation," ibid., 43 (1929–30): 426. If they proved less than publishable, Frankfurter often salvaged the best parts and used them in his own articles, acknowledging his students' contributions. See, for ex-

ample, Felix Frankfurter, "Distribution of Judicial Power between the United States and State Courts," *Cornell Law Quarterly* 13 (1928): 499, acknowledging a seminar paper by A. H. Feller and N. Jacobs on limitation of diversity jurisdiction.

42. Felix Frankfurter, "Taft and the Supreme Court," in Philip B. Kurland, ed., *Felix Frankfurter on the Supreme Court: Extrajudicial Essays on the Court and the Constitution* (Cambridge, Mass.: Harvard University Press, 1970), 59–60. The piece originally appeared in a series of unsigned editorials in the *New Republic* in October 1920 and January 1922.

43. *Pierce v. Society of Sisters*, 268 U.S. 510 (1925); Felix Frankfurter, "Can the Supreme Court Guarantee Toleration?" in Kurland, *Frankfurter on the Supreme Court*, 174. The piece originally appeared as an unsigned editorial in the *New Republic*, 17 June 1925.

44. Frankfurter to Hand, 11 April 1923, quoted in Parrish, *Frankfurter*, 165.

45. See, for example, the essays on these men in Kurland, *Frankfurter on the Supreme Court*, as well as the lectures Frankfurter delivered in 1938, published as *Mr. Justice Holmes and the Supreme Court* (Cambridge, Mass.: Harvard University Press, 1938).

46. Laski to Holmes, 18 February 1920, in Howe, *Holmes-Laski Letters*, 1:245.

47. Phillips, *Frankfurter Reminisces*, 300.

48. James Bradley Thayer, "The Origin and Scope of the American Doctrine of Constitutional Law," *Harvard Law Review* 7 (1893): 129.

49. Frankfurter to Robert Jackson, 11 April 1942, FF-HLS.

50. Thayer, "Origin and Scope," 144.

51. Felix Frankfurter, "The Nomination of Mr. Justice Brandeis," in Kurland, *Frankfurter on the Supreme Court*, 43. The piece originally appeared as an unsigned editorial in the *New Republic* (5 February 1916).

52. Legal realism refers to a jurisprudential theory, developed mainly at the Yale Law School, that, as opposed to abstract idealism, emphasized the role of human idiosyncrasy in legal decision-making, stressed the utility of social sciences in understanding the law, and called for greater efficiency and certainty in administration of the law. See Wilfred E. Rumble, Jr., *American Legal Realism* (Ithaca, N.Y.: Cornell University Press, 1968).

53. Frankfurter, to A. T. Mason, 27 May 1940, quoted in Sanford V. Levinson, "Skepticism, Democracy, and Judicial Restraint: An Essay on the Thought of Oliver Wendell Holmes and Felix Frankfurter" (Ph.D. diss., Harvard University, 1969), 215.

54. Mark Silverstein, *Constitutional Faiths: Felix Frankfurter, Hugo Black, and the Process of Judicial Decision-Making* (Ithaca, N.Y.: Cornell University Press, 1984), 79.

55. Felix Frankfurter, *The Public and Its Government* (New Haven, Conn.: Yale University Press, 1930), 160.

56. Ibid., 79–80; cf. Brandeis's dissent in *New State Ice Co. v. Liebmann*, 285 U.S. 262, 280 at 311 (1932).

CHAPTER 3

1. Phillips, *Frankfurter Reminisces*, 233.

2. Ibid., 234.

3. Robert A. Burt suggests that even at this early time Frankfurter felt the conflicts that would plague his years on the Supreme Court: the desire on the one hand to be

accepted, to be an "insider," and the deep-rooted conception of himself as the eternal "outsider" who, much as he might want to do so, could never fit in. *Two Jewish Justices: Outcasts in the Promised Land* (Berkeley: University of California Press, 1988), 53–54.

4. Leonard Baker, *Brandeis and Frankfurter: A Dual Biography* (New York: Harper & Row, 1984), 271.

5. *Boston Evening Transcript*, 23 June 1932. This charge, ironically, was also hurled at Brandeis in 1916 during his confirmation hearings.

6. Parrish, *Frankfurter*, 210.

7. Frankfurter to Joseph B. Ely, 29 June 1932, printed copy in FF-HLS.

8. Phillips, *Frankfurter Reminisces*, 235.

9. Murphy alleges that Brandeis encouraged Frankfurter to renew his relationship with Roosevelt and to educate this promising new political figure along the "right lines" (Brandeis to Frankfurter, 4 and 14 November 1928, FF-LC); "Though he had not seen FDR for a decade, the Harvard professor went to work to promote a relationship between his two friends" (*The Brandeis/Frankfurter Connection*, 100). Murphy relies on the fact that two prolific correspondents did not write to each other for nearly nine years. Max Freedman reports, however, that Frankfurter did keep in touch with Roosevelt during these years. *Roosevelt and Frankfurter: Their Correspondence, 1928–1945* (Boston: Atlantic/Little, Brown, 1967), 12.

10. "Were I God, of course," Frankfurter wrote to the historian Wallace Notestein, "I should want more of a fellow to guide our destinies during the next four years than is Roosevelt." Quoted in Nelson L. Dawson, *Louis D. Brandeis, Felix Frankfurter, and the New Deal* (Hamden, Conn.: Archon Books, 1980), 8–9.

11. The full extent of Frankfurter's involvement in the New Deal exceeds the scope of this book. The interested reader is referred to Urofsky and Levy, *"Half-Son, Half-Brother"*; Murphy, *The Brandeis/Frankfurter Connection*; and Freedman, *Roosevelt and Frankfurter*.

12. Felix Frankfurter, memorandum of visit with Roosevelt, 8 March 1933, FF-HLS; Frankfurter to Roosevelt, 14 March 1933, and Roosevelt to Frankfurter, 5 April 1933, in Freedman, *Roosevelt and Frankfurter*, 120–21, 123–24; Phillips, *Frankfurter Reminisces*, 242–47.

13. Freedman, *Roosevelt and Frankfurter*, 7; Arthur M. Schlesinger, Jr., *The Coming of the New Deal* (Boston: Houghton Mifflin, 1958), 16.

14. Arthur M. Schlesinger, Jr., *The Politics of Upheaval* (Boston: Houghton Mifflin, 1960), 392; William E. Leuchtenburg, *Franklin D. Roosevelt and the New Deal, 1932–1940* (New York: Harper & Row, 1963), 162–63.

15. A good analysis of the Roosevelt administration's efforts to develop a policy toward big business is Ellis Wayne Hawley, *The New Deal and the Problem of Monopoly: A Study in Economic Ambivalence* (Princeton, N.J.: Princeton University Press, 1966).

16. Elliot Janeway, *Struggle for Survival* (New Haven, Conn.: Yale University Press, 1951), 140–41; "Felix Frankfurter," *Fortune* 13 (1936): 83, 90.

17. One should remember that Harvard Law School at this time accepted only males, nearly all of whom were white, and as a result, all of the people Frankfurter placed were white males. In 1947, however, he took William T. Coleman, Jr. as his clerk, the first black clerk employed by the Court in its history.

18. Murphy, *The Brandeis/Frankfurter Connection*, ch. 4; Dawson, *Brandeis, Frankfurter, and the New Deal*, ch. 4; Urofsky and Levy, *"Half-Son, Half-Brother,"* passim.

19. G. Edward White, "Felix Frankfurter, the Old Boy Network, and the New Deal: The Placement of Elite Lawyers in Public Service in the 1930s," *Arkansas Law Review* 39 (1986): 631. I am indebted to Professor White's discussion of Frankfurter and the idea of a network for much of this section.

20. Frankfurter had been one of the first to teach administrative law in a major law school, and he had shocked many of his colleagues by insisting that administrative law was also constitutional law. In a textbook he coauthored with J. Forrester Davison on the subject, *Cases and Other Materials on the Administrative Process* (New York: Commerce Clearing House, 1932), he devoted nearly two-thirds of the text to separation of powers, a subject traditionalists considered part of constitutional law; they demanded that administrative law be restricted to nonconstitutional procedural matters. But Frankfurter's approach was vindicated by the Supreme Court itself when it struck down the administrative procedures of the National Industrial Recovery Act because they violated separation of powers. *Schecter v. United States*, 295 U.S. 495 (1935).

21. Frankfurter to Holmes, 6 September 1913, quoted in Hirsch, *Enigma*, 41.

22. Parrish, *Frankfurter*, 108. Parrish's claim, however, that during the First World War "Frankfurter's 'boys'. . . formed a network of intelligence and intrigue that stretched from the Justice Department to the Emergency Fleet Corporation," is somewhat exaggerated.

23. White, "Placement of Elite Lawyers," 651. According to Jerold Auerbach, "The Depression generation of talented Jewish lawyers was saved from professional extinction, insofar as it was saved at all, only by the New Deal alphabet agencies." "From Rags to Robes: The Legal Profession, Social Mobility and the American Jewish Experience," *American Jewish Historical Quarterly* 66 (1976): 249, 266.

24. The issue of how much Frankfurter's Jewishness affected his behavior is one that has become the focus of some scholarly debate; to my mind, no definite conclusion can be made on the basis of either the evidence or the arguments put forward by the protagonists. See, for example, Donna E. Arzt, "The People's Lawyers: The Predominance of Jews in Public Interest Law," *Judaism* 35 (1986): 47, and the response by Jerold Auerbach, "Prophets or Profits? Liberal Lawyers and Jewish Tradition," ibid. 36 (1987): 360. See also the controversial essay by Robert Burt in Burt, *Two Jewish Justices*.

25. White, "Placement of Elite Lawyers," 659.

26. Thus, if Roosevelt or someone acting at the President's request asked for Frankfurter's advice on who could fill a certain position, his nominee would receive serious consideration. But when Frankfurter tried to get Learned Hand appointed to the Supreme Court, Roosevelt refused to go along, even though he recognized Hand's abilities. William O. Douglas, *Go East, Young Man* (New York: Random House, 1974), 332.

27. Dawson, *Brandeis, Frankfurter, and the New Deal*, 169–70.

28. Murphy, *The Brandeis/Frankfurter Connection*, 185.

29. Parrish, *Frankfurter*, 251.

30. A good précis of the Brandeisian plan can be found in a memorandum prepared for Frankfurter by Harry Shulman, a Frankfurter protégé and former Brandeis clerk, following a conversation with Brandeis, 8 December 1933, FF-HLS.

31. I am not suggesting that Frankfurter did not try to carry out Brandeis's objectives; the works of Murphy, Dawson, Parrish, and others, as well as the correspondence between the two men, show Frankfurter to have been, at least through 1936, a loyal and devoted lieutenant. Rather, it strikes me that Frankfurter never believed wholeheartedly

in the Brandeisian vision so much as he believed in Brandeis. He had been loyal to Stimson, to Brandeis, and to Roosevelt; he would, in the future, get on well even with some people whose ideas he did not share, because people always mattered most to him.

32. For a variety of perspectives, see Edward S. Corwin, *Court over Constitution* (Princeton, N.J.: Princeton University Press, 1938); Leonard Baker, *Back to Back: The Duel between FDR and the Supreme Court* (New York: Macmillan, 1967); William E. Leuchtenburg, "The Origins of Franklin D. Roosevelt's 'Court-Packing' Plan," *Supreme Court Review* 347 (1966); and Charles A. Leonard, *A Search for a Judicial Philosophy: Mr. Justice Roberts and the Constitutional Revolution of 1937* (Port Washington, N.Y.: Kennikat, 1971).

33. *New York Times,* 11 June 1936.

34. Frankfurter to Harlan Fiske Stone, 29 February 1932, quoted in Parrish, *Frankfurter,* 258. Stone had dissented along with Brandeis and Cardozo in *Crowell* v. *Benson,* 285 U.S. 22 (1932).

35. Murphy, *Constitution in Crisis Times,* 136; *Panama Refining Co.* v. *Ryan,* 293, U.S. 388 (1935).

36. Brandeis to Frankfurter, 13 June 1933, FF-LC.

37. *Schechter* v. *United States,* 295 U.S. 495 (1935) (see note 20 above); Chief Justice Hughes's opinion for a unanimous Court also imposed a narrow view of the commerce clause.

38. *Louisville Joint Stock Bank* v. *Radford,* 295 U.S. 555 (1935).

39. *Humphrey's Executor* v. *United States,* 295 U.S. 602 (1935).

40. Quoted in Murphy, *The Brandeis/Frankfurter Connection,* 156.

41. Roosevelt to Frankfurter, 15 January 1937, in Freedman, *Roosevelt and Frankfurter,* 377.

42. Frankfurter to Roosevelt, 7 February 1937, in ibid., 380–81.

43. Frankfurter "United States Supreme Court," 474, 478–79.

44. Frankfurter to Roosevelt, 18 February 1937, in Freedman, *Roosevelt and Frankfurter,* 383–87; Roosevelt incorporated some of these ideas into his fireside chat to the nation on 9 March 1937.

45. Frankfurter to Roosevelt, 30 March 1937, in ibid., 392.

46. Parrish, *Frankfurter,* 269–70.

47. Mason, *Stone,* 450–53.

48. Frankfurter to Brandeis, 26 March 1937, FF-LC.

49. Brandeis to Frankfurter, 5 April 1937, and Frankfurter to Brandeis, 1 April and 15 July 1937, FF-LC. Frankfurter also let his feelings be known to others whom he could count on to relay the information to Brandeis (Murphy, *The Brandeis/Frankfurter Connection,* 183–84).

50. *West Coast Hotel* v. *Parrish,* 300 U.S. 379 (1937); by a similar 5–4 vote, it had invalidated a New York law in *Morehead* v. *New York ex rel. Tipaldo,* 298 U.S. 587 (1936). The overturn came with the change of Justice Roberts's vote, leading wits to comment that "a switch in time saves nine." In fact, as later evidence has shown, Roberts had decided to vote for the measure well before Roosevelt announced his plan. See John W. Chambers, "The Big Switch: Justice Roberts and the Minimum Wage Cases," *Labor History* 10 (1969): 44.

51. *National Labor Relations Board* v. *Jones & Laughlin Steel Co.,* 301 U.S. 1 (1937).

52. *Stewart Machine Co.* v. *Davis,* 301 U.S. 548 (1937), and *Helvering* v. *Davis,* 301 U.S. 619 (1937).

53. Frankfurter to Roosevelt, "Notes for an Address on the State of the Union," 10 August 1937, and draft of Roosevelt's Constitution Day speech, for delivery on 17 September 1937, in Freedman, *Roosevelt and Frankfurter,* 404–6, 409–17.

54. Frankfurter to Charles Wyzanski, 13 April 1937, quoted in Parrish, *Frankfurter,* 272.

CHAPTER 4

1. Quoted in Dennis J. Hutchinson, "Felix Frankfurter and the Business of the Supreme Court, O.T. 1946–O.T. 1961," *Supreme Court Review* (1980): 143.

2. Alexander Bickel, "Applied Policies and the Science of Law: Writings of the Harvard Period," in Wallace Mendelson, ed., *Felix Frankfurter: A Tribute* (New York: Reynal, 1964), 197.

3. Quoted in Mason, *Stone,* 469.

4. Ibid., 469–70.

5. Frankfurter to Brandeis, 28 May 1938, FF-LC.

6. The relationship between Frankfurter and Douglas is more fully explored in Melvin I. Urofsky, "Conflict among the Brethren: Felix Frankfurter, William O. Douglas, and the Clash of Personalities and Philosophies on the United States Supreme Court," *Duke Law Journal* (1988): 71.

7. Quoted in Hirsch, *Enigma,* 145.

8. Frankfurter to William O. Douglas, 3 January 1941, in the Hugo LaFayette Black Papers, Manuscript Division, Library of Congress.

9. Frankfurter to Stanley Reed, 2 December 1941, FF-LC.

10. Frankfurter to Robert H. Jackson, 29 January 1953, quoted in Bernard Schwartz, *Super Chief: Earl Warren and His Supreme Court* (New York: New York University Press, 1983), 39.

11. Frankfurter to Reed, 2 December 1941, FF-LC.

12. Quoted in Schwartz, *Super Chief,* 39.

13. William O. Douglas, *The Court Years, 1939–1975* (New York: Random House, 1980), 180. Douglas also claimed that some of the justices often squirmed at Frankfurter's intense grillings of counsel. One day Frankfurter kept shouting repeatedly at a lawyer, "Give me a case that stands for that proposition!" Finally, Douglas claimed, he could take no more, and he leaned over and said, "Don't bother to send Justice Frankfurter the list he wants. I'll be happy to do it myself." Ibid., 181.

14. Hutchinson, "Frankfurter and Business of the Supreme Court," 205.

15. Sidney Fine, *Frank Murphy: The Washington Years* (Ann Arbor: University of Michigan Press, 1984), 159. After Frankfurter came on the Court, Chief Justice Hughes continued to call him "Professor Frankfurter."

16. Quoted in Bernard Schwartz with Stephan Leshar, *Inside the Warren Court* (Garden City, N.Y.: Doubleday, 1983), 24.

17. Quoted in Fine, *Murphy,* 258–59.

18. Frankfurter to Hand, 5 November 1954, quoted in ibid., 251.

19. James F. Simon, *Independent Journey: The Life of William O. Douglas* (New York: Harper & Row, 1980), 9.

20. Louis L. Jaffe, "The Judicial Universe of Mr. Justice Frankfurter," *Harvard Law Review* 62 (1949): 357, 358.

21. Thomas Reed Powell, "Judicial Protection of Civil Rights," *Iowa Law Review* 29 (1944): 383, 395.

22. "It's easy to write opinions," Frankfurter told a friend, "if one only writes what one thinks is right. But here, I suppose, naiveté is not a virtue but a handicap, or, at best, a habit." Frankfurter to Powell, 29 January 1941, Powell Papers.

23. Fred Rodell, "Felix Frankfurter, Conservative," *Harper's* 183 (October 1941): 449, 453.

24. Kalman, *Legal Realism at Yale* 51.

25. Frankfurter to Jackson, 23 February 1944, FF-LC. Frankfurter captioned this letter, which dealt with a question of statutory interpretation, "Some Reflections of an Unashamed Professor."

26. From Ngaio Marsh, *Death at the Bar*, quoted in Frankfurter to Powell, 6 May 1940, Powell Papers.

27. For the striking temperamental differences between Holmes and Frankfurter, see Lash, *Diaries*, 77. Frankfurter himself admitted that he lacked Brandeis's "austerity." Frankfurter to Powell, 13 February 1942, Powell Papers.

28. Schwartz, *Super Chief*, 40.

29. Douglas, *Court Years*, 33–34.

30. *Minersville School District v. Gobitis*, 310 U.S. 586 (1940).

31. Fine, *Murphy*, 185.

32. Mason, *Stone*, 514.

33. Fine, *Murphy*, 185.

34. Douglas, *Court Years*, 45.

35. Quoted in Hirsch, *Enigma*, 150.

36. 310 U.S. at 597–98, 600.

37. Ibid.; see also Levinson, "Skepticism, Democracy, and Judicial Restraint," 225–26.

38. There is little question but that Frankfurter's own experience as an immigrant boy Americanized in the New York public school system, and his intense patriotic fervor, played a significant role in how he saw the facts of the two cases. See the interesting discussion in Richard Danzig, "Justice Frankfurter's Opinions in the Flag Salute Cases: Blending Logic and Psychologic in Constitutional Decisionmaking," *Stanford Law Review* 36 (1984): 675.

39. 310 U.S. at 601.

40. Mason, *Stone*, 532.

41. Ickes, *Secret Diaries*, 3:199.

42. Frankfurter to Alice Hamilton, 13 June 1940, FF-HLS.

43. Fine, *Murphy*, 185. Murphy had even prepared a dissent but reluctantly decided to go with the majority.

44. Ibid., 187.

45. *Gilbert v. Minnesota*, 245 U.S. 325, 334, 343 (1920), Brandeis, J., dissenting.

46. *Gitlow v. New York*, 268 U.S. 562 (1925), speech; *Near v. Minnesota*, 283 U.S. 697 (1931), press; and *Powell v. Alabama*, 287 U.S. 45 (1932), right to counsel.

47. 302 U.S. 319 (1937); see discussion in chapter 6.

48. Ibid., at 325.

49. Ibid., citing *Snyder v. Massachusetts*, 291 U.S. 97, 105 (1934).

50. *Bridges v. California*, and *Times-Mirror Co. v. Superior Court of California*, decided together at 314 U.S. 252 (1941).

51. Fine, *Murphy*, 269.

52. 314 U.S. at 263.

53. Ibid., at 270.

54. Ibid., at 279.

55. Frankfurter to S. E. Morison, 6 January 1942 [misdated 1941], FF-HLS.

56. 316 U.S. 584 (1942).

57. Ibid., at 623–24.

58. Frankfurter to Stone, 21 Oct. 1942, Harlan Fiske Stone Papers, Manuscript Division, Library of Congress. A few months later Frankfurter noted in his diary: "We were . . . in Conference for almost eight hours, a perfectly indefensible way of deliberating on the kind of stiff issues with which we are concerned"; Lash, *Diaries*, 217, entry for 15 March 1943. Frankfurter later claimed that Stone's personal defects greatly exacerbated the problems. "He was fundamentally a petty character, self-aggrandizing and ungenerous. . . . Hardly anybody was any good, hardly any lawyer was any good, hardly any argument was adequate, hardly anybody ever saw the real point of a case, etc., etc." Frankfurter to Powell, 21 December 1953, Powell Papers.

59. Douglas to Fred Rodell, 25 October 1843, quoted in Fine, *Murphy*, 243.

60. C. Herman Pritchett, *The Roosevelt Court: A Study in Judicial Values and Politics* (New York: Macmillan, 1948), 39–41.

61. Mason, *Stone*, 605.

62. *Wall Street Journal*, 25 November 1941.

63. Murphy, *The Brandeis/Frankfurter Connection*, 266–67.

64. There is no question that Hugo Black was the intellectual leader of "the Axis," but he had found a friend and potent ally in Douglas. During their first three terms together the two did not vote apart on a single case, and throughout the more than three decades they sat together on the Court, they became linked in the public mind. A Black biographer believes they shared a "sense of alienation toward both the social order and the conventional wisdom into which they had been born"; Dunne, *Black*, 193. Although Frankfurter detested both men's judicial philosophy and derided their abilities, he never felt toward Black the hatred he had for Douglas, with whom he barely talked after 1948. Black, on the spur of the moment in 1957, slipped Frankfurter a note on the bench, stating that he hoped "nothing will happen that causes you to leave the Court." After Frankfurter's retirement in 1962 because of illness, Black often dropped in to visit him and discuss law. Lash, *Diaries*, 78.

65. The case of *Johnson v. United States*, 318 U.S. 189 (1943), is a good example; see Lash, *Diaries*, 177–80, entry for 2 Feb. 1943.

66. *West Virginia Board of Education v. Barnette*, 319 U.S. 624 (1943).

67. Ibid., at 642.

68. Douglas, *Court Years*, 45.

69. 319 U.S. at 646.

70. Ibid., at 653.

71. Frankfurter to Jackson, 4 June 1943, FF-HLS. Frankfurter evidently had a diffi-

cult time in writing the opinion. As he told Jackson, "perhaps [it is] because it is credo and not research that the expression of it is so recalcitrant."

72. 319 U.S. at 649.

73. Ibid., at 653.

74. Levinson, "Skepticism, Democracy, and Judicial Restraint," 232.

75. Frankfurter to C.E. Hughes, 15 June 1943, FF-HLS; Frankfurter to Roosevelt, 3 May 1943, in Freedman, *Roosevelt and Frankfurter*, 699. Frankfurter must have sent the president an early draft of his dissent, since the final decision did not come down for another month.

76. Quoted in Hirsch, *Enigma*, 175. See Hirsch's interesting footnote to this passage, however, indicating that Brandeis may not have been as supportive of the *Gobitis* opinion as Frankfurter claimed. Ibid., 243, n. 190.

77. Lash, *Diaries*, 175, entry for 30 January 1943.

78. Robert Burt believes that the flag salute cases epitomized Frankfurter's role as the outsider become insider, and that all he would offer to the Jehovah's Witnesses was an invitation that they give up their absurd practices and become full-fledged Americans, as he had. *Two Jewish Justices*, 44–45.

79. *Lochner* v. *New York*, 198 U.S. 45 (1905); *New State Ice Co.* v. *Liebmann*, 285 U.S. 262 (1932); See Paul L. Murphy, *World War I and the Origins of Civil Liberties in the United States* (New York: Norton, 1979). One might also compare Frankfurter's earlier comments on Holmes and free speech, which can almost be read as implying that Holmes supported a "preferred position" for First Amendment rights, and Frankfurter's own more cramped views as expressed in the flag salute cases. Frankfurter, *Mr. Justice Holmes and the Supreme Court* 84–85.

80. In *Gitlow* v. *New York*, 268 U.S. 562 (1925).

81. In *Palko* v. *Connecticut*, 302 U.S. 319 (1937).

82. *United States* v. *Carolene Products Co.*, 304 U.S. 144, 152, n. 4 (1938).

83. 198 U.S. at 75.

84. Louis D. Brandeis, "The Living Law," 10 *Illinois Law Review* 461, 464 (1916).

85. Chief Justice Stone, in a conversation with writer Irving Brant, said (although not in connection with *Gobitis*), "I believe the Court should correct its own errors, even when I help to make them." Mason, *Stone*, 589.

86. On controversial issues such as school desegregation, in *Brown* v. *Board of Education*, 347 U.S. 483 (1954); school prayer, in *Engel* v. *Vitale*, 370 U.S. 421 (1962); rights of the accused, in *Miranda* v. *Arizona*, 384 U.S. 436 (1966); and abortion, in *Roe* v. *Wade*, 410 U.S. 113 (1973).

87. *Williamson* v. *Lee Optical Co.*, 348 U.S. 483 (1955).

88. See the interesting comment on this issue by Paul Freund, Frankfurter's friend and student, in his portrait of Frankfurter, *Dictionary of American Biography*, suppl. 7 (New York: Scribner's, 1981), 260, 264. Frankfurter, however, was not as completely rigid across his entire judicial career as he appeared in these early years. In 1949, for example, he flatly denied the idea that First Amendment speech protections have a special or preferred value, in *Kovacs* v. *Cooper*, 336 U.S. 77 (1949). Two years later, however, in *Dennis* v. *United States*, 341 U.S. 494 (1951), he recanted this view and acknowledged the importance of courts providing extra protection to speech.

89. In *The Commerce Clause under Marshall, Taney and Waite* (Chapel Hill: Univer-

sity of North Carolina Press, 1937), Frankfurter wrote quite persuasively about the need for the Constitution to adapt to changing conditions.

90. Pritchett, *Roosevelt Court,* 42.

91. Fine, *Murphy,* 244.

92. 320 U.S. 661 (1944): A similar alignment can be seen in *Federal Power Commission* v. *Hope Natural Gas Co.,* 320 U.S. 591 (1944), handed down the same day. *Mercoid* involved questions of how much power a patent-holder had over users in terms of nonpatented items.

93. Quoted in Mason, *Stone,* 589.

94. Hand to Frankfurter, 6 February 1944, FF-LC.

95. Quoted in Fine, *Murphy,* 245.

96. Hirsch, *Enigma,* 177.

97. See, for example, the semihumorous memo addressed to "Mr. Justice of New Jersey," who, Frankfurter said, may one day become "Mr. Justice of the United States," as soon as he recognizes it is the U.S. Constitution and not New Jersey law that governs at the federal level. Frankfurter to William J. Brennan, 25 October 1957, FF-HLS.

98. G. Edward White, *Earl Warren: A Public Life* (New York: Oxford, 1982), 179; Warren quoted in Schwartz, *Super Chief,* 25–27.

99. See Bernard Schwartz, "Felix Frankfurter and Earl Warren: A Study of a Deteriorating Relationship," *Supreme Court Review* (1980): 115.

100. Hutchinson, "Frankfurter and Business of the Supreme Court."

101. Quoted in ibid., 182–83.

102. William O. Douglas to Conference, 13 October 1960, William O. Douglas Papers, Manuscript Division, Library of Congress (hereafter cited as Douglas Papers).

103. Douglas to Conference, 23 October 1961, Douglas Papers.

104. Douglas, memorandum to Conference, 15 June 1949, quoted in Fine, *Murphy,* 254.

105. Quoted in Murphy, *The Brandeis/Frankfurter Connection,* 191.

106. Quoted in Fine, *Murphy,* 255.

107. Douglas, *Court Years,* 243; see also Walton Hamilton, book review, *Yale Law Journal* 56 (1947): 1458, 1459–60.

CHAPTER 5

1. Freedman, *Roosevelt and Frankfurter,* 744.

2. Frankfurter to Roosevelt, 25 November 1938, in ibid., 466. For the failure of Britain to live up to the Balfour promise, see Urofsky, *American Zionism,* ch. 10.

3. Lash, *Diaries,* 73.

4. Murphy, *The Brandeis/Frankfurter Connection,* 187–88.

5. Frankfurter to Roosevelt, 8 and 14 March 1939, and Roosevelt to Frankfurter, 14 March 1939, in Freedman, *Roosevelt and Frankfurter,* 488–89. Frankfurter did go on the inactive reserve list in 1943.

6. See especially Murphy, *Brandeis/Frankfurter Connection,* chs. 6–8.

7. Grace Tully, *F.D.R. My Boss* (New York: Scribner's, 1949), 290.

8. Frankfurter to Roosevelt, 11 May 1939, in Freedman, *Roosevelt and Frankfurter,* 492–94.

9. The other conditions were, first, that as a Republican he be released from the traditional political loyalty demanded of Cabinet members; second, that the War Department adopt a draft system immediately; and third, that he have absolute freedom to advocate that the United States aid the Allies then fighting the Axis. Roosevelt had no trouble with the first and third, but the second appeared politically risky in an election year.

10. Freedman, *Roosevelt and Frankfurter*, 521–30; Murphy, *The Brandeis/Frankfurter Connection*, 197–200.

11. Murphy, *The Brandeis/Frankfurter Connection*, 201–3.

12. James F. Simon, *The Antagonists* (New York: Simon & Schuster, 1989), 133; Freedman, *Roosevelt and Frankfurter*, 582–86; Murphy, *The Brandeis/Frankfurter Connection*, 216–20.

13. Frankfurter to John M. Maguire, 5 June 1943, FF-HLS.

14. Lash, *Diaries*, 155, entry for 11 January 1943.

15. Simon, *Antagonists*, 133.

16. Paul L. Murphy, *The Constitution in Crisis Times, 1918–1969* (New York: Harper & Row, 1972), 176–78; Frank Murphy's tenure as attorney general is detailed in Fine, *Murphy*, chs. i–vii.

17. *Schneiderman v. United States*, 320 U.S. 119 (1943).

18. Summary of discussion at Conference, 5 December 1942, FF-HLS.

19. *United States v. Schwimmer*, 279 U.S. 644, 653, 654–55 (1929), Holmes dissenting.

20. Summary of discussion at Conference, 5 December 1942, FF-HLS.

21. Frankfurter to Murphy, 31 May and 2 June 1943, FF-HLS.

22. 320 U.S. at 181.

23. Felix Frankfurter, "Notes on the Schneiderman case," 1 June 1943, FF-HLS.

24. Frankfurter to Stone, 31 May 1943, FF-HLS.

25. *Baumgartner v. United States*, 322 U.S. 665 (1944); the Murphy concurrence is at 678. Not until 1946 did the Court uphold a denaturalization order. In that case, *Knauer v. United States*, 328 U.S. 654 (1946), the government presented conclusive evidence that at the time Knauer sought American citizenship, he had been seeking to promote Nazism in the United States.

26. *Bridges v. Wixon*, 326 U.S. 135 (1945). The effort to deport Bridges is told in Stanley I. Kutler, *The American Inquisition: Justice and Injustice in the Cold War* (New York: Hill & Wang, 1982), ch. 5.

27. 326 U.S. at 135.

28. 250 U.S. 616, 624 (1919).

29. *Hartzel v. United States*, 322 U.S. 680 (1944).

30. Ibid., at 689.

31. In another denaturalization case a year later, Frankfurter joined with a slim majority to set aside the conviction on the grounds of insufficient evidence. *Keegan v. United States*, 325 U.S. 478 (1945).

32. For the story of the internment, and the resulting legal battles, see Peter Irons, *Justice at War* (New York: Oxford, 1983), and U.S. Commission on Wartime Relocation, *Personal Justice Denied* (Washington, D.C.: Government Printing Office, 1983).

33. Quoted in Irons, *Justice at War*, 60–61.

34. Ibid., 38.

35. *Hirabayashi v. United States*, 320 U.S. 81 (1943).

36. Irons, *Justice at War*, 235.

37. 320 U.S. at 93.

38. Ibid., at 102.

39. Douglas to Stone, 31 May 1943, Douglas Papers; see also the discussion of Douglas's conflicting views in Irons, *Justice at War*, 237–39.

40. Frankfurter to Stone, 4 June 1943 (two letters), Stone Papers.

41. Murphy, draft opinion, quoted in Irons, *Justice at War*, 244.

42. Frankfurter to Murphy, 10 June 1943, FF-HLS.

43. Quoted in Irons, *Justice at War*, 250.

44. *Korematsu v. United States*, 323 U.S. 214 (1944).

45. Minutes of Conference, 16 October 1944, in Irons, *Justice at War*, 322.

46. Frankfurter to Black, 9 November 1944, FF-HLS.

47. 323 U.S. at 230.

48. Ibid., at 224–25; Irons, *Justice at War*, 340–41.

49. Alexander Meiklejohn to Frankfurter, 3 January 1945, and Frankfurter to Meiklejohn, 8 January 1945, FF-HLS.

50. Douglas wrote in his memoirs that he always regretted not dissenting in the relocation cases, which were "ever on my conscience" (*Court Years*, 279–80).

51. Simon, *Antagonists*, 155. Commentators condemned the decisions right from the beginning. One of the earliest and still one of the best critiques is that of Eugene V. Rostow, "The Japanese-American Cases—A Disaster," *Yale Law Journal* 54 (1945): 489.

52. Dunne, *Black*, 213.

53. There was one other case, *Ex parte Endo*, 323 U.S. 283 (1944), in which a Japanese-American woman of proven loyalty continued to be detained at the camp in Topaz, Utah. The Court voted unanimously to free her, and Douglas quickly prepared the opinion. But Stone held up the announcement until after the election so as not to embarrass the administration.

54. *Trop v. Dulles*, 356 U.S. 86 (1958).

55. *Perez v. Brownell*, 356 U.S. 44 (1958).

56. Ibid., at 64–65. Nearly a decade later the Court reversed the Frankfurter holding in *Perez*. In *Afroyim v. Rusk*, 387 U.S. 253 (1967), Justice Black overturned a State Department effort to take away the citizenship of a naturalized citizen who had voted in an Israeli election. The citizen provisions of the Fourteenth Amendment, Black held, protect citizens against forcible destruction of their citizenship. Unless a person voluntarily relinquishes his or her citizenship, it cannot be removed.

57. 356 U.S. at 101. The three dissenters in *Perez* were joined by Justice Whitaker, who while concurring in the result had questioned the scope of the expatriation power, and by Justice Brennan, who believed expatriation for desertion too harsh a punishment. See the illuminating discussion of these cases in White, *American Judicial Tradition*, 346–51.

58. Simon, *Antagonists*, 238. Brennan told Simon that the vote in *Trop* marked the "parting of the ways" for the two men, and "when Felix didn't get his way, he was like a child."

59. 356 U.S. at 127–28.

60. To view denaturalization as cruel and unusual, Frankfurter wrote, was "to stretch that concept beyond the breaking point." In fact, Frankfurter denied that denaturalization in this context even constituted a punishment. Ibid., at 124–25.

61. Burt, *Two Jewish Justices*, 96–97.

62. *Schaefer* v. *United States*, 251 U.S. 466, 495 (1920), Brandeis dissenting.

CHAPTER 6

1. Frankfurter was not totally without influence, if for no other reason than his membership on the Supreme Court, but his status as a close friend of the President, his easy access to the White House and to Cabinet members, quickly evaporated. For an account of his political activity during these years, see Murphy *The Brandeis/Frankfurter Connection*, ch. 9.

2. Frankfurter to Paul Freund, 18 December 1947, FF-HLS.

3. Copies of the memoranda, marked "To be passed on and kept up to date," are in FF-HLS.

4. There are at least 40 such research memoranda in FF-HLS, with titles such as "United States Supreme Court Cases, 1792–1900, Federal Judicial Power: Suits to Which a State Is a Party."

5. Baker, *Brandeis and Frankfurter*, 415.

6. Ibid., 415–16.

7. Interview with Lewis Hankin, New York, 1 July 1988.

8. *Williamson* v. *Lee Optical Company*, 348 U.S. 483, 488 (1955).

9. Frankfurter to Murphy, 10 June 1946, FF-LC.

10. Leuchtenburg, *FDR and the New Deal*, 261–62.

11. *Jewell Ridge Coal Corp.* v. *Local 6167 United Mine Workers*, 325 U.S. 161 (1945).

12. The personal and professional relations between Black and Harris are explained in Dunne, *Black*, 234.

13. Murphy had written an expansive interpretation of the same act a year earlier in another case in which the union had also been represented by Harris, *Tennessee Coal, Iron & Railroad Co.* v. *Muscada Local 123*, 321 U.S. 590 (1944).

14. 325 U.S. at 170; FF voted with Jackson.

15. *Jewell Ridge Coal Corp.* v. *Local 6167, United Mine Workers*, 325 U.S. 897 (1945). The story of the internal friction on the Court arising from this case can be found in Mason, *Stone*, 642–45; Dunne, *Black*, 233–40; and Lash, *Diaries*, 265.

16. Frankfurter to Black, 9 June 1945, FF-LC.

17. See, for example, the editorial in the *New York Times*, 12 June 1945: "It seems to us that Justice Jackson has committed an error in taste and that Justice Black has committed the worse offense of lowering judicial standards."

18. Despite Frankfurter's frustration with Roberts during the 1930s, he had evidently regarded his colleague highly for many years; in 1930 he had written warmly, congratulating Roberts on his appointment to the Court. At that time he had said that although there was a great deal of loose talk about "conservatives" and "liberals," what really "divides men much more decisively is the extent to which they are free—free from a dogmatic outlook on life, free from fears. You have, I believe, no skeletons in the closet of

your mind, and are a servant neither of blind traditionalism nor of blind indifference to historic wisdom." Frankfurter to Roberts, 10 May 1930, FF-LC.

19. See his bitter dissent in *Mahnich v. Southern Steamship Co.*, 321 U.S. 96, 113 (1944), encouraged by and joined in by Frankfurter.

20. The original draft of the letter, with Black's deletions, dated 20 August 1945, and with Douglas's comments that the changes were "wholly agreeable" to him, is in the Stone Papers.

21. Frankfurter to Conference, 30 August 1945, *Stone Papers*. It is possible that Brandeis may have said something of this nature to Frankfurter, but I have seen nothing in either the Frankfurter or Brandeis papers to support his assertion.

22. Mason, *Stone*, 768.

23. Robert H. Jackson, oral history interview at Columbia University, quoted in Dennis J. Hutchinson, "The Black-Jackson Feud," *Supreme Court Review* (1988): 203, 209. I am indebted to Professor Hutchinson for the opportunity to use his work in an earlier manuscript form and have relied on it for much of this section.

24. Quoted in Simon, *Antagonists*, 158.

25. The debate is beyond the scope of this book, but the reader is referred to William J. Bosch, *Judgment on Nuremberg: American Attitudes toward the Major War-Crimes Trials* (Chapel Hill: University of North Carolina Press, 1970); Ann and John Tusa, *The Nuremberg Trial* (New York: Atheneum, 1983); and the highly polemical and critical Richard H. Minear, *Victor's Justice: The Tokyo War Crimes Trial* (Princeton, N.J.: Princeton University Press, 1971).

26. The justices did agree to hear an appeal from the court set up to try Japanese accused of war crimes, which had been established by Gen. Douglas MacArthur in his capacity as military commander under the aegis of the Allied powers. In the end, however, the Court denied the appeal and in a brief per curiam held that, as an international tribunal, that court's decisions could not be reviewed by American courts; *Hirota v. MacArthur*, 338 U.S. 197 (1948). The issues of this case are discussed in Fine, *Murphy*, 522–26, and in C. Herman Pritchett, *Civil Liberties and the Vinson Court* (Chicago: University of Chicago Press, 1954), 171–73. Frankfurter in all instances voted to deny jurisdiction.

27. Mason, *Stone*, 714–19.

28. Frankfurter to Jackson, 6 February 1946, FF-HLS.

29. Frankfurter to Jackson, 11 May 1946, FF-HLS. According to Bruce Murphy, Frankfurter was quite sincere in his reassurances to Jackson and defended Jackson's role at Nuremberg to other acquaintances (*The Brandeis/Frankfurter Connection*, 306).

30. Mason, *Stone*, 566–67.

31. *New York Times*, 11 June 1946.

32. Robert S. Allen and William V. Shannon, *The Truman Merry-Go-Round* (New York: Vanguard, 1950), 366–67.

33. Frankfurter to Black, 30 September 1950, FF-LC. Black at the time told his son that he was sure Felix had in fact done it. Simon, *Antagonists*, 169; Hugo Black, "Mr. Justice Frankfurter," *Harvard Law Review* 78 (1965): 1522.

34. *The Brandeis/Frankfurter Connection*, 306–7.

35. Hutchinson, "Black-Jackson Feud," 216–17. Hutchinson also presents evidence supporting his claim that William O. Douglas, in his effort to sink the Jackson candidacy,

leaked information about the *Jewell Ridge* confrontation to Doris Fleeson and also to Drew Pearson.

36. See, for example, Frankfurter to Freund, 29 October 1946, FF-HLS, objecting to a letter critical of Jackson that was published in the *Washington Post* by Louis L. Jaffe, a former Frankfurter student and Brandeis clerk.

37. *Colgrove v. Green*, 328 U.S. 549 (1946).

38. *Nixon v. Herndon*, 273 U.S. 536 (1927); *Nixon v. Condon*, 286 U.S. 73 (1932); *Smith v. Allwright*, 321 U.S. 649 (1944).

39. *United States v. Classic*, 313 U.S. 299 (1941).

40. *Wood v. Broom*, 287 U.S. 1, 8 (1932).

41. *Luther v. Borden*, 7 How. 1 (1849); see also Charles Gordon Post, Jr., *The Supreme Court and Political Questions* (Baltimore: Johns Hopkins University Press, 1969).

42. In *Nixon v. Herndon*, 273 U.S. at 540.

43. 328 U.S. at 552. For details on this case, see Richard C. Cortner, *The Apportionment Cases* (New York: Norton, 1970), ch. 1.

44. 328 U.S. at 565–66.

45. Tinsley E. Yarbrough, *Mr. Justice Black and His Critics* (Durham, N.C.: Duke University Press, 1988), 229–30.

46. 328 U.S. at 569.

47. *Adamson v. California*, 332 U.S. 46 (1947).

48. *Gitlow v. New York*, 268 U.S. 562 (1925).

49. *Near v. Minnesota*, 283 U.S. 697 (1931).

50. *Palko v. Connecticut*, 302 U.S. 319 (1937).

51. Ibid., at 325, 327, 328.

52. *Johnson v. Zerbst*, 304 U.S. 458 (1938).

53. Dunne, *Black*, 257–61; Simon, *Antagonists*, 172–76.

54. 7 Pet. 243 (1833).

55. Frankfurter to Black, 31 October 1939, FF-HLS.

56. 316 U.S. 455 (1942).

57. Quoted in Yarbrough, *Black and His Critics*, 87. The reference here is to Holmes's alleged comment that his test for whether a state had violated procedural fairness is whether the action made him want to puke.

58. Frankfurter to Black, 13 November 1943, FF-HLS.

59. Black to Conference, 23 March 1945, FF-HLS.

60. 211 U.S. 78 (1908).

61. 332 U.S. at 54.

62. Black's essay in history started a minicontroversy of its own. Charles Fairman attacked Black's interpretation in "Does the Fourteenth Amendment Incorporate the Bill of Rights? The Original Understanding," *Stanford Law Review* 2 (1949): 5, to which Black responded more than 20 years later in his concurrence in *Duncan v. Louisiana*, 391 U.S. 145, 162 (1968). Other historians have found the evidence far from conclusive on either side; for two recent expositions, see Michael Kent Curtis, *No State Shall Abridge: The Fourteenth Amendment and the Bill of Rights* (Durham, N.C.: Duke University Press, 1986) and William E. Nelson, *The Fourteenth Amendment: From Political Principle to Judicial Doctrine* (Cambridge, Mass.: Harvard University Press, 1988).

63. 332 U.S. at 68, 70.

64. L. A. Powe, Jr., "Justice Douglas after Fifty Years: The First Amendment, McCarthyism and Rights," *Constitutional Commentary* 6 (1989): 267, 278.

65. 332 U.S. at 59, 65.

66. Ibid., at 67–68.

67. *Rochin v. California,* 342 U.S. 165, 172 (1952).

68. *Uveges v. Pennsylvania,* 335 U.S. 437, 449–50 (1948).

69. See Black's dissent in *Griswold v. Connecticut,* 381 U.S. 479, 507 (1965).

70. See, for example, Wallace Mendelson, *Justices Black and Frankfurter: Conflict in the Court* (Chicago: University of Chicago Press, 1961).

71. 316 U.S. 455 (1942).

72. Mendelson, *Justices Black and Frankfurter,* 69, relying on William Beany, *The Right to Counsel in American Courts* (Ann Arbor: University of Michigan Press, 1955), 27–44.

73. 316 U.S. at 476.

74. For an analysis of these decisions, see Yale Kamisar, "Betts v. Brady Twenty Years Later," *Michigan Law Review* 61 (1962): 219.

75. *Gideon v. Wainwright,* 372 U.S. 335 (1963); the story of this case is magnificently told in Anthony Lewis, *Gideon's Trumpet* (New York: Random House, 1964).

76. *Malloy v. Hogan,* 378 U.S. 1, 6 (1964).

77. *Griffin v. California,* 380 U.S. 609 (1965).

78. 338 U.S. 25 (1949).

79. *Weeks v. United States,* 232 U.S. 383 (1914).

80. 338 U.S. at 27–28.

81. Mendelson, *Justices Black and Frankfurter,* 71–72.

82. 338 U.S. at 41. In his dissent Murphy analyzed the merits of two proposed alternatives to the exclusionary rule—criminal prosecution of police, and civil actions in trespass—and found both remedies to be "illusory" in terms of deterring illegal searches. Justice Douglas dissented separately, on the sole ground that no other effective remedy existed. Justice Black concurred with the majority opinion, since his strict reading of the Fourth Amendment found no plain command for an exclusionary rule. Over the next dozen years, however, Black gradually came to believe not only that the exclusionary rule was efficacious but that it could be supported by a liberal reading of the Fourth Amendment. See his concurrence in *Mapp v. Ohio,* 367 U.S. 643, 662 (1961).

83. Roger Traynor, "Mapp v. Ohio at Large in the 50 States," *Duke Law Journal* (1962): 391, 324. In the article, Traynor, the highly respected member of the California Supreme Court, explained the shift in his own thinking; he came around to accepting the exclusionary rule on grounds very similar to the Murphy dissent—it is the only thing that works.

84. 342 U.S. 165 (1952).

85. *Irvine v. California,* 347 U.S. 128 (1954).

CHAPTER 7

1. Douglas, *Court Years,* 57.

2. *Schaefer v. United States,* 251 U.S. 466, 482–83 (1920), Brandeis dissenting.

3. *Dennis v. United States,* 341 U.S. 494, 525 (1951), Frankfurter concurring.

4. Powe, "Douglas after Fifty Years," 267, 277–79.

5. The genesis and provisions of the Smith Act are detailed in Michael R. Belknap, *Cold War Political Justice: The Smith Act, the Communist Party, and American Civil Liberties* (Westport, Conn.: Greenwood, 1977), ch. 1.

6. See, for example, Francis Biddle, *In Brief Authority* (Garden City, N.Y.: Doubleday, 1962), 233–51.

7. The Justice Department did invoke the Smith Act against a group of Trotskyites and convicted them for activities designed to effect insubordination in the armed forces. *Dunn v. United States*, 138 F.2d 137 (8th Cir. 1941), certiorari denied, 329 U.S. 790 (1941).

8. *Hines v. Davidowitz*, 312 U.S. 52 (1941). The decision allayed the fears of Justice Department officials that state action might not only impede the federal program but lead to the heavy-handed purges that had marked World War I state efforts.

9. See Chapter 4. The Court did have the chance to deal with the Smith Act directly in the October 1943 term in a case entitled *Dunne v. United States*, 320 U.S. 790 (1943), but only three members of the Court, Murphy, Rutledge, and Black, voted to grant certiorari. Douglas later explained his decision to vote against certiorari on the grounds that the remaining five members of the Court would have voted to affirm the Smith Act's constitutionality. "It seemed to me at that particular point in history unwise to put the Court's seal of approval on that doctrine" (Douglas, *Court Years*, 94).

10. Murphy, *Constitution in Crisis Times*, 256–57.

11. *Joint Anti-Fascist Refugee Committee v. McGrath*, 341 U.S. 123 (1949).

12. Ibid., at 149, 171–72.

13. Ibid., at 142, 143.

14. Murphy, *Constitution in Crisis Times*, 256–57.

15. Belknap, *Cold War Political Justice*, 51.

16. Douglas made his comment in his concurrence in *Brandenburg v. Ohio*, 395 U.S. 444, 452 (1969). The Holmes dissent is at 268 U.S. 652, 672 (1925).

17. 395 U.S. at 454, Douglas concurring.

18. Hugo L. Black, *A Constitutional Faith* (New York: Knopf, 1968), 50, 52.

19. Frankfurter to Reed, 7 February 1956, FF-LC.

20. Douglas, *Court Years*, 47.

21. 334 U.S. 558 (1948).

22. 336 U.S. 77 (1949).

23. Frankfurter to Fred Vinson, 29 November 1948, FF-HLS.

24. 336 U.S. at 89, 90, 95–96.

25. *Terminiello v. Chicago*, 337 U.S. 1 (1949).

26. The Court had unanimously held, in *Chaplinsky v. New Hampshire*, 315 U.S. 568 (1942), that insults and "fighting" words "are no essential part of any exposition of ideas" and are of so little social value as to warrant no First Amendment protection.

27. *Niemotko v. Maryland*, 340 U.S. 268 (1951).

28. *Kunz v. New York*, 340 U.S. 290 (1951).

29. *Feiner v. New York*, 340 U.S. 315 (1951).

30. Ibid., at 320.

31. Ibid., at 273; Pritchett, *Civil Liberties and Vinson Court*, 62.

32. 340 U.S. at 289.

33. *Beauharnais v. Illinois*, 343 U.S. 250 (1952).

34. Ibid., at 253–64.

35. 341 U.S. at 541.

36. 339 U.S. 382 (1950). Frankfurter had concurred in all but one section of Chief Justice Vinson's opinion. He and Jackson rejected that provision covering people who "believe in" the overthrow of the government by force or unconstitutional methods, since "probing into men's thoughts trenches on those aspects of individual freedom which we rightly regard as the most cherished aspects of Western civilization." 339 U.S. at 415, 421.

37. 341 U.S. 918 (1951). *Bailey* relied heavily on the attorney general's list of suspected organizations, which had been upheld in *Joint Anti-Fascist Refugee Committee* v. *McGrath* (1949).

38. *United States* v. *Dennis*, 183 F.2d 201, 212 (2d Cir. 1950). Hand personally disliked the Smith Act and under his own earlier formulation of the test would have limited restriction of speech only to those instances where the speech constitutes a direct incitement to illegal action. But that test had never won widespread approval, and Hand felt constrained to follow recent Supreme Court decisions such as *Douds*. See Belknap, *Cold War Political Justice*, 123–32, for the case in the Court of Appeals.

39. 341 U.S. at 509.

40. For this distortion of the original Holmes-Brandeis formulation, see Louis B. Boudin, "'Seditious Doctrines' and the 'Clear and Present Danger' Rule," *Virginia Law Review* 38 (1952): 143, 315. The decision is defended by Wallace Mendelson, "Clear and Present Danger—From Schenck to Dennis," *Columbia Law Review* 52 (1952): 52.

41. Belknap, *Cold War Political Justice*, 145.

42. 341 U.S. at 517, 525.

43. Paul A. Freund, *On Understanding the Supreme Court* (Boston: Little, Brown, 1949), 27.

44. 341 U.S. at 544, 550.

45. Ibid., at 581, 591.

46. Belknap, *Cold War Political Justice*, ch. 4, details the trial; Dennis not only was one of the defendants but had served as his own lawyer.

47. American Bar Association, *Model Code of Professional Responsibility and Code of Judicial Conduct* (Chicago: ABA, 1980), canon 2, ethical consideration 2–27.

48. Ibid., canon 3.A.1.

49. For the travail of the lawyers, see Kutler, *American Inquisition*, ch. 6.

50. *Sacher et al.* v. *United States*, 341 U.S. 952 (1951).

51. Medina, however, was a hero to many Americans at the time; mail came addressed to him as "The *American* Judge." For a sympathetic portrait, see Daniel Hawthorne, *Judge Medina: A Biography* (New York: Funk, 1952).

52. Kutler, *American Inquisition*, 267, n. 21.

53. *Sacher et al.* v. *United States*, 343 U.S. 1, 5, 11–14 (1952). Justice Clark, who had been the attorney general at the time of the *Dennis* case and therefore nominally responsible for its prosecution, did not participate in either the certiorari or decisional aspects of this case.

54. Ibid., at 14.

55. Ibid., at 25.

56. *Offutt* v. *United States*, 348 U.S. 11 (1954). The Court heard one more case involving a *Dennis* attorney, an appeal from the New York disbarment ruling of Abraham J. Isserman on the basis of his conviction for contempt of court. The Court declined to overturn the disbarment, and under its own rules also disbarred Isserman from Supreme Court practice. The Court split on the issue. Vinson, Reed, Burton, and Minton upheld the disbarment, while Black, Frankfurter, Douglas, and Jackson voted the other way. Clark recused, and the 4-4 split left the state ruling intact. *In re Isserman*, 345 U.S. 286 (1953).

57. *United States* v. *Rosenberg*, 195 F.2d 583 (2d Cir. 1952). The literature on the Rosenberg case is enormous, and the controversy continues over whether they were in fact innocent or guilty, and whether they, like Sacco and Vanzetti in the 1920s, had been convicted and executed not for their alleged crime but for their political beliefs. We are here primarily concerned with how the Supreme Court in general, and Felix Frankfurter in particular, responded to their appeals. For this section I have relied on Michael E. Parrish, "Cold War Justice: The Supreme Court and the Rosenbergs," *American Historical Review* 82 (1977): 805. In that article Parrish strongly criticizes Justice Douglas; his criticism is challenged by William Cohen, "Justice Douglas and the *Rosenberg* Case: Setting the Record Straight," *Cornell Law Review* 70 (1985): 211. See Parrish's rejoinder, ibid., 1056.

58. Frankfurter, memorandum to Conference, 20 May 1953, FF-HLS.

59. Douglas, memorandum to Conference, 22 May 1953, Douglas Papers. The court of appeals had agreed that some of the U.S. attorney's conduct had been inappropriate but concluded that it had not prejudiced the defendants' case.

60. Simon, *Independent Journey*, 303.

61. Frankfurter to Burton, 23 May 1953, quoted in Parrish, "Cold War Justice," 824.

62. *Rosenberg et ux.* v. *United States*, 345 U.S. 989 (1953).

63. For details of this evidence, see Parrish, "Cold War Justice," 828–31.

64. They claimed that the 1917 Espionage Act had been superseded by the Atomic Energy Act of 1946. Under the latter statute, a death sentence for espionage could be imposed only with a jury's recommendation and if it had been proved that the crime was committed with the intent to injure the United States.

65. Individual justices can, if they believe circumstances warrant it, issue stays of execution pending review by the full Court. At this point only an individual stay could possibly have saved the Rosenbergs.

66. Douglas, *Court Years*, 80–81.

67. *Rosenberg* v. *United States*, 346 U.S. 273, 309 (1953).

68. Parrish, "Cold War Justice," 842.

69. Simon, *Antagonists*, 192–93.

70. 342 U.S. 485 (1952).

71. Black to John Frank, 26 November 1952, quoted in Simon, *Antagonists*, 202. The two men had dissented together in another First Amendment case that term, *Zorach* v. *Clauson*, 343 U.S. 306 (1952), in which the majority had held that religious studies for public school students held during school hours but not on school grounds did not violate the separation of church and state.

72. 341 U.S. at 525.

73. Conference notes, *Scales* v. *United States*, 367 U.S. 203 (1961), Douglas Papers. The efficacy of that act had been seriously eroded in *Yates* v. *United States*, 354 U.S. 298

(1957), in which the Court had set aside the conviction of 14 lower echelon Communist leaders. Justice Harlan, along with Frankfurter, had urged that the convictions be set aside on technical grounds; his majority opinion avoided questions of speech and association.

74. Murphy, *Constitution in Crisis Times*, 291.

75. Black, *Constitutional Faith*, 16. For an example of a case decided on narrow procedural grounds, see *Peters v. Hobby*, 349 U.S. 331 (1955).

76. *Communist Party v. SACB*, 367 U.S. 1 (1961).

77. 367 U.S. 203 (1961).

78. *Noto v. United States*, 367 U.S. 290 (1961).

79. *Gibson v. Florida Legislative Committee*, 372 U.S. 539 (1963). For details of the conference proceedings and the original vote in the case, see Schwartz, *Super Chief*, 452–53.

CHAPTER 8

1. Parrish, *Frankfurter*, 155–59.

2. Frankfurter to Freund, 18 December 1947, FF-HLS.

3. Frankfurter to William Coleman, Jr., 27 August 1949, quoted in William T. Coleman, Jr., "Mr. Justice Felix Frankfurter: Civil Libertarian as Lawyer and as Justice . . . ," in Ronald D. Rotunda, ed., *Six Justices on Civil Rights* (New York: Oceana, 1983), 90, n. 22.

4. Frankfurter, "Can the Supreme Court Guarantee Toleration?" 176.

5. C. Vann Woodward, *The Strange Career of Jim Crow*, 2d ed. (New York: Oxford, 1966), chs. 2 and 3.

6. 109 U.S. 3 (1883).

7. 163 U.S. 537 (1896).

8. Mark V. Tushnet, *The NAACP's Strategy against Segregated Education, 1925–1950* (Chapel Hill: University of North Carolina Press, 1987).

9. 305 U.S. 339 (1938).

10. This is not the place to review the NAACP campaign. The interested reader is referred to Tushnet, *NAACP Strategy*; Loren Miller, *The Petitioners: The Story of the Supreme Court of the United States and the Negro* (Cleveland: World, 1966); and above all, the magisterial study by Richard Kluger, *Simple Justice: The History of Brown v. Board of Education and Black America's Struggle for Equality* (New York: Knopf, 1976).

11. 321 U.S. 649 (1944).

12. *Grovey v. Townsend*, 295 U.S. 45 (1936).

13. *United States v. Classic*, 313 U.S. 299 (1941).

14. Felix Frankfurter "Memorandum on Smith v. Allwright," 10 April 1944, FF-HLS.

15. *Buchanan v. Warley*, 245 U.S. 600 (1917).

16. 334 U.S. 1 (1948). Justices Reed, Jackson, and Rutledge did not participate in this case, presumably because each owned property covered by a restrictive covenant.

17. *Hurd v. Hodge*, 334 U.S. 24 (1948).

18. Ibid., at 36.

19. Frankfurter to Vinson, 27 April 1948, FF-HLS.

20. *Barrows* v. *Jackson*, 346 U.S. 249 (1953).

21. *Brotherhood of Railway Trainmen* v. *Howard*, 343 U.S. 768 (1952).

22. *Sipuel* v. *Oklahoma State Board of Regents*, 332 U.S. 631 (1948).

23. *McLaurin* v. *Oklahoma State Regents*, 339 U.S. 637 (1950).

24. 339 U.S. 816 (1950).

25. *Sweatt* v. *Painter*, 339 U.S. 626 (1950).

26. Frankfurter to Vinson, 19 May 1950, quoted in Kluger, *Simple Justice*, 281.

27. 339 U.S. at 634; Tushnet, *NAACP Strategy*, 131–37.

28. Simon, *Antagonists*, 216–17.

29. Kluger, *Simple Justice*, 655–56.

30. Mark Tushnet, with Katga Lezin, "What Really Happened in *Brown* v. *Board of Education.*" I am grateful to Prof. Tushnet for sharing this manuscript article with me.

31. The piece was so good that Bickel, with Frankfurter's blessing and encouragement, published it in slightly modified form as "The Original Understanding and the Segregation Decision," *Harvard Law Review* 69 (1955): 1.

32. Baker, *Brandeis and Frankfurter*, 479.

33. Philip Elman, "The Solicitor General's Office, Justice Frankfurter and Civil Rights Litigation, 1946–1960: An Oral History," *Harvard Law Review* 100 (1987): 817, 832. See also Kluger, *Simple Justice*, chs. 23 and 24.

34. Kluger, *Simple Justice*, 656.

35. Felix Frankfurter, memorandum on discrimination, 26 September 1952, FF-HLS.

36. Kluger, *Simple Justice*, 664. G. Edward White, *Earl Warren: A Public Life* (New York: Oxford, 1982), 177–78, also reports that Frankfurter had been concerned about Warren's lack of legal experience and his political background.

37. Frankfurter to Sylvester Gates, 29 October 1953, quoted in Simon, *Antagonists*, 221.

38. Author's interview with Gerald Gunther, 14 August 1988, Palo Alto, California. Hugo Black, on the other hand, held back from pushing Warren, certain that their common political backgrounds and interests would eventually lead them down the same path. One day Warren came to Black's chambers and asked if the senior justice could recommend a book on opinion writing. Black suggested Aristotle's *On Rhetoric*, which deals with the art of analyzing and making arguments. Simon, *Antagonists*, 223.

39. White, *Warren*, 165.

40. Kluger, *Simple Justice*, 683.

41. Frankfurter, Memorandum to Conference, 15 January 1954, FF-HLS.

42. Elman, "Solicitor General's Office," 844.

43. Frankfurter to McGeorge Bundy, 15 May 1964, quoted in ibid., 845. Elman's view of his own importance in the case, as well as the aspersions he casts on the NAACP legal team, are vigorously criticized in Randall Kennedy, "A Reply to Philip Elman," *Harvard Law Review* 100 (1987): 1938.

44. White, *Warren*, ch. 6; Kluger, *Simple Justice*, ch. 25.

45. Frankfurter to Earl Warren, 17 May 1954, Earl Warren Papers, Manuscript Division, Library of Congress (hereafter cited as Warren Papers).

46. Quoted in Kluger, *Simple Justice*, 711.

47. Frankfurter to Warren, 5 July 1954, quoted in Simon, *Antagonists*, 224.

48. Michael Parrish, "Felix Frankfurter," paper delivered at Georgetown University Law Center conference on the Warren Court, Washington, D.C., 27 January 1990.

49. Quoted in J. Harvie Wilkinson III, *From Brown to Bakke: The Supreme Court and School Integration, 1954–1978* (New York: Oxford, 1979), 63; see also the description of the oral argument in Kluger, *Simple Justice*, 730–36.

50. Kluger, *Simple Justice*, 736–37.

51. Frankfurter, memorandum to Conference, November 1954, FF-HLS.

52. Frankfurter had quoted the phrase from an earlier Holmes opinion and used it himself in three or four previous cases. He wanted Warren to cite the Holmes case, on the grounds that citing precedent would make the decree stronger, but Warren refused.

53. *Brown v. Board of Education (Brown II)*, 349 U.S. 294 (1955).

54. See the discussion of *Brown II* and the response to it in Wilkinson, *From Brown to Bakke*, ch. 4.

55. G. Edward White suggests that Frankfurter realized his support of desegregation ran counter to his often and loudly proclaimed theories of judicial restraint, and that he did not want to cast a spotlight on that inconsistency. *Warren*, 166.

56. Frankfurter to Hand, 21 July 1954, FF-LC.

57. White notes that Frankfurter may have been responsible for the plan of rearguing the case and separating the decision from the decree but reminds us that it succeeded only because of Warren's patient, step-by-step conversion of the doubtful members of the Court to support of the decision (*Warren*, 168).

58. Frankfurter to Hand, 12 October 1957, quoted in Kluger, *Simple Justice*, 603. Philip Kurland, ever Frankfurter's champion, argues that Warren only came into the picture toward the end of a process of consensus building that had started under Vinson and therefore deserves little of the credit for the unanimity in *Brown*. "Earl Warren, the 'Warren Court,' and the Warren Myths," *Michigan Law Review* 67 (1968): 353.

59. Warren to Frankfurter, 6 August 1954, FF-LC.

60. See, for example, the undated note Frankfurter sent to Warren sometime in 1957: (FF-LC)

> Dear Chief: I have not been left unaware that from time to time you have been rather puzzled by what you deem my technicalities, in the derogatory sense of the term. A study of this book, when time permits, will perhaps make some of my attitudes less mystifying. What is more important, it may help to establish that these technicalities are bound up with the greatest safeguards for the Court's future because they are indispensable to the wise exercise of its powers.

61. Clyde Jacobs, "The Warren Court—after Three Terms," *Western Political Quarterly* 10 (1956): 937. There has been some debate over the validity of Jacobs's use of terms such as "liberal" and "center," but the figures do indicate a shift away from a nonideological center toward a more activist and liberal orientation.

62. Frankfurter to Hand, 30 June 1957, quoted in White, *Warren*, 181; White also notes that Hand was very critical of Warren, and that his constant denigration of the chief may have played a role in Frankfurter's lowered estimation of Warren.

Interestingly enough, Frankfurter's hero, Louis Brandeis, was a great admirer of Jefferson. After a visit to Monticello, Brandeis wrote to Frankfurter: "I have spent a day at

Charlottesville to see Monticello & the University. It is strong confirmation that T.J. was greatly civilized. Washington, Jefferson, Franklin, Hamilton were indeed a Big Four." Brandeis to Frankfurter, 22 September 1927, FF-LC.

63. Eisenhower believed that one cannot "change the hearts of men with laws or decisions"—a legitimate enough sentiment, but moral leadership can sometimes help the process along. He also evaded comment on desegregation, except to sympathize from time to time with the "great emotional strains" endured by the white South. Wilkinson, *From Brown to Bakke,* 76.

64. For the Little Rock story and the subsequent Supreme Court decision, see Tony A. Freyer, *The Little Rock Crisis: A Constitutional Interpretation* (Westport, Conn.: Greenwood, 1984).

65. Frankfurter to Warren, 11 September 1958, FF-LC.

66. Frankfurter to Harlan, 12 September 1958, FF-HLS.

67. Earl Warren, *The Memoirs of Earl Warren* (Garden City, N.Y.: Doubleday, 1977), 298.

68. *Cooper v. Aaron,* 358 U.S. 1 (1958).

69. Quoted in Simon, *Antagonists,* 232.

70. Warren, *Memoirs,* 298–99.

71. Frankfurter to C. C. Burlingham, 12 November 1958, quoted in Dennis Hutchinson, "Unanimity and Desegregation: Decisionmaking in the Supreme Court, 1948–1958" *Georgetown Law Journal* 68 (1979) 1, 84.

72. 358 U.S. at 16.

73. Ibid., at 22.

74. Simon, *Antagonists,* 232–33; White, *Warren,* 183–84. Although Warren did not comment on Frankfurter, the latter kept up a running criticism of the chief in his remaining years on the Court and on into his retirement. White, *Warren,* 181–82.

CHAPTER 9

1. See, for example, Fred P. Graham, *The Self-Inflicted Wound* (New York: Macmillan, 1970), ch. 3.

2. I am greatly indebted to the discussion of this question in Silverstein, *Constitutional Faiths,* esp. ch. 4.

3. Ibid., 128–29.

4. Ibid., 129–30.

5. Frankfurter to Black, 15 December 1939, FF-HLS.

6. Frankfurter had long believed that, as he put it in 1925, "the real battles of liberalism are not won in the Supreme Court" but through "a persistent, positive translation of the liberal faith into the thoughts and acts of the community"; "Can the Supreme Court Guarantee Toleration?" 197. He repeated this sentiment in even stronger terms in 1937 and again in 1950. Silverstein, *Constitutional Faiths,* 145, 146, n. 44.

7. See Louis H. Pollak, "Mr. Justice Frankfurter: Judgment and the Fourteenth Amendment," *Yale Law Journal* 67 (1957): 304.

8. *Watts v. Indiana,* 338 U.S. 49, 54 (1949).

9. Quoted in Graham, *Self-Inflicted Wound,* 57–58.

10. *Adamson v. California,* 332 U.S. at 67–68.

11. *Rochin* v. *California,* 342 U.S. 165, 172, 173 (1952).

12. Silverstein, *Constitutional Faiths,* 151, n. 60.

13. *Buchalter* v. *New York,* 312 U.S. 780 (1943).

14. Lash, 241–42, entry for 15 May 1943.

15. *Stein* v. *New York,* 346 U.S. 156, 199 (1953), Frankfurter dissenting.

16. *Powell* v. *Alabama,* 287 U.S. 45 (1932).

17. *Johnson* v. *Zerbst,* 304 U.S. 458 (1938); Justice Black wrote for the Court in this case, his first great criminal procedure opinion.

18. See, for example, *Hudson* v. *North Carolina,* 363 U.S. 697 (1960), and *Chewning* v. *Cunningham,* 368 U.S. 443 (1962). By the early 1960s, as Jerold Israel points out, "the Court had consistently whittled away at the *Betts* rule until . . . it was almost completely eroded." "Gideon v. Wainwright: The 'Art' of Overruling," *Supreme Court Review* (1963): 211, 260.

19. *Gideon* v. *Wainwright,* 372 U.S. 355 (1963).

20. 324 U.S. 401 (1945).

21. Frankfurter to Douglas [no date, 1945], quoted in Silverstein, *Constitutional Faiths,* 157.

22. 324 U.S. at 414–17.

23. Yarbrough, *Black and His Critics,* 90.

24. Graham, *Self-Inflicted Wound,* 2.

25. 324 U.S. at 417.

26. In 1950 Frankfurter testified before the Royal Commission on Capital Punishment in London; he explained that he was opposed to the death penalty not for humanitarian or even penological reasons but because of the deleterious effects on the trial system caused by the sensationalism surrounding a potential death sentence. Copy of Frankfurter testimony, 21 July 1950, FF-HLS.

27. *Louisiana ex rel. Francis* v. *Resweber,* 329 U.S. 459 (1947).

28. Frankfurter to Burton, 13 December 1946, quoted in Silverstein, *Constitutional Faiths,* 160.

29. Frankfurter to Hand, 6 December 1947, FF-LC.

30. 329 U.S. at 471.

31. Pritchett, *Civil Liberties and Vinson Court,* 246.

32. *Haley* v. *Ohio,* 332 U.S. 596 (1947).

33. Ibid., at 603.

34. Mendelson, *Justices Black and Frankfurter,* 41.

35. *Stein* v. *New York,* 346 U.S. 156, 200 (1953).

36. Frankfurter to Murphy, 15 February 1947, quoted in Silverstein, *Constitutional Faiths,* 149, n. 54. Frankfurter said essentially the same thing in *Harris* v. *United States,* 331 U.S. 145, 156 (1947).

37. *H. P. Hood and Sons* v. *Du Mond,* 336 U.S. 525, 564 (1949), Frankfurter dissenting.

38. *Griswold* v. *Connecticut,* 381 U.S. 479 (1965). In 1961 Frankfurter wrote the plurality opinion dismissing an earlier challenge to the Connecticut ban on contraceptives. Since there had been only one prosecution in 80 years, he deemed the claim not yet ripe for adjudication. *Poe* v. *Ullman,* 367 U.S. 497 (1961).

39. This is not the "original intent" argument used by conservatives such as Edwin

Meese or Robert Bork. Frankfurter did not believe that the "unreasonable" standard should be the one in use in 1776 or 1787, but rather that the purpose of the Fourth Amendment was to protect people and their privacy from unlawful police conduct. Judges need to interpret "unreasonable" in contemporary terms, but always keeping in mind the strong feelings the colonists had on this subject.

40. Silverstein, *Constitutional Faiths*, 213.

41. 331 U.S. 145 (1947).

42. Ibid., at 161.

43. *United States v. Di Re*, 332 U.S. 581 (1948); *Johnson v. United States*, 333 U.S. 10 (1948); and *Trupiano v. United States*, 334 U.S. 699 (1948). In all three cases Frankfurter voted with the majority to restrict the seized evidence.

44. 339 U.S. 25 (1950).

45. *On Lee v. United States*, 343 U.S. 747 (1952).

46. Graham, *Self-Inflicted Wound*, 208.

47. 232 U.S. 383 (1914). The Court reiterated its opposition to violation of the Fourth Amendment in *Silverthorne Lumber Co. v. United States*, 251 U.S. 385 (1919), when Justice Holmes, branding the government's actions an "outrage," blocked *any* use of the illegally seized materials by the government in any court action.

48. *Byars v. United States*, 273 U.S. 28 (1927), and *Gambino v. United States*, 275 U.S. 310 (1927).

49. 338 U.S. 25 (1949). The case involved conviction of an abortionist on evidence seized without a warrant.

50. Ibid., at 27.

51. Ibid., at 33. All nine members of the Court agreed that the Fourth Amendment should apply to the states; Douglas, Murphy, and Rutledge, however, believed that the exclusionary rule should also apply, for without it the amendment was essentially a dead letter.

52. Mendelson, *Justices Black and Frankfurter*, 71 (emphasis in the original).

53. *Rochin v. California*, 342 U.S. 165 (1952).

54. *Irvine v. California*, 347 U.S. 128 (1954).

55. *Elkins v. United States*, 364 U.S. 206, 217 (1960).

56. 367 U.S. 643 (1961).

57. The five also picked up Justice Clark, who normally favored the state in criminal procedure cases but who had also come to believe in the need for the exclusionary rule.

58. Roger Traynor, "Mapp v. Ohio at Large in the 50 States," *Duke Law Journal* (1962): 319, 324.

59. See, for example, *Fikes v. Alabama*, 352 U.S. 191 (1957), and *Payne, v. Arkansas*, 356 U.S. 560 (1958). The Court's shift is explored in Otis H. Stephens, Jr., *The Supreme Court and Confessions of Guilt* (Knoxville: University of Tennessee Press, 1973), chs. 4 and 5. Frankfurter wrote to Black on 18 May 1951: "Once you admit, as you must admit, that the mere claim of privilege cannot compel acceptance, you are necessarily presented with the problem of deciding when the situation, on the face of it, makes the claim of privilege proof of the validity of the claim." FF-HLS.

60. 337 U.S. 201 (1964).

61. Melvin I. Urofsky, *The Continuity of Change: The Supreme Court and Individual Liberties, 1953–1986* (Belmont, Calif.: Wadsworth, 1990), ch. 7.

CHAPTER 10

1. Simon, *Antagonists*, 179–80.

2. *Everson v. Board of Education*, 330 U.S. 1 (1947).

3. *Cantwell v. Connecticut*, 310 U.S. 296 (1940). There is, of course, a lively debate over just what the framers meant by the phrase, and whether the First Amendment requires a high wall of separation or allows accommodation between the state and religion. See Leonard W. Levy, *The Establishment Clause: Religion and the First Amendment* (New York: Macmillan, 1986).

4. 330 U.S. at 15.

5. Ibid., at 19.

6. Dunne, *Black*, 264; Yarbrough, *Black and His Critics*, 154.

7. Frankfurter to Grenville Clark, 6 March 1937, quoted in Dunne, *Black*, 264–65.

8. Black, "Mr. Justice Frankfurter," 1521.

9. Frankfurter to Murphy, undated, FF-LC.

10. Fine, *Murphy*, 569. Fine notes that "although Murphy did not normally permit his religion to influence his behavior as a public official, his *Everson* vote may have been one of those rare instances when his Catholicism tipped the scales for him." Ibid., 571.

11. Lash, *Diaries*, 343; entry for 9 March 1948.

12. *McCollum v. Board of Education*, 333 U.S. 203 (1948).

13. Lash, *Diaries*, 343, entry for 9 March 1948.

14. Simon, *Antagonists*, 182–83. The infighting is detailed in Fine, *Murphy*, 571–75.

15. Phillips, *Frankfurter Remembers*, 4–5.

16. 333 U.S. at 216–17. Rutledge, Jackson, and Burton joined in the concurrence.

17. Both quoted in Pritchett, *Civil Liberties and Vinson Court*, 12.

18. *Zorach v. Clauson*, 343 U.S. 306 (1952).

19. Ibid., at 313–14.

20. Jackson thought the Court opinion a disaster and in an emotional letter to Frankfurter declared that "the battle for *separation* of Church and State is lost. From here on it is only a question of how far the intermixture will go." Jackson to Frankfurter, 30 April 1952, FF-LC.

21. 343 U.S. at 320, 321.

22. Frankfurter to Black, 5 March 1952, quoted in Simon, *Antagonists*, 202.

23. *McGowan v. Maryland*, 366 U.S. 420, 444 (1961). One of the cases involved a free exercise claim by Jewish merchants, *Braunfeld v. Brown*, 366 U.S. 599 (1961), in which Warren sidestepped the central issue. Within a few years the Court would reverse the philosophy behind these decisions, in *Sherbert v. Verner*, 374 U.S. 398 (1963).

24. Justices Brennan and Stewart dissented only in *Braunfeld*, in the free exercise case.

25. 366 U.S. at 459. One can speculate that Frankfurter distinguished between religious or semireligious activities taking place in the school, which he held as inviolable, and those taking place in the market, even if sanctioned by the state.

26. *Engel v. Vitale*, 370 U.S. 421 (1962).

27. 364 U.S. 339 (1960).

28. 364 U.S. at 346–47. Frankfurter spoke for a unanimous Court, but Douglas and Whittaker both filed brief concurring opinions. Douglas reiterated his adherence to his

dissent in *Colgrove;* Whittaker believed the decision should have been grounded in the equal protection clause rather than in the Fifteenth Amendment.

29. *Baker v. Carr,* 364 U.S. 898 (1961), probable jurisdiction noted; case decided at 369 U.S. 186 (1962).

30. For oral arguments before the Court, see Richard C. Cortner, *The Apportionment Cases* (New York: Norton, 1970), ch. 5.

31. Quoted in ibid., 140. The youngest member, of course, was Brennan.

32. 369 U.S. at 269, 321.

33. *Gray v. Sanders,* 372 U.S. 368 (1963).

34. 377 U.S. 533 (1964).

35. 369 U.S. at 266, 270.

36. *Bell v. Maryland,* 378 U.S. 226 (1964).

37. Simon, *Antagonists,* 255–60.

38. Lash, *Diaries,* 89.

39. Baker, *Brandeis and Frankfurter,* 491; Simon, *Antagonists,* 260.

40. The view of judicial restraint as democratic in nature is explored in Sanford V. Levinson, "The Democratic Faith of Felix Frankfurter," *Stanford Law Review* 25 (1973): 430. Levinson also concludes that Frankfurter's views on judicial restraint and its relation to democracy were forged in his academic years.

41. *United States v. United Mine Workers,* 330 U.S. 250, 308 (1947).

42. Frankfurter, *Commerce Clause under Marshall, Taney and Waite.*

BIBLIOGRAPHIC ESSAY

Manuscripts

Frankfurter left an enormous collection of papers, divided into three parts. The largest section, which deals with his legal career as a scholar at Harvard and then as a justice, is in the Manuscript Collections at Harvard Law School; it is also available on microfilm. The second part, covering his reform work and his extensive nonlegal correspondence, is deposited in the Manuscript Division of the Library of Congress. The smallest part, relating to his work with the Zionist Organization, can be found in the Central Zionist Archives in Jerusalem, Israel.

Frankfurter papers can be found in literally hundreds of manuscript depositories in the United States and abroad, but for the purposes of this study certain collections have proven the most useful. First, there are the Harvard Law School Library's Learned Hand Papers, which contain hundreds of letters in which Frankfurter unburdened himself of his real and imagined travails on the bench. Similar complaints, as well as some gossip about the Court, may be found in his correspondence with Thomas Reed Powell, also in the Harvard Law School Library.

The Louis D. Brandeis Papers are housed at the Law School of the University of Louisville and are helpful in filling in many of the details of Frankfurter's reform career. The one obvious gap in the Brandeis Papers is the lack of letters *from* Frankfurter. The late Pearl von Allman, longtime law librarian at Louisville, said that Frankfurter came down to Louisville shortly after Brandeis's death and removed most of his letters because he did not want Alpheus Mason (then working on a Brandeis biography) to see them. The letters to Frankfurter from Brandeis are in the Frankfurter Papers at the Library of Congress and are essential to understanding their relationship. With David W. Levy, I have edited a selection of them, *"Half-Son, Half-Brother": The Letters of Louis D. Brandeis to Felix Frankfurter* (Norman: University of Oklahoma Press, 1991). Also useful are the notes Frankfurter made of his conversations with Brandeis in the 1920s and

1930s. The originals are in the Frankfurter Papers at Harvard Law School; I have transcribed and annotated them in *Supreme Court Review* (1985): 299–340.

A number of the men with whom Frankfurter served on the bench left their papers, which have proven a treasure trove for scholars. The most useful are those of Harlan Fiske Stone and William O. Douglas, but those of Robert Jackson, Earl Warren, and Hugo Black are also helpful. All of them are in the Manuscript Division of the Library of Congress.

Works by Frankfurter

An extremely prolific writer, Frankfurter's pieces, both those he signed and those he published anonymously, are scattered throughout America's periodical literature for nearly a half-century. Many of these have been collected and are readily available in the following collections: Archibald MacLeish and E. F. Pritchard, Jr., eds., *Law and Politics: Occasional Papers of Felix Frankfurter, 1913–1938* (New York: Harcourt Brace, 1939); Philip H. Kurland, ed., *Felix Frankfurter on the Supreme Court: Extrajudicial Essays on the Court and the Constitution* (Cambridge, Mass.: Harvard University Press, 1970); and Philip Elman, ed., *Of Law and Men: Papers and Addresses of Felix Frankfurter, 1939–1956* (New York: Harcourt Brace, 1956).

In reading these collections, one can easily see, I believe, that Frankfurter's jurisprudential ideas were well set by the time he took his seat on the Court, and that he did not significantly change them afterwards. In this connection, see the various essays on Frankfurter, especially that of Alexander Bickel, in Wallace Mendelson, ed., *Felix Frankfurter: A Tribute* (New York: Reynal, 1964). Samplings of some of Frankfurter's early opinions can be found in Samuel J. Konefsky, ed., *The Constitutional World of Mr. Justice Frankfurter* (New York: Macmillan, 1949).

The two most important books that Frankfurter wrote before taking a seat on the high court would have to be *The Case of Sacco and Vanzetti: A Critical Analysis for Lawyers and Laymen* (Boston: Little, Brown, 1927) and *The Business of the Supreme Court: A Study in the Federal Judicial System* (New York: Macmillan, 1927), which he wrote with James M. Landis. He summed up his philosophy of government in *The Public and Its Government* (New Haven, Conn.: Yale University Press, 1930). His comments in *Mr. Justice Holmes and the Supreme Court* (Cambridge, Mass.: Harvard University Press, 1939) are indicative of Frankfurter's philosophy of judicial restraint.

Works about Frankfurter

Michael Parrish, *Felix Frankfurter and His Times: The Reform Years* (New York: Free Press, 1982), the first of two volumes, is a model biography that covers the period up to Frankfurter's taking his seat on the Court. I have profited greatly from this book, as well as from conversations with Professor Parrish about Frankfurter. An interesting application of psychological theory to biography can be found in H. N. Hirsch, *The Enigma of Felix Frankfurter* (New York: Basic Books, 1981); Hirsch does present some new information, but for the most part he takes well-known facts about Frankfurter and reinterprets them from a psychological perspective. An older, but at times still useful study is Liva Baker, *Felix Frankfurter* (New York: Coward-McCann, 1969).

Frankfurter never wrote an autobiography, but he did allow extensive portions of his oral history memoir at Columbia University to be published as *Felix Frankfurter Reminisces*, ed. Harlan Philips (New York: Reynal, 1960). While there are some fascinating vignettes in these recollections, the scholar must approach them circumspectly, to say the least. Much more revealing of the man are his occasional diary entries, which have been gathered in Joseph P. Lash, ed., *From the Diaries of Felix Frankfurter* (New York: Norton, 1975). Lash's biographical essay on Frankfurter is absolutely one of the best pieces available on this complex and contradictory character.

Frankfurter's relations with Brandeis are the subject of Bruce Allan Murphy, *The Brandeis/Frankfurter Connection* (New York: Oxford, 1982). The controversy stirred up by the alleged sensationalism of both author and publisher obscured the fact that Murphy does present some extremely valuable findings and raises a number of disturbing questions about the proper role of Supreme Court justices. Nelson L. Dawson also examines the efforts of the two men to influence government agencies in *Louis Brandeis, Felix Frankfurter, and the New Deal* (Hamden, Conn.: Archon Books, 1980); while his conclusions are generally the same, the book lacks the richer texture and broader scope of Murphy's work. Leonard Baker, *Brandeis and Frankfurter: A Dual Biography* (New York: Harper & Row, 1984) is an effort to "respond" to Murphy's accusation; while it has some interesting anecdotes, it does not measure up to Baker's other work.

Frankfurter's relations with Brandeis are explored in a far different manner in Robert A. Burt, *Two Jewish Justices: Outcasts in the Promised Land* (Berkeley: University of California Press, 1988). Burt offers a number of very useful insights, but in the end his argument is far from convincing. Frankfurter's close ties to Franklin Roosevelt are well documented in Max Freedman, ed., *Roosevelt and Frankfurter: Their Correspondence, 1928–1945* (Boston: Atlantic/Little, Brown, 1967).

Frankfurter and the "brethren"

There have been a number of books about the members of the Court during this era, and nearly all of them have some sections dealing with Frankfurter. Of special value is James F. Simon, *The Antagonists: Hugo Black, Felix Frankfurter and Civil Liberties in Modern America* (New York: Simon & Schuster, 1989), which explores the ambivalent relationship between the two. For Black, see also Gerald T. Dunne, *Hugo L. Black and the Judicial Revolution* (New York: Simon & Schuster, 1977); Toney Freyer, *Hugo Black and the Dilemma of American Liberalism* (Boston: Little, Brown, 1990); and Tinsley E. Yarbrough, *Mr. Justice Black and His Critics* (Durham, N.C.: Duke University Press, 1988).

In the jurisprudential battle between Black and Frankfurter, the latter has had a powerful advocate in Wallace Mendelson, author of *Justices Black and Frankfurter: Conflict in the Court* (Chicago: University of Chicago Press, 1961), but I prefer what I consider the more balanced approach in Mark Silverstein, *Constitutional Faiths: Felix Frankfurter, Hugo Black, and the Process of Judicial Decision-Making* (Ithaca, N.Y.: Cornell University Press, 1984).

James F. Simon has also written a biography of William O. Douglas, *Independent Journey* (New York: Harper & Row, 1980), which well captures both the virtues and blemishes of Douglas's character. A good sampling of the man can be found in Melvin I. and Philip E. Urofsky, eds., *The Douglas Letters* (Washington, D.C.: Adler & Adler, 1987). The last volume of Douglas's memoirs, *The Court Years, 1939–1975* (New York: Random House, 1980), was written when he was quite ill and is not always reliable. For the ongoing feud with Frankfurter, see my "Felix Frankfurter, William O. Douglas, and the Clash of Personalities and Philosophies on the United States Supreme Court," *Duke Law Journal* (1988): 71–113.

Sidney Fine, *Frank Murphy: The Washington Years* (Ann Arbor: University of Michigan Press, 1984) and Alpheus Thomas Mason, *Harlan Fiske Stone: Pillar of the Law* (New York: Viking, 1956) both shed a great deal of light on the Court in the 1940s, and on the disruptive role Frankfurter played. There is, at present, no good biography of Robert Jackson; Dennis Hutchinson is at work on one, and his article, "The Black-Jackson Feud" *Supreme Court Review* (1988): 203–44, is pertinent to Frankfurter.

Frankfurter's problems with Earl Warren are examined in G. Edward White, *Earl Warren: A Public Life* (New York: Oxford, 1982), ch. 7, as well as in Bernard Schwartz, *Super Chief: Earl Warren and His Supreme Court* (New York: New York University Press, 1983), and in Schwartz's article, "Felix Frankfurter and Earl Warren: A Study of a Deteriorating Relationship," *Supreme Court Review* (1980): 115–42. There is, unfortunately, no biography of Frankfurter's closest ally on the Warren Court, John Marshall Harlan.

An extremely useful article detailing how Frankfurter's poor relations with his colleagues defeated him even when he had good ideas is Dennis J. Hutchinson, "Felix Frankfurter and the Business of the Supreme Court, O.T. 1946–O.T. 1961," *Supreme Court Review* (1980): 143–210.

The Pre-Court Years

For the status of the legal profession at the beginning of Frankfurter's career, see Jerald Auerbach, *Unequal Justice: Lawyers and Social Change in Modern America* (New York: Oxford, 1976). Harvard Law School during Frankfurter's years as a student and teacher is described in Arthur E. Sutherland, *The Law at Harvard* (Cambridge, Mass.: Harvard University Press, 1967); one should also see David Wigder, *Roscoe Pound: Philosopher of Law* (Westport, Conn.: Greenwood, 1974). There is no specific study of Frankfurter's relationship with Holmes, but the great importance of Holmes to many young reformers of that time is described in Gary J. Aichele, *Oliver Wendell Holmes, Jr.: Soldier, Scholar, Judge* (Boston: Twayne, 1989).

Two of the great cases that occupied Frankfurter's attention during World War I are detailed in James W. Byrkit, *Forging the Copper Collar: Arizona's Labor-Management War of 1901–1921* (Tuscon: University of Arizona Press, 1982) and Richard Frost, *The Mooney Case* (Stanford, Calif.: Stanford University Press, 1968). The problems with Judge Gary and the steel industry are best explained in David Brody, *Labor in Crisis: The Steel Strike of 1919* (Philadelphia: Lippincott, 1965). Life at the House of Truth is examined in Jeffrey O'Connell and Nancy Dart, "The House of Truth: Home of the Young Frankfurter and Lippmann," *Catholic University Law Review* 35 (1985): 79–95, while Zionist activities are the subject of my *American Zionism from Herzl to the Holocaust* (Garden City, N.Y.: Doubleday/Anchor, 1975). Frankfurter's role in the early days of the *New Republic* is discussed in Charles Forcey, *The Crossroads of Liberalism: Croly, Weyl, Lippmann and the Progressive Era, 1900–1925* (New York: Oxford, 1961).

William E. Leuchtenburg, *The Perils of Prosperity* (Chicago: University of Chicago Press, 1958) remains the best overview of the turbulent twenties. The decade began badly for liberals, as Robert K. Murray shows in *The Red Scare: A Study in National Hysteria* (New York: McGraw-Hill, 1955), and got worse with the Sacco-Vanzetti case. There are numerous studies of this event and its significance, such as Robert S. Feuerlicht, *Justice Crucified: The Story of Sacco and Vanzetti* (New York: Farrar, Straus & Giroux, 1977) and Francis Russell, *Tragedy in Dedham: The Story of Sacco and Vanzetti* (New York: Harper & Row, 1962). Herbert B. Ehrmann, who worked with Frankfurter to try to save the two men, tells his side of the story in *The Case That Will Not Die: Commonwealth v. Sacco and Vanzetti* (Boston: Little, Brown, 1969).

The conflicting currents in constitutional developments are examined in

Paul L. Murphy, *The Constitution in Crisis Times, 1918–1969* (New York: Harper & Row, 1972). Joel Paschal, *Mr. Justice Sutherland: A Man against the State* (Princeton: Princeton University Press, 1951), captures well the conservative mind-set of the times. For the debate over Legal Realism, which found Frankfurter an interested observer, see Wilfred E. Rumble, Jr., *American Legal Realism* (Ithaca, N.Y.: Cornell University Press, 1968) and Laura Kalman, *Legal Realism at Yale, 1927–1960* (Chapel Hill: University of North Carolina Press, 1986).

For the 1930s, one can begin with William E. Leuchtenburg, *Franklin D. Roosevelt and the New Deal* (New York: Harper & Row, 1963). The economic problems that so concerned Brandeis and Frankfurter are perceptively explored in Ellis Wayne Hawley, *The New Deal and the Problem of Monopoly: A Study in Economic Ambivalence* (Princeton, N.J.: Princeton University Press, 1966). Frankfurter's role as mentor and employment agency is examined in G. Edward White, "Felix Frankfurter, the Old Boy Network, and the New Deal: The Placement of Elite Lawyers in Public Service in the 1930s," *Arkansas Law Review* 39 (1986): 631–67.

The Court Years—World War and Cold War

An overall examination of the Court during Frankfurter's first years can be found in C. Herman Pritchett, *The Roosevelt Court: A Study in Judicial Values and Politics* (New York: Macmillan, 1948). Civil liberties during wartime in general are assessed in Edward S. Corwin, *Total War and the Constitution* (New York: Knopf, 1947). The justice's ongoing relationship with President Roosevelt is well documented in Murphy, *The Brandeis/Frankfurter Connection* and Freedman, *Roosevelt and Frankfurter*, cited earlier.

The first issue to arise before the Court during Frankfurter's tenure, the flag salute cases, is the subject of David Manwaring, *Render unto Caesar: The Flag Salute Controversy* (Chicago: University of Chicago Press, 1962). Richard Danzig has examined Frankfurter's position in two articles: "How Question Begot Answers in Felix Frankfurter's First Flag Salute Opinion," *Supreme Court Review* (1977): 257–74, and "Justice Frankfurter's Opinions in the Flag Salute Cases: Blending Logic and Psychologic in Constitutional Decisionmaking," *Stanford Law Review* 36 (1984): 675–723. The Court's approval of Japanese relocation has had few defenders, and it is blisteringly attacked in Peter Irons, *Justice at War* (New York: Oxford, 1983).

The single best book on the Court during the cold war is Michael R. Belknap, *Cold War Political Justice: The Smith Act, the Communist Party, and American Civil Liberties* (Westport, Conn.: Greenwood, 1977), which can be supplemented by Stanley I. Kutler, *The American Inquisition: Justice and Injustice in the Cold War* (New York: Hill & Wang, 1982); both books deal extensively with the Dennis trial. The debate over the proper test for free speech can be found in many articles: Louis B. Boudin attacks what he sees as the Court's distortion of the original Holmes-Brandeis test in "'Seditious Doctrines' and the 'Clear and Present Danger' Rule," *Virginia Law Review*, 38 (1952): 143–86 and 315–56. The Court, and Frankfurter, are defended by Wallace Mendelson in "Clear and Present Danger—From Schenck to Dennis," *Columbia Law Review* 52 (1952): 313–33.

The Black and Douglas dissents, derided at the time by Frankfurter's champions, have over time come to be recognized as courageous responses to the hysteria of the times. See Harry Kalven, Jr., "Upon Rereading Mr. Justice Black on the First Amendment," *UCLA Law Review* 14 (1967): 428–53, and Lucas A. Powe, Jr., "Justice Douglas after Fifty Years: The First Amendment, Mc-Carthyism and Rights," *Constitutional Commentary* 6 (1989): 267–87.

The Court Years—Incorporation and Civil Rights

The debate over whether or not the Fourteenth Amendment "incorporates" the guarantees of the Bill of Rights has been going on ever since Justice Brandeis first made the suggestion in the 1920s. For a good discussion, see Richard C. Cortner, *The Supreme Court and the Second Bill of Rights* (Madison: University of Wisconsin Press, 1981), as well as the excellent essay by John Hart Ely, *Democracy and Distrust: A Theory of Judicial Review* (Cambridge, Mass.: Harvard University Press, 1980). Justice Black's dissent in *Adamson* drew forth a critique from Charles A. Fairman, "Does the Fourteenth Amendment Incorporate the Bill of Rights? The Original Understanding," *Stanford Law Review* 2 (1949): 5–139, and the answering critique by William W. Crosskey in *University of Chicago Law Review* 22 (1954): 1–143. Frankfurter prepared a memorandum expressing his own views, and this was published after his death as "Memorandum on 'Incorporation' of the Bill of Rights into the Due Process Clause of the Fourteenth Amendment," *Harvard Law Review* 78 (1965): 746–83. The latest word on the subject is the prizewinning study by William E. Nelson, *The Fourteenth Amendment: From Political Principle to Judicial Doctrine* (Cambridge, Mass.: Harvard University Press, 1988).

A general view of rights in the later 1940s and early 1950s is C. Herman Pritchett, *Civil Liberties and the Vinson Court* (Chicago: University of Chicago Press, 1954). For apportionment, see Richard C. Cortner, *The Apportionment Cases* (New York: Norton, 1970) and Charles G. Post, Jr., *The Supreme Court and Political Questions* (Baltimore: Johns Hopkins University Press, 1969). The groundlessness of Frankfurter's fears are well documented in Robert McKay, "Reapportionment: Success Story of the Warren Court," *Michigan Law Review* 67 (1968): 223–36.

For cases and problems arising out of the religion clauses, see Richard E. Morgan, *The Supreme Court and Religion* (New York: Free Press, 1972); Frank J.

Sorauf, *The Wall of Separation* (Princeton, N.J.: Princeton University Press, 1976); and Candida Lund, "Religion and Commerce—The Sunday Closing Cases," in C. Herman Pritchett and Alan F. Westin, eds., *The Third Branch of Government*, 275–308 (New York: Harcourt Brace & World, 1963).

The literature on the Warren Court and its activism is large and growing. Critics range from the polemical Raoul Berger, *Government by Judiciary* (Cambridge, Mass.: Harvard University Press, 1977) to the thoughtful and perceptive Alexander M. Bickel, *The Least Dangerous Branch* (New Haven, Conn.: Yale University Press, 1962) and *Politics and the Warren Court* (New York: Harper & Row, 1965). For a defense, see Archibald Cox, *The Warren Court: Constitutional Decision as an Instrument of Social Reform* (Cambridge, Mass.: Harvard University Press, 1968). Frankfurter's departure, which opened the way for the appointment of the liberal Arthur Goldberg as his replacement, ushered in the most activist years of the Warren era.

The desegregation cases, arguably the most important of all Warren Court decisions, are examined in numerous works, but the definitive study is Richard Kluger, *Simple Justice: The History of Brown v. Board of Education and Black America's Struggle for Equality* (New York: Knopf, 1976), which also looks at the problems associated with the implementation decision. During the deliberations over *Brown*, Frankfurter put his law clerk to work researching what, if anything, history had to say about the Fourteenth Amendment and education—and then encouraged its publication: see Alexander M. Bickel, "The Original Understanding and the Desegregation Decision," *Harvard Law Review* 69 (1955): 1–65. Frankfurter's questionable manipulations during this time are discussed in Philip Elman, "The Solicitor General's Office, Justice Frankfurter and Civil Rights Litigation, 1946–1960: An Oral History," *Harvard Law Review* 100 (1982): 817–52. But see Randall Kennedy's critique of Ellman in ibid. at 1938–48.

Frankfurter's role in the desegregation cases is amplified and defended in Philip Kurland, "Earl Warren, the Warren Court, and the Warren Myth," *Michigan Law Review* 67 (1968): 353–58. As a corrective see Dennis J. Hutchinson, "Unanimity and Desegregation: Decisionmaking in the Supreme Court," *Georgetown Law Journal* 68 (1979): 1–96. Tony A. Freyer has examined the *Cooper* case, including Frankfurter's somewhat inexplicable actions, in *The Little Rock Crisis: A Constitutional Interpretation* (Westport, Conn.: Greenwood, 1984).

Frankfurter's role and reputation as a civil libertarian are discussed in Joseph L. Rauh, Jr., "Felix Frankfurter: Civil Libertarian," *Harvard Civil Rights—Civil Liberties Law Review* 11 (1976): 496–520, and in William T. Coleman, Jr., "Mr. Justice Frankfurter: Civil Libertarian as Lawyer and as Justice," in Donald D. Rotunda, ed., *Six Justices on Civil Rights*, 85–106 (New York: Oceana, 1983). The view that judicial restraint is democratic in nature is argued in Sanford V. Levinson, "The Democratic Faith of Felix Frankfurter," *Stanford Law Review* 25 (1973): 430–48.

INDEX

THE AUTHOR

Melvin I. Urofsky is professor of history at Virginia Commonwealth University. His previous works include *Big Steel and the Wilson Administration* (1969), the prizewinning *American Zionism from Herzl to the Holocaust* (1975), *Louis D. Brandeis and the Progressive Tradition* (1981), and *A March of Liberty* (1988). He has edited the letters of William O. Douglas and, with David W. Levy, five volumes of Louis D. Brandeis letters. He is currently working on a study of death, dying, and the law. His wife, Susan, is Commissioner of Rehabilitative Services for the Commonwealth of Virginia, and they have two sons, Philip, a lawyer in New York, and Robert, a teacher in Virginia.